And The Oscar

Goes To...

Tim J. Culbertson

Published by Book Writing Pioneer

Cover design by Book Writing Pioneer

ISBN: Printed in the United States

Dedication

I would like to dedicate this book to all the people around the world who enjoy the arts, especially cinema. Most importantly, to my immediate family, my friends, and especially to my husband, companion, fellow movie-goer and DVD-Blu-ray collector of thirty years, Gary LaPalombara.

Table Of Contents

About the Author

Allow me to introduce myself. I am Tim J. Culbertson. Born in Sikeston, Missouri, a small town of approximately 17,000 people in Southeast Missouri located on the mighty Mississippi River located approximately between 140-145 miles from St. Louis and Memphis. I was born the third son, the fifth child, in 1959. I was fortunate to attend parochial school in first grade but then switched to public schools till graduation. I attended Southeast Missouri State University located in Cape Girardeau, 35 miles from Sikeston, and graduated in 1982 with a degree in Education specializing in Library Science. After graduation, I switched careers by immediately turning to restaurants and retail. I retired from retail grocery in March 2022.

As you see, the title And the Oscar Goes To is a manuscript filled with Oscar trivia from 1959-2000 and the forty-year friendship of six individuals trying to make it big working behind the camera instead of in front of the camera and their obsession and ability to attend Oscar ceremonies. I also have the privilege to attach an appendix of Oscar winners from 1929-present of the categories *Best Picture, Best Director, Best Actor, Best Actress, Best Supporting Actor, and Best Supporting Actress.*

I have been a lifelong fan of movies since conception, LOL. I have been interested in celebrities' lives, the Oscars and watching movies on television and screen forever. I read books about and by celebrities at every opportunity I get, see films all the time, as well collect favorites on Blu-ray and DVD format. Don't ever get me started on asking who my favorite celebrity, film genre, or film is. I couldn't begin to compile a favorite list if asked to do so.

I am ever so thankful to my late mother, Jane Culbertson, for my introduction to the love of cinema. Ever-fond memories of going to see Sound of Music with her and my Godmother, Wilma Rogers, at the Rialto Theatre in Cape Girardeau and watching old movies like Back Street, Imitation of Life, and Madame X, starring some of my faves, Susan Hayward and Lana Turner. I also treasure my celebrity biographies/memoirs I still have on Judy Garland, Doris Day, Susan Hayward and countless others we shared the 17 years we had together as mother and son.

Secondly, I am thankful for having a wonderful soulmate of 30 years, Gary LaPalombara, an East Coast gentleman who loves the cinema, too. Big kudos to him.

Hopefully, as you read the Oscar trivia bits I include in this manuscript, I hope you will enjoy it coupled with the story of the six friends and their friendship.

As Bette Davis said in All About Eve,

"Buckle Your Seats, It's Gonna Be a Bumpy Ride!"

Tim J. Culbertson

July 2024

Disclaimer

This book includes references to the Academy Awards® (also known as the Oscars®), which is a registered trademark of the Academy of Motion Picture Arts and Sciences (AMPAS). The use of the Academy Awards® name and related trademarks is for descriptive purposes only and does not imply any affiliation with or endorsement by AMPAS. This book is not authorized, approved, licensed, or endorsed by AMPAS.

The content of this book is intended solely for educational and informational purposes and is based on publicly available information. The author has made every effort to ensure the accuracy of the information herein; however, the author and publisher assume no responsibility for errors, inaccuracies, omissions, or any consequences arising from the use of this book. All opinions expressed in this book are solely those of the author and do not reflect the views or opinions of AMPAS.

PLEASE NOTE:

Some drug and sexual references aren't made purposely to upset the reader but in hopes of enhancing the story because Hollywood wasn't all glitz and glamour. It was filled with ambition fueled with greed coupled with combined drugs and sex. LOL. Enjoy!

Page Blank Intentionally

Introduction

Author's Notes

A ND THE OSCAR GOES TO …...those five words are just as infamous in any Academy Award ceremony as …. AND THE NOMINEES FOR … whatever category being presented.

The Academy Awards, or Oscars as most known, are given annually to artists for acting and technical merit in the film industry and presented by the voting membership of the (AMPAS) Academy of Motion Picture Arts and Sciences.

For Oscar trivia, I used Wikipedia, Chat GPT, and Chris Strodder's Parts One and Two of The Academy Awards Book of Lists: An Unauthorized, Unofficial, and Unprecedented History of the Oscars to highlight nominees and winners.

The Oscars began in 1929. There were only two handfuls of winners; the categories were as few as eleven, and the best director was divided into two categories: comedy and drama. According to Chris Strodder's Oscar research, in the first and only year, there were two top awards. The 1st award was called Outstanding Picture, which went to Wings, and the other Unique and Artistic Picture went to Sunrise. Both films were made in 1927. From 2010 to 2022, nominees for Best Picture ranged anywhere from five to eight to nine to ten and, at one time, highlighted from Twitter, voted "two fan favorites."

Best Picture of the Year was called different names over the years. Starting in 1930, it was called Outstanding Production, followed in 1942 by Outstanding Motion Picture. Again, in 1945, the word "Best" was first used, and finally, for what it is known today as Best Picture in 1962. The Best Supporting Category for Actor and Actress wasn't introduced till 1937. In 1978, the Best Actor and Actress added a Leading Role to its name. There were often Juvenile Awards presented to younger performers, a few were Shirley Temple, Judy Garland, and Hayley Mills, as well as Honorary and the Irving G. Thalberg Memorial Award presented to directors, performers, and companies for their contributions to the filmmaking process and the inspiration as well as entertainment to worldwide audiences.

In the beginning, the best acting category for actors and actresses was nominated for one or sometimes two or three. Eighteen Oscars from the Academy of Motion Picture Arts and

AND THE OSCAR GOES TO...

Sciences or the acronym AMPAS, for movies made between August 1, 1927, and July 31, 1928, taking place with a private dinner held in the Blossom Room of the Hollywood Roosevelt Hotel in Los Angeles, California on May 16, 1929, hosted by Douglas Fairbanks and only 270 attendees.

Several locations for ceremonies changed over the years from various rooms in venues like the Hollywood Roohitlt, Biltmore Hotel in downtown Los Angeles, the Ambassador Hotel, Shrine Auditorium, Santa Monica Civic Auditorium, Dorothy Chandler Pavilion, and presently the Dolby Theatre. When COVID hit in 2020, a much smaller venue at Union Station was used. Broadcasting went to high scales with television rights. The Oscars were first telecast in 1953 on NBC bicoastal from New York and

Los Angeles till 1957. Eventually, between NBC and ABC, unbelievably, there was a radio broadcast in 1968. ABC has broadcast the Oscar telecast since 1976, and for the first time was colorized in 1966.

Over the years, other award ceremonies began celebrating film excellence. These were the Golden Globe Awards, Screen Actors Guild Awards, Directors Guild Awards, and sometimes the Los Angeles and New York Film Critics Association Awards.

Hosting, producing, and musical directing the Academy Awards became quite a chore. Academy Awards hosts certainly changed over the years, ranging from Douglas Fairbanks, Bob Hope, Johnny Carson, Billy Crystal, David Letterman, Whoopi Goldberg, and often alternating performers to the present day, Jimmy Kimmel. Apparently, when performers hosted, it was either to promote their movies or to be nominated that evening.

I have been a movie buff all my life. My late mother and I would often watch movies late on Friday and Saturday nights and read about movies, their performers, gossip, relationships, and trivia. Over the years, I have collected media like DVDs and Blu-rays, music, and books on my favorite movies and their performers. Sadly, she passed when I was seventeen and didn't have the opportunity to have cable, streaming devices, or Turner Classic Movies.

AND THE OSCAR GOES TO...

After retirement in 2022, I toyed with ideas of writing about my two loves of baseball and Hollywood. Choosing the latter is filled with Oscar trivia through the years, real-life stars, and fictional names mixed with fame and fortune amidst the glitz and glamour of Hollywood.

Growing up in a small town in Missouri, we had two theatres, and eventually, by leaving for Texas, there were more or drive thirty-five miles to see something. One of my fondest memories is the Malone Theatre in downtown Sikeston, charging thirty-five cents for children eighteen years of age and seventy-five cents to a dollar for adults over eighteen. Cherished memories were interacting with elderly usher Hodge Decker and "ticket lady" Dorothy DeMaris before attending high school athletic events. We elementary and junior high students flocked to the theater on Friday nights, often a Saturday double feature, trying to sneak someone from the alley in the side door and sometimes getting caught. If you were caught, discipline was either a call to your parents for them to get you or sitting in the lobby until the movie ended to wait for your friends. Everyone knew everyone in Sikeston, so it was no secret we knew who was in trouble with talk on the school bus on Monday morning. The Malone Theatre was where I saw my first R-rated film there, one of Bruce Lee's kung fu paired as a double feature with the original Texas Chainsaw Massacre.

Ironically, my hometown had a church fire, leading them to

rent out the Rex Theatre, infamous for showing X-rated movies. This rattled older members of the conservative community of over 16,000 people gasping with disbelief and caused a movement for showing dirty movies at the Delta Drive-In located out in the country.

I dedicate this to all my friends and family, but most importantly, to my mother, the late Jane Culbertson, who introduced me to movies, my husband, Gary LaPalombara, a patient soul allowing me to use the computer more, and not to forget a few of my Facebook acquaintances, friend and mentor, authors Richard Bassett, Charles Casillo, David Davis, Matthew Rettenmund, Randy Schmidt, William J. Mann, and J. Randy Taraborelli and a family friend, Ron Senciboy inspiring me to attempt writing. On a personal note, not counting the above, four very dear friends and many others, far too many mentioning here, have inspired me to get a "wild hair" to write and deserve recognition as well. They are Gary Crouch, Carol Mahan, Paula Laminack McArthur, and John Reichle Jr. I couldn't have completed this journey without them either. An extra special shout out to Vickie and Steven Traylor, who both went beyond our wildest dreams, assisting in making this dream a reality. I will forever be most grateful.

A little bit of me: I was born Sunday, March 1, 1959, at 4:03 am to Edgar and Jane Culbertson, the third son and fifth child in Sikeston, Missouri, a small USA town infamous for farming, construction, and other businesses. Sikeston is approximately seventy-six miles from Blytheville, Arkansas, 140 miles from Memphis, Tennessee, and 145 miles from St. Louis, home of my lifetime favorite baseball team, the St. Louis Cardinals.

The title reads, AND THE OSCAR GOES TO; it is those five words that come babbling out of a Hollywood performer's mouth announcing the winner in a specific category at the Academy Awards ceremony.

Let us begin with how Jackie Gleason would start his variety show .... AND AWAY WE GO!

Disclaimer: I divided this into movie award seasons, when ceremonies were held in the first quarter of the year, usually in March or April, and nominations were announced in February for movies made the previous year. When reading about my characters and their work on films, it may include their post-production work, often given the time of year may or may not coincide with a film's release date. Usually, it is the year of contention to secure the Oscar nomination.

Thank you for reading!

In loving memory of:

M. Jane Culbertson 1929-1976

Eric D. Coy 1968-2024

TIM J. CULBERTSON

Carol Brewer 1938-2019

Cathy Mims McElroy 1957-2020

Chapter One

T his is the story of six individuals who, behind the scenes, obsess themselves with the glitz and glamour of Hollywood after chance meetings at a common studio commissary for lunch and conversation. Throughout this novel, they will love, hate, and fight for anything and everything for success. In the interim, they will embark on adventures you will never dream possible, from attending Oscar ceremonies for many years, traveling to exotic locations, and experiencing life-changing events to make them better people and long-term friendships/relationships with others.

1. Cole Forrester
2. Ashlee Guthrey
3. Beau Madison
4. Carole Ziegler
5. Keller, and
6. Janine Wallace

First up is Cole Forrester. Cole was born and raised with a silver spoon in Beverly Hills to a hospitality tycoon in 1933 and tried desperately to make it on his own in Hollywood. After attending Hollywood High with better-known celebrities' children and choosing not to attend college, he opted to get a job at Warner Brothers studio. Cole was willing to do anything entry-level, even if it was sweeping the lot, parking cars, the cafeteria, etc. Cole was a very handsome young man, 6'3, 175, blond, blue eyes, all American good looks, but he couldn't talk to save his life. Everything out of his mouth sounded like talking with a lisp, and his walk was all wrong, a swish here and there. Cole was determined not to sleep on his way to landing his first break, but if push came to shove, he might. Being "different," Cole did not label himself as gay in Hollywood and taboo; he certainly didn't have luck with ladies either. Working at the studio, Cole met famous performers, catching his eye but not making it known he wasn't blowing his way to the top. Right before Christmas 1958, he met a trio looking to make it big, too. They were Ashlee Guthrey, Beau Madison, and Carole Ziegler.

Ashlee Guthrey is next. Ashlee was born and raised in Davenport, Iowa, to a single mom trying to make ends meet by cleaning the offices of studios in 1935, who eventually made it to the secretarial steno pool. Ashlee couldn't type fifty words a minute nor claim fame for not having the "look" on the Warner Brothers lot from stars like Grace Kelly, Marilyn Monroe, and Elizabeth Taylor. Ashlee had flaws, and her "attitude" wasn't what they were looking for at the time. Ashlee decided to be a secretary to the big brass with her crass, foul mouth cussing like a sailor, and big boobs would get her ahead at the steno pool. You could easily find Cole, Ashlee, Beau, and Carole drinking their small studio fortunes away at the Coconut Grove in the Ambassador Hotel.

Beau Madison is next. Beau was born in 1937 to a sports-oriented but strictly guarded Pentecostal family in Memphis, Tennessee (before Elvis moved to Graceland). He hoped to become a professional basketball star with a scholarship to UCLA, but Hollywood caught his eye. Beau was famous for his love of ladies. They seemed to love him for his tanned good looks and his endowment. Word on the street was Beau made lots of ladies' heads and some guys' turn every time walking on the studio lot in his tight jeans and bulge in his crotch. Beau couldn't catch the acting bug, so he opted for behind-the-scenes as a lighting assistant. This is where he met the love of his life, an older woman, Carole Ziegler, a script girl and make-up artist to the stars.

Carole Ziegler is next. Carole was born in 1934 in Chicago, Illinois, to immigrant German and Jewish parents who relished bakery goods. Carole was a stunning dark-haired beauty like Elizabeth Taylor. The Zeiglers came to California with the dream of owning a bakery, but their dreams were dashed when their establishment was robbed and murdered in 1956. After this tragedy, Ashlee kept her figure delivering food to the studio cafeterias, where she met and fell in love with lighting assistant Beau Madison. Eventually, Carole got her foot in the door as make-up assistant to the stars and script girl. Warner Brothers and other studios allowed Carole as a "borrow" or "loan," alternating between positions with no problem.

As luck had it, the four became inseparable, doing a cocktail happy hour circuit from open to close, somehow making it to work the next day. The 1958 film season was ending, and these friendships brought something exciting to them in April 1959. Totally, expectations didn't let it bother them. Fame wasn't in their favor.

Keller and Janine Wallace were a brother and sister duo from St. Louis. They arrived in California on a whim to get away from their so-called "clingy" parents. Keller was gay like Cole, very closeted, and interested in learning new trades of the business, possibly accounting, sound effects, etc., just about anything he could learn, he was willing. Janine was his youngest, who knew her way around the secretarial aspect of business, a business school graduate, and would not take NO for an answer. Janine was determined to do anything or anybody to get results. We will learn more about them later.

AND THE OSCAR GOES TO…

Everyone's dream in Hollywood is to work in front of the camera and get recognized, star in a feature film, and possibly win an Academy Award. Right? Behind the scenes is exactly what these people wanted; they could care less for the glitz and glamour but enjoyed working closely with the best. The day would soon arrive. Ashlee, working in the steno pool of the common studios, would receive a "lifetime gift," forever changing her life. One of the common studio heads asked her if she liked the Oscars. Ashlee told them she would dress up and watch the Oscars all the time. The big brass rewarded Ashlee with Oscar tickets. Ashlee accepted them and gratefully inquired if she could have extra. It would be no problem. The rest is history.

Going to the Oscars was an important thing for Ashlee. Coming from the cornfields of Iowa, she couldn't believe it when the studio head handed the tickets to her and her friends. Ashlee told her mom, "Momma, you aren't going to fucking believe this, but your little girl, yes me, is going to the Oscars." Of course, her mom would nod her head in between drinks of scotch. By this time, Ashlee was watching her mom in the throes of early alcoholism, drinking from sunup to sundown. Ashlee felt so isolated and alone, but when she was in the company of the trio, she had no care in the world. Beau couldn't be happier attending as well, a "first" big date with Carole and being with Cole and Ashlee, just not romantically involved yet. The youngest of the foursome, Beau was giddy as a star athlete escorting the homecoming queen to the winter sports prom. Beau called home to his parents in Memphis and told them the good news. They tried being excited without showing deep concern. The Madison family wanted him to play basketball. Mr. Madison was furious, saying to him, "You know you aren't going to make it in the movies; might as well get an education and make a name for yourself." Beau finally had the balls and told them to fuck off. Not too happy with that kind of language, they abruptly cut him off.

Rent was high, and salaries for studio personnel were not extremely high dollars, so it was hard to live alone. Before the Oscar's attendance, Beau and Cole decided to forgo a platonic friendship as roommates on the Sunset Strip. They found a bungalow for $225 a month, near eight hundred square feet, small but roomy enough to make it home. It was a matter of time before Cole started a phase of bringing home every Tom, Dick, and Harry when the foursome would have drinks. Beau didn't let it bother him, only having eyes on Carole, but was too shy to express his feelings. Carole was equally excited about attending the Oscars, trying to be a "mother figure" to Ashlee or a role model. Ashlee wanted to be the "party girl." Carole was aloof, being very professional in her job, either as a make-up artist assistant or a script girl. Carole accepted what came her way and tried not to let it go to her head when sometimes the trio would stop her in her tracks. Cloud nine would sometimes come out of nowhere when one night she announced at the top of her lungs in a drunken stupor, "I got to help with Lana Turner's make-up for Peyton Place." They were so drunk to say, "Who the fuck is Lana Turner?" Once said, they all four broke up in laughter.

The friendship continued with lunches in the main commissary, fitting for shy Beau Madison, who had enough nerve to say to Carole, "Hey, since Ashlee got tickets for the four of us to the Oscars, will you be my date? I mean, a real date, just not like the weekly nights at the Grove drinking?" Carole, being cool and calculated and high and mighty as one of the oldest, said in her sultry voice, "Oh, you are just a boy, but a handsome boy. At that point, everyone will think I am paying you to be my date, especially if they see what I see through your trousers. Let it be known I don't date boys. I date men!"

What a bitch, why was Carole treating Beau like this. You would think she imitates Elizabeth Taylor in Cat on a Hot Tin Roof, but then, she gave in with her Elizabethan voice, "Yes, we can go on a date; just this once."

Fame is the name of the game in Hollywood – being at the right place at the right time. Does it look like I am trying to remind everyone of Julia Jean Turner, also known as Lana Turner, who sealed her fate and ticket to fame at Schwab's Drug Store on Sunset

Boulevard? It was here. Oscar Night 1959 rewarding excellence for movies made in 1958. Information given about this perfect night you had dueling divas Hedda Hopper and Louella Parsons laced with the word BITCH written all over their faces.

Ashlee was at Carole's apartment further down on Sunset, several blocks from Cole and Beau's bungalow, busily making their final changes to their dresses and make-up when the phone rang. It was Cole. Cole would say in his effeminate voice, "You bitches ready?" Nervously, Beau was fixing his tie, changing his shirt five times, and splashing plenty of Old Spice, drowning himself. Beau cleared with Cole, asking, "Do I look all right?" Cole waltzed over, hugging Beau with a pat on the mid-section of his tux and feeling him up to say, "Yes, princess, you look very handsome; Carole will be very happy." Pushing Cole away, Beau laughed to remind him he would never have him. Cole would be left sulking in the corner, fantasizing about Beau. The two men climbed in Beau's Cadillac Coup de Ville, the car received upon signing his letter of intent to UCLA. UCLA let Beau keep the car after he dropped out. To recall, the Cadillac Coup de Ville had 325 horsepower, a V-8 engine, and protruding from the end of the vehicle, were fine like brake light missiles. As the men pulled up to the curb of her apartment, Cole jumped out, leading the ladies by chanting. "Mi ladies, your chariot awaits." The two ladies were dressed to the nines in their as Beau couldn't take his eyes off Carole with Ashlee. They settled for second best, and they were off to the RKO Pantages Theatre. With all eyes focused on celebrities nominated this year, like Susan Hayward in I Want to Live, Paul Newman and Elizabeth Taylor in Cat on a Hot Tin Roof, Spencer Tracy in The Old Man and the Sea, and Tony Curtis and Sidney Poitier in The Defiant Ones. Who would take the prize?

The four Musketeers arrived in style, and as the valet parked their car, they stood ogling as their first adventure to the Oscars and stalked their favorite stars arriving in their limousines. Nobody stood out more than Ashlee. Her virginal white gown stood out only by her statuesque figure pushed up by her hefty breasts. As reporters and photographers waited impatiently for the arrival of celebrities, some looked more focused on Ashlee. You would wonder if there were conversations about "Who's that beauty?" to Carole appearing unfazed, walking with Beau in his tight-fitting tuxedo pants, proudly showing his endowment. Fame certainly wasn't the four playing the game. They were on cloud nine, having the time of their lives, their first Oscar ceremony, and more to come. Nobody had any significant rewards, just four simple folks living the dream of seeing Oscar history right in front of their eyes. Once in the Pantages theatre, the four snuggled in their seats. The 31st Academy Awards was about to begin with an ensemble of hosts for their pleasure. Bob Hope, Jerry Lewis, David Niven, a nominee for Separate Tables, Laurence Olivier, Tony Randall, and Mort Sahl. The Oscars began with serious banter from Niven and Olivier, but nothing could be funnier than laughter from the crowd when Hope, Lewis, Randall, and Sahl took the stage. Everyone was having a wonderful time; Cole turned Ashlee into a fag hag showing her sexy guys who were gay or bi ogling over the stars walking to their seats. Their "free" tickets were not the best, but did have a view of who's who in Hollywood. Anxiously looking at the guys hiding an erection, Cole often excused himself to the gentleman's lounge. Beau, on the first date with Carole, became nothing at first but, by evening's end, appeared quite chummy. Carole was shocked to find out Beau was only twenty-two, moved to tears upon hearing about his family estrangement, her German-Jewish upbringing, and her parents' senseless tragedy.

The awards presentation made history. Gigi, a musical, won all nine of its nominations with odd rarity and no major acting nominations. David Niven, being a host, was awarded best actor for Separate Tables; beautiful Susan Hayward won best actress for I Want to Live; Burl Ives won best-supporting actor for Big Country; the shy waif Wendy Hiller won best supporting actress for Separate Tables. The major award of best picture and director went to Gigi and Vincente Minnelli. Jerry Wald, the show's producer, cut numbers to ensure it ends on time. Luck showed too much was cut, ending thirty minutes early; asked Jerry Lewis to fill in the remainder.

AND THE OSCAR GOES TO...

With the year now a quarter over, back to work even with the Oscars on a Monday, there is no next day off. The four headed to Carole's place for a few nightcaps to hash out what they thought of their first Oscar attendance. Ashlee remarked the fashions were the bomb. Cole mentioned in an effeminate giggle the opportunity on his gentleman lounge visits. He saw a few stars' cocks at the urinal. Ignoring Cole and Ashlee, new friends, Beau and Carole couldn't keep their hands off each other. Carole busily rubbed her hands over Beau, but being a gentleman, he expressed himself by stroking her silky, beautiful hair. Cole and Ashlee, feeling left out, cleared their throat, "Beau, I think it's time we let these beauties sleep and head home. Whatcha think?"

Work started the next day, Cole parking the executive's cars at the studio lot, Ashlee back at the typewriter, taking notes from her steno pad detailing rejection letters telling them they weren't fit for the studio. Beau was learning his craft on a new film, The Apartment, a Billy Wilder comedy with Jack Lemmon, Fred MacMurray, and Shirley MacLaine. Carole had been asked to step in on a make-up stint for the new film Butterfield 8, a drama with Elizabeth Taylor and Laurence Harvey based on the John O'Hara novel. They were to meet at the common commissary for lunch. Ashlee called the gate, but Cole couldn't get away. He was "busy." This means Cole cruised the studio lot for executives, bumping into Henry Willson, a talent agent to big-name male stars who invited him over to a discrete, secluded place on the lot for a quick blow-and-go. Luck would have it; production was halted for a couple of hours on both sets, and Beau and Carole were able to catch lunch in the common. It looks like Slim Pickings is opting for sandwiches and chips. The two lovebirds sat outside catching sunny California rays. The romance was in full swing.

April's love certainly was in the air for Carole and Beau, with no beds and roses for Ashlee and Cole. Cole, being gay, doing whoever and whenever taking, he could get it. Slowly being labeled a hustler, not a male prostitute per se, but occasionally, he met an executive honcho or male star who would float him some sugar to help on rent. Poor Ashlee, between caring for her drunk mother and not wanting to go home, it was either meeting the trio for drinks at the Grove or becoming friends with other secretaries at work. As of late, staying late working on projects with studio heads provided other ulterior motives. Ashlee, going with the flow, slowly found herself being used and abused by many with nobody to talk to. In her case, crying rape or anything foul, who would believe her? For her best interest, she kept her trap shut.

Chapter Two

A s days and months passed into the new Oscar season, Carole and Beau appeared to be smitten in love with each other. At their ages, time was of the essence to stop the hand-holding and heavy petting stage to have hot sex. Who was the holdout? Cole was Cole, still not ready for a relationship, doing what was best for everyone and everywhere! Poor Ashlee, her life was in a downward spiral. Having hardly any friends besides the trio, she was through the various studios' secretarial pools. Ashlee was lonely, her alcoholic mom would not listen, and Carole was busy with Beau all the time. She was losing her only friend. Every time Oscar season rolled around, tickets became available, she saved for the trio. They were the first batch of friends she made upon her arrival to Hollywood, destined to be her last.

Oscar buzz was circulating, lots of comedies and dramas, to name a few, Some Like It Hot, one of my favorites, Imitation of

Life, Pillow Talk, the Nun's Story, Ben-Hur, etc.

Ashlee called Carole earlier to ask if waiting again for the boys at her place was ok and apologized for not connecting sooner. Carole said, "Oh, it's quite ok, Ash. I have been so busy with Beau. Between work, we only have a few hours every night." Beau often would stay late because Cole was always "busy." Carole wanted Beau so badly to commit but was patient and didn't ask any questions.

As they climbed in the car, Cole was holding the doors open for the ladies, and in a fun way, he mumbled to Beau, "So stud, when you going to get down on that?" Quite embarrassed, Beau told Cole to mind his own business and that he would get to it. At the same venue as last, the RKO Pantages Theatre with a solo host, Bob Hope, was on the dais. Doris Day was a shoo-in for Pillow Talk, Audrey Hepburn for The Nun's Story, Katharine Hepburn and Elizabeth Taylor canceled each other for Suddenly, Last Summer, and not forget sultry Simone Signoret for Room at the Top. The Oscar went to Simone. Best Actor was more demanding, Laurence Harvey for Room at the Top, Charlton Heston for Ben-Hur, Jack Lemmon for Some Like It Hot, Paul Muni for The Last Angry Man, and James Stewart for Anatomy of a Murder. Ending with a big win of eleven Oscars, surpassing last year's Gigi's nine, Ben-Hur made history with Heston taking the golden statue. Keeping the streak alive, Heston's co-stars, Hugh Griffith for Ben-Hur and Shelley Winters, won Diary of Anne Frank for Supporting Actor and Actress, respectively. Alas, no surprise Best Picture and Best Director were awarded to Ben-Hur and William Wyler.

There was time for lunch. Carole rang Ashlee over and said, "Hun, you have time for lunch, the two of us. I have something to talk about!" Ashlee replied. "Sure, doll, anything for you, I will be happy to." The two met promptly at noon in Commissary B, away from the noise and other studio personnel, for a much-overdue lunch and much-needed girl talk. They went through the buffet, opting for salads to keep their girlish figures. Between munching on salads and small talk, Ashlee spoke first, "Carole, my friend, please forgive me for rambling. I need to go elsewhere; meeting executives and actors ogles me like a piece of meat. It doesn't do any good to stay late to get ahead. Men are animals; massage my shoulders when I work, can't concentrate, and the next thing, we are in their offices with the doors locked and skirts up."

Turning red, Carole replied, "OMG, my darling, you have it bad, that's taking way advantage. Speak up for yourself and just say NO, those animals don't think twice about what they are doing." Ashlee asked what was new with Beau. Carole rambled, saying, "He won't touch me. Is it I'm too old, or is he gay? We kiss, nothing more. I feel him against my clothes when cuddling and watching TV or listening to music and dancing. I need to be aggressive with him." Carole recommended Ashlee to find another job, get a lawyer, and rid herself of these show business shenanigans. Ashlee admitted fearing coming forward and fearing the consequences of never working again in Hollywood, besides, who would believe her, like his word over hers? Carole wondered if she was helping Ashlee. Carole admired Ashlee's beautiful looks without the buxom chest, feeling she didn't have a chance. Ashlee was pouring out her heart when she said, "You there?"

Later that evening, Carole fixed a romantic dinner for Beau. Chicken Piccata over pasta, garlic bread, and tossed salad. Discussing their mutual workday over a glass of wine. Beau said, "How was your day, did you script or make up today?" Carole replied, "An easy day. I observed the lead make-up artist with Elizabeth Taylor and co-stars' had lunch with Ashlee at Commissary B?" Carole told Beau Ashlee was having a sad time both at home and at work; the poor girl just didn't know what to do. Beau, being coy, said, "My dear Carole, what are you ever thinking about? "Carole mentioned I am beginning to think you see me as a friend or don't like women. Are you gay? Beau was embarrassed to say, "No, I am not gay. You may now know the truth. I have found you sexy ever since I laid eyes on you." Carole said, "Don't worry, my darling, I think I love you!" Beau is reaching for his handkerchief and crying, "Oh, Carole, I am falling in love with you too. I didn't know how to tell you." Beau was tongue-tied and started to stutter, "I'm a virgin. I never have had sex with a girl!" Carole consoles him, "Oh baby, it is okay," and starts kissing his sweet face to reassure him everything will be okay. Whew! It took two years to get that out in the open.

What a relief that Beau isn't gay! At least they also finally told each other I LOVE YOU, which meant something to the friendship, leading to a relationship. Dinner was wonderful; the salad and pasta dishes were equally outstanding. Carole apologized there wasn't any time to stop for dessert. Beau said it was quite all right; the only thing was her by his side now and forever. Carole assured him nothing and nobody would ever come between them. You are right! Our two lovebirds made love not just once but three times until the wee hours of the morning! A night to remember and a smile on his face! The day after shines a glow; how these two lovebirds gave way to desire and hot sex. Let's hope this is the beginning of a beautiful relationship, destined forever as anything is possible. Especially for people behind the scenes, you need not worry about gossip leaked to the tabloids and paparazzi.

Chapter Three

B eau found love with Carole, and it's time to take their friendship to the next level. They are in love, and nobody is going to take it from them – a fairy tale love in Hollywood akin to Paul Newman-Joanne Woodward, Robert Wagner-Natalie Wood, or a future Richard Burton-Elizabeth Taylor. Love is in the air! Calmer times for Ashlee, she threatened the studio execs calling them out for rape and sexual harassment. Cole appeared calm, too. Beau moved in with Carole and spent more time after work watching TV or listening to music. Ashlee's mother was an alcoholic, throwing shade at her by claiming she was no good for anyone, pushing her into more despair. Cole said there were flakes in Hollywood! Certainly, didn't keep Cole from loitering at adult bookstores or the occasional gay bar. Will Cole ever understand there is more in life than just sex?

Let's hope 1961 is another good year for movies. Especially

great for Beau, who is diligently working on a new film nominated for a slew of awards. The film was Billy Wilder's The Apartment, starring nominees Jack Lemmon and Shirley MacLaine. Beau praised them for being nice to him during the shoot. It was also a night for Carole, acknowledging doing make-up for Elizabeth Taylor and her co-stars in Butterfield 8. Ashlee was still able to receive her tickets but seriously thought with name-calling and threats, she wouldn't get anything. To shut Ashlee up, these execs figured that one way to stop the bleeding would be to keep giving her tickets. This was the first year the Oscars were aired on ABC, and they took place at the Santa Monica Civic Auditorium hosted by Bob Hope. It was held on Monday, April 17th. With the lovebirds shacking up, Cole didn't mind walking down the several blocks, and Carole reminded Ashlee she could get ready over at their place. Beau and Carole were nervous. Something else brewing? The quartet arrived at the auditorium, noticing walking down and around the corner. It was the red carpet, the first time in Oscar history, and when Beau saw this, he thought no time than the present. Walking down amongst the celebrities, the execs, and nobodies like themselves, Beau yelled out, "Hey gang, wait a minute, I forgot something!"

Cole said, "Princess, what you forget now?"

Ashlee said, "Please hurry. I want to see if Elizabeth Taylor shows up!"

Beau couldn't stop himself to say, "Fuck you all, want to see some romance here?"

A few feet from Cole and Ashlee, Beau twirled Carole in his arms, yelling, "Carole Ziegler, make me the luckiest man in the world. I love you with all my heart; will you MARRY ME?" Ashlee nudged Cole. Beau, on bent knee and ring in hand, crying and laughing at the same time.

Carole screamed out, "YES OH GOD, YES, Beau Madison, I love you too, I'll marry you!" Ashlee fell, grabbing Cole's arm in excitement, hearing and seeing what had just happened. Upon stopping to their seats, Cole spotted an open cash bar and said, "Hey, let's celebrate the lovebirds with a glass of bubbly!" Carole assured the three it was ok. Standing with glasses in hand, Cole exclaimed, "To the nicest people in the world, I am happy to be your friend. Congratulations and best wishes for many years of happiness. I love you both!" Ashlee acknowledged in unison, "To my best friends, I couldn't be happier for you both!"

The award presentation was running quite smoothly until a gasp in the auditorium. Shirley Jones won Best Supporting Actress for Elmer Gantry. Shirley cast against type, given her musical background, and against front-runner Janet Leigh for the shower thriller Alfred Hitchcock's Psycho. Peter Ustinov won Best Supporting Actor for Spartacus, Burt Lancaster carried Elmer

AND THE OSCAR GOES TO…

Gantry to a gold statuette as Elizabeth Taylor for Butterfield 8 was the sentimental winner after losing her husband Mike Todd in a plane crash and her near-fatal illness resulting in a tracheotomy. The last two awards, Best Picture and Best Director, went to Billy Wilder for directing the comedy-drama The Apartment.

The Oscar season ended beautifully. Carole was busy planning a June wedding. Right as the rain, summer blockbuster movies were rolling. Carole was assigned script girl for the Robert Wise musical West Side Story, while Beau was doing a Paul Newman drama, The Hustler. The movie schedules were tightly set, and Beau and Carole quickly had to "I do" or wait for Carole on location with West Side Story. The early buzz generated West Side Story was going to sweep next year's Oscar season! West Side Story was HUGE, with lots of work to be done in New York City. Carole feared Beau would succumb to Cole's flirtatious ways. Production on West Side Story pushed forward faster. Wise requested crew on location by April's end.

After many months on location, Carole was so happy to see Beau, pressured to set a wedding date. Beau, so lonely in Carole's absence, stayed quite busy with his blockbuster, The Hustler, working with his idol, blue-eyed Adonis, Paul Newman. Sitting down for dinner, Beau asked Carole, "Sweetheart, before we start the next year, you think we need to set a date?" Carole replied with excitement, "Yes darling, I think, why don't we ask Cole and Ashlee to drive to Vegas with us, and we get married in one of those wedding chapels!" It would give Ashlee a change of scenery after the months of her forever mother issues. Ashlee's mother would be better off dead, the way she has been treating her! It isn't fair. A weekend getaway would do some good. It was set to celebrate Christmas and New Year's Eve, drive to Vegas and get married. Looking at the calendar, New Year's Eve, 1961, was a Sunday. Lovebirds thought they could drive Friday after work, get married Saturday evening, and drive back late Sunday afternoon, just in time to go back to work on Tuesday, January 2, 1962. Beau asked a studio friend to call Flamingo to make reservations for two rooms. The ladies could sleep in one and then switch for the wedding night. Don't think it would hurt Cole to be straight for one night, letting Ashlee sleep with him, LOL. Ashlee assured Cole that she wouldn't change him.

Upon arrival, the quartet settled into their rooms after a four-hour drive from Hollywood and time for a quick stroll around the strip and dinner. Beau promised Cole and Ashlee they were standing for him and Carole. Room was on him, meals, drinks, the whole nine yards. Despite wages not being the best for studio help, Beau reassured all monies had been saved and determined to make Carole his bride. Saturday afternoon, December 30, 1961, the lovebirds and friends drove over to the Little Chapel of Flowers. As the owner of the chapel pronounced husband and wife, all you could hear was loud crying. LOL. The quartet was singing and laughing like old times on the drive back to Hollywood. Their friendship was three years, growing strong, wondering what was in store for the rest of their lives. Where were they going with their careers in Hollywood? How many celebrities were they going to meet and still enjoy their fun at the Academy Awards?

Chapter Four

P reparing for award season, speculation perked for well-deserved performances this year, having two or three films worthy of consideration. Case in point, exquisite Audrey Hepburn made Breakfast at Tiffany's and The Children's Hour, and Natalie Wood made Splendor in the Grass and West Side Story. Sure-fire nods were certain to go to the heavy drama Judgement at Nuremberg and the musical West Side Story, scoring twelve nominations. The 34th annual Academy Awards were presented on Monday, April 9, 1962, at the Santa Monica Civic Auditorium (again) and again hosted by Bob Hope. As the norm, Ashlee scored tickets for the quartet to attend. Carole was stoked to see Natalie Wood with her Splendor co-star, Warren Beatty, fresh from her break up with Robert Wagner. Tongues were wagging everywhere, and not to mention Cole was on the prowl! Grr. Joan Crawford was on hand to present Maximilian Schell for his stirring turn in Judgment at

AND THE OSCAR GOES TO...

Nuremberg, Burt Lancaster presented Sophia Loren a surprise win for Two Women over Natalie Wood for Splendor in the Grass, and Audrey Hepburn a hopeful for Breakfast at Tiffany's. A sheer delight was Andy Williams singing "Moon River," giving Henry Mancini an Oscar for Best Song. West Side Story had heavy momentum, winning eleven of twelve nominations; both supporting awards went to George Chakiris and Rita Moreno and co-directors Jerome Robbins and Robert Wise. Nobody could be happier than Carole, who had a challenging time cheering the sulking Beau, whose work on The Hustler went unnoticed, drinking at the cash bar with a Vodka tonic. Let's hope Beau will get his due soon so as not to cause a rift in the early months of wedded bliss!

As fate would have it, turnabout fair play, Beau landed the job of a lifetime, meaning possible separations for the newlyweds. Carole had several projects in the works to keep her busy and prevent her from missing her man. Carole was doing make-up on The Miracle Worker, Whatever Happened to Baby Jane, and Days of Wine and Roses; she was thoroughly excited because she worked with two legends (drum roll please), Bette Davis and Joan Crawford. Preliminary work had already begun, but there were lots of people working on the next blockbuster. David Lean was requesting extra lighting in exotic Jordan, Morocco, London, and Spain for Lawrence of Arabia. Luck would have it; there was a delay in filming, and most didn't have passports. Time was essential, preparing Beau to leave, passport first, and, secondly, asking Ashlee to come and stay with Carole. Ashlee obliged, and even Cole said he would stop by to check on the "bitches" in between his trysts. Cole was slowing down with a new job at one of the studios. Cole wasn't going to be parking cars or ogling the kingpins, actors, etc. There was a new job working in the accounting department as an accounting clerk.

Beau promised he would write and cable Carole as much he could from the grueling locations. Little did he know the fictional "attack" scene of the film was located on the beach called Playa del Algarrobico near Carboneras, which is close to Almeria in Southern Spain. Beau was excited he was going to meet famous actors from his generation like O'Toole, Guinness, and Quinn. This is the first film of its genre to have no female speaking roles. As filming started late fall, studios panicked it wouldn't receive the praise in time for Oscar nominations being released in early 1963.

Carole stayed busy working on the films mentioned above as the dynamic duo of Ashlee and Cole kept her company. Evenings in between, Ashlee watched her mother continue to drink herself in a stupor slowly and Cole working feverishly overtime in the accounting department to learn the "ropes." Fall weather fell in California with lots of cool rain in the evenings and sunny skies by day. The trio did the best they could under the circumstances. Never in his wildest, Beau thought he would want to do that again. David Lean enjoyed Beau's hard work ethic and later asked for his services for the next shoot, Doctor Zhivago in Russia. Beau appreciated the offer and told Lean he needed to spend more time with his wife.

The holiday movie season was amongst us as Carole's work on The Miracle Worker was completed and released in late July. Whatever Happened to Baby Jane was released on Halloween, and the drama Days of Wine and Roses was set to be released before the end of the year. Many others were vying for the nominations to be announced in February 1963.

Chapter Five

The season promised an epic of all epics, heavy dramas tackling courtroom drama, alcoholism, sister rivalries, the correctional system involving real people, and, end of all, a wonderful drama based on real-life characters in performances resonating with others for a lifetime. Critics were buzzing about who would get the much-needed momentum to sway the Academy voters. Will all the challenging work Beau put in Lawrence of Arabia pay off as the three films that Carole tirelessly put her heart and soul into their short marriage separated from afar stand the test? Nominees ranged from Jack Lemmon and Lee Remick for the raw Days of Wine and Roses, Anne Bancroft and Patty Duke for The Miracle Worker, Burt Lancaster in the real-life prison drama, Birdman of Alcatraz and Gregory Peck in the courtroom drama, To Kill a Mockingbird based on the best-selling novel by Harper Lee.

Ashlee accepted a new position; beaming with pride and

victory in her heart, she felt accomplished, dusting herself off and starting over. The position was in part of an agreement not to squeal on the men who sexually, physically, and emotionally harassed her; Ashlee asked keeping lifetime tickets to the Oscars would sweeten the deal to keep her trap shut. The studio executives didn't think twice; this was the easiest way out of a tricky situation. Ashlee promised if they didn't cooperate with her not-so-ordinary request, they would have hell to pay by screaming at the tabloid queens of gossip. You knew you would have been had if Louella and Hedda got the scoop.

Cole was enjoying his new job, learning something new, by keeping his dick in his pants at least during daytime hours. Cole was beginning to collect knowledge of deep studio secrets, their financial highs and lows, being resourceful for Beau and Carole in their decision-making process on a studio producing the latest blockbusters.

The 35th Academy Awards ceremony was held Monday, April 8, 1963, at the Santa Monica Civic Auditorium (again). The host this year was Frank Sinatra. Last year's supporting actor winner, George Chakiris, presented favorite Patty Duke with her stunning performance as a young Helen Keller for The Miracle Worker. To keep with Oscar tradition, last year's supporting actress, Rita Moreno, presented Ed Begley for Sweet Bird of Youth. Critics' darling epic Lawrence of Arabia won both Best Picture and Best

Director, and David Lean won seven of ten nominations. It was no surprise to members that handsome Gregory Peck received the Best Actor award as Atticus Finch for To Kill a Mockingbird. Drawing close to the Best Actress award, tense moments were created. Joan Crawford, who was subbed a nod when co-star Bette Davis received a final career nod for Whatever Happened to Baby Jane, graciously told the other actresses' nominees that if absent, she would accept on their behalf. Maximillian Schell announced Anne Bancroft as Helen Keller's teacher and Annie Sullivan in The Miracle Worker as Best Actress. Crawford had the last laugh upstaging Davis accepting for Bancroft, who had a Broadway commitment. Davis and Crawford were to star in Hush, Hush Sweet Charlotte to continue the supposed feud, but Crawford fell ill and abruptly left production and was replaced by Olivia De Havilland. Before year's end, the Academy announced a new award would be added: best sound effects. This proves beneficial for Cole to better his resume with more behind-the-scenes work on the soundstage for the first time, assisting on a slew of future films.

1963 was quite a year, with Cleopatra starting to garner quite a buzz not so soon after the ceremony was over. Cleopatra started filming back in September 1960 with Elizabeth Taylor in the lead, being paid, at the time, a record-setting salary of a million dollars. Due to Taylor's health and other executive decisions, the film was in jeopardy. The film restarted production in late 1961 and was made ready for the public in 1962, but fate had many reshoots stretched into early 1963. Massive production costs surpassed millions after grossing almost fifty-eight million United States, Canada, and worldwide receipts termed it a hit. Several years later, critics labeled it a bomb. The best way to summarize the ordeal was to pair Taylor with Welsh actor Richard Burton. It was the beginning of a torrid yet troublesome love affair developed in one of the greatest acting duos. Leaving question marks unanswered for future audiences was the duo a real deal. In between the Hollywood nonsense, our quartet decided to work on fewer extravaganzas with different genres, targeting audiences for enjoyment at a grander scale.

Back at work, the quartet was available to occasionally meet for lunches and after-work happy-hours dinners at the Grove. The newlyweds, still in the honeymoon phase, were teased by Ashlee and Cole for being fuddy-duddies and staying home more. Politics was taking over Beau, being both mesmerized and infatuated with the presidency of one John F. Kennedy. Beau imitated the way Kennedy talked with a Boston accent and emulated his sexual prowess as a stud. Carole was in stitches with laughter. Beau didn't let the Hollywood gossip affect his Kennedy obsession. As everyone knew, being a Kennedy, as well as John and his younger brother, Robert, vied for bombshell Marilyn Monroe's attention, ending in tragedy. There was circulated gossip Robert F. Kennedy was in Hollywood talking to his brother, John, on the ill-fated August night Monroe ended her life with a barbiturate overdose. In November

1963, Beau's impersonation of political satire was tarnished when John F. Kennedy was assassinated by Lee Harvey Oswald, leaving the entire world in shock for days, weeks, months, and years to come. United States history would never be the same. Beau moped around like a little puppy dog for weeks, leaving Carole for the remainder of 1963 to get him out of his funk.

Chapter Six

T he Oscar nominations were announced in February 1964 with few notable surprises. Tom Jones, the historical comedy farce, had three, yes, three supporting actress nominations, and Sidney Poitier became the first African American male to be nominated for Best Actor in a Leading Role. Several films got five or more nominations: Tom Jones led with ten, Cleopatra with nine, How the West was Won with eight, and rounding out another popular favorite with seven was Hud. Two older nominees over seventy were vying for best-supporting roles, Margaret Rutherford for the VIPs and Melvyn Douglas for Hud. It looked like Newman was a lock for Best Actor; would he spoil the Poiter momentum and secure his first win over his former co-star?

To keep their marriage fresh, an opportunity for Carole to put the finishing touches on Cleopatra, but Carole politely refused by shifting gears as an assistant writer for Lilies of the Field and

Love with a Proper Stranger. Beau secured lighting jobs for Hud and Captain Newman, M.D. Cole was reeling in his new sound effects position working on the Air Force testosterone-fueled drama, A Gathering of Eagles, starring studs in Hollywood, handsome Rock Hudson, and sexy Australian hunk Rod Taylor.

Around Easter Sunday, the ladies spent the weekend shopping for new dresses as the men tagged along for shits and grins. Hating shopping, it gave the men time for a stroll down Rodeo Drive, scoping out celebrities with luck on their side; out of the corner of Beau's eye, they noticed Natalie Wood with her sister, Lana.

Oscar evening approached April 13th, 1964; the lights shined bright on the Santa Monica Civic Auditorium. Celebrities started their way for a fun night with Jack Lemmon selected to host. Beau was excited to meet Paul Newman and his wife, the lovely Joanne Woodward, and bumped into Sidney Poitier and Natalie Wood. Cole was hoping to see either or both Rock Hudson and Rod Taylor in the men's lounge. History was made this year; Poitier was the first African American male nominated for winning Best Actor. Patricia Neal and Melvyn Douglas won their respective Best Actress and Best Supporting Actor awards for Hud. Margaret Rutherford won Best Supporting Actress for the VIPs, being one of the oldest winners, and Tom Jones won Best Picture.

AND THE OSCAR GOES TO...

Business as usual, the studios rushed back to work after last night's ceremony, and Ashlee returned to the offices earlier than usual. Carole and Beau offered a sleepover on the couch and a ride to work in the morning, but she politely declined to say she needed to check on her mother. Being the gentleman, Beau graciously walked her to the door. No sooner than Ashlee turned the key, loud music came from inside out to the street. Ashlee, so embarrassed, you heard a scream, "Ashlee, it's about time you got your ass home; get in here and fix me another drink," Beau asked Ashlee if it was ok to leave her and reaffirm the offer to stay with them. Ashlee nodded, and it was ok. The next morning as Ashlee prepared for work, her mom staggered to yell, "Well, you little whore, how was the Oscars? Did you let anyone fuck you in the powder room?" Ashlee said, "Mom, leave me alone. I am running late for the bus and work; I need to get there early." Ashlee's mom screeched, pulling on her hair to ask her to please stay home. Ashlee reassured her mom she would leave early and come straight home. Startled from earlier, worried about her Mom, Ashlee started typing her daily assignments. Ashlee decided to take a breather around 10:15 after being there for almost three hours. The studio head left her urgent instructions: travel plans needed to be made with itineraries sent to the United States film crew in Naples, Italy, making Marriage, Italian Style. Ashlee called home on her break and found it odd; nobody answered. Ashlee became very worried. Finally, Ashlee went to the ladies' room to freshen her make-up; she went to the lead secretary of the steno pool and said, "I came in earlier to ready travel documents, but it's very necessary; I need to check on my mom." Trying not to bring the feel sorry for me pity look, Ashlee told the lead her mom was an alcoholic and needed some assistance. The lead took one look up with glasses down to her nose and said, "Oh darling, I am so sorry we are so behind in these docs. If you must go, go, but please let me know if there is anything we can do; call us, OK?" Ashlee said, "I am sorry. I will let you know." Ashlee grabbed her purse from the desk drawer and scurried out of the office to the sidewalk. A guard nodded to say, "Have a great day!" Reciprocating the nod, she hurried down the sidewalk as fast as her legs carried her. The next bus was another five minutes, as this was going to be the longest five minutes of Ashlee's life. Riding on the bus, Ashlee sat across the aisle from a smiley drunk bum, making sexist remarks about her looks, making her three shades of red. Walking three blocks down from the bus stop, Ashlee noticed a few police cars out front. Assuming the worst, Ashlee walked down the sidewalk, head held high, met at the front by a police officer and the apartment manager, old fart Louie Freeman. Louie stopped Ashlee in her tracks and told her not to go any further. Ashlee screamed, "OH NO, Mommy, NO!" Running down the sidewalk to the apartment, Ashlee saw the front door wide open and policemen wrapping yellow tape around the front door. Ashlee politely told the officer she lived there and needed to go inside. One of the officers told Ashlee it was not pretty. As Ashlee pushed the officer aside, she walked inside to find her mom lying on the couch in her robe and nightgown wrapped tightly around her cold body. Ashlee's mother was dead. Sobbing uncontrollably, Ashlee thought to herself why her mother would do this to her. Ashlee stared at the floor in front of the couch; there were scotch and vodka bottles, one empty and the other half full. Looks like Ashlee's mother had drunk herself to a fast way out with an empty Seconal bottle near her outstretched hand. Shocked beyond disbelief, Ashlee was relieved her mom was gone. The way she died, but why did she do it? Ashlee figured it was a blessing, no more loud curdling screams of whore and slut coming from moms' lips. Now, Ashlee could get on with life and make something out of it. Ashlee wept; she let the police officers call an ambulance to get her mom. Still a bit shocked, where could they take the body? The attendants told Ashlee they were going to the Coroner's office in Los Angeles.

First things first, Ashlee called at work, telling them that she would take the next several days off to arrange everything. Julie, the steno pool lead, gave her some numbers to call and plan. Julie told Ashlee to contact a studio head as they would help with some expenses. Ashlee called to find where Carole was. Carole was working on the set, doing make-up and scripting girl tasks for Where Love Has Gone, a vehicle starring Susan Hayward and Bette Davis.

Carole was at a loss for words. She said when she finished dallies, she would stop to find Cole and come over for company while Beau was working late on the comedy What a Way to Go! Ashlee sounded a bit better after talking to Carole. Julie followed up with Ashlee, and the studio president said anything Ashlee needed would be taken care of. It's the least they could do for what she has in the studios. Ashlee settled on the suggested Pierce Brothers Mortuary and Forest Lawn as the cemetery in the Hollywood Hills. The only reason to gain attention and have a father figure, Ashlee was raised by a single mother, coming to Hollywood from Iowa in hopes of getting her foot in the door and making a splash on the big screen. Rejection after rejection, Ashlee's mother made commercials to get by, hoping for that big break, but nothing came her way. Besides all these rejections, trying to stay optimistic, Ashlee's mother attempted to sleep her way to the top, but when rejected, the drinking began, taking Ashlee to clubs or being left at home alone. Jeez, Louise, what a downward spiral she would weave. Living from paycheck to paycheck, the family ended up close to being homeless, but an anonymous studio head gave her mother an offer not to be refused. This gentleman offered to pay their rent on condition that she didn't spill any malicious words about him or any other studio's wrongdoings. This wasn't known to Ashlee until after her mother was six feet under. Ashlee claimed she would never look back and keep her lips sealed what her mother had done and duplicated before her eyes. Ashlee found it hard to face either failure or success but decided to take charge of her life and learn to say NO.

The movie season was full of music in the ears of moviegoers. The Beatles made a movie, Broadway's Darling; Julie Andrews was snubbed from being cast in My Fair Lady. However, she eventually signed with Disney to do the children's favorite, Mary Poppins and Debbie Reynolds became the Unsinkable Molly Brown. Heavy dramas were headliners: Dr. Strangelove, Becket, Seven Days in May, The Chalk Garden, and The Night of the Iguana.

Chapter Seven

W ouldn't It Be Loverly, one of everyone's favorite songs from the musical My Fair Lady, led the way, swooning in the academy members' hearts as the nominations were announced in February 1965. History continued to be made as three of the five Best Picture nominations scored more than ten, Mary Poppins led with thirteen, and My Fair Lady and Becket scored twelve.

Julie Andrews and Debbie Reynolds scored Best Actress nominations, including dramatic turns for men such as Richard Burton, Peter O'Toole, and Peter Sellers, and with musicals scoring many nominations, it is interesting who will win. As mentioned, Audrey Hepburn, taking over the role in the film version of My Fair Lady from Julie Andrews, was snubbed in the Best Actress category; Julie got the last laugh singing in Mary Poppins. George Cukor asked Marni Nixon to sing for Hepburn, who also dubbed for Natalie Wood in West Side Story.

AND THE OSCAR GOES TO...

The ceremony grew closer, with Ashlee still withdrawn over the death of her mother. Beau and Carole stayed busy working, and Cole was relishing his new work adventure. Sound effects were becoming a following, and he found his work assignments quite challenging. But forever as a horned dog, Cole couldn't stop talking about the hotness he worked with. Cole wondered what would be any hotter than Hudson or Taylor; his second gig assigned him to The Lively Set. The movie was set around the car racing circuit, leaving it to the imagination to ogle over James Darren and Doug McClure. Over cocktails with the trio, Cole couldn't stop talking about the two hunks rising in the ranks of heartthrobs for teenage girls around the world. Ashlee was trying her best not to let the first anniversary of her mom's death rattle her. Ashlee focused on working hard in the studio steno pool by finding time to have lunch and the occasional after-work happy hour with the trio. Friends are what she needed now, more than ever. And their annual trek to the Academy Awards was more fun.

For the 14th time and a couple of year's absence, Bob Hope was selected to host the 37th Academy Awards (again) being held at the Santa Monica Civic Auditorium in Santa Monica. As the stars hurried into the auditorium, the quartet was running a tad late; Beau took Ashlee to Forest Lawn to place flowers on her mom's grave. All was okay; Beau wanted to ensure all four were ready for a fun-filled with music in the air piping from the speakers outside from

My Fair Lady and Mary Poppins soundtracks. Running to the doors, you could hear A Spoonful of Sugar leaving to the imagination of the quartet kicking their heels in unison. As the awards were presented, My Fair Lady outshined Mary Poppins, not showing any ill feelings; it proved a reunion for Broadway co-stars Rex Harrison won Best Actor for My Fair Lady and Julie Andrews won Best Actress for Mary Poppins. Peter Ustinov won Best Supporting Actor for Topkapi, and Lila Kedrova won Best Supporting Actress for Zorba the Greek. My Fair Lady slayed the competition, winning eight out of twelve statues, including Best Picture and Best Director George Cukor.

Ashlee decided to call out the day after the Oscars. Ashlee said to herself, "I must find a new place. I can't stay here forever." Ashlee asked Cole and Carole if any apartments were available at their complexes. Cole said he would check but was on his way to Austria finishing sound effects for Blake Edwards' The Great Race starring Tony Curtis, Natalie Wood, and Jack Lemmon. Carole would check at her complex while doing script girl duties for A Patch of Blue starring Sidney Poitier, and Beau was doing lighting for A Thousand Clowns.

Ashlee had become good friends with one of the newest steno pool secretaries, Janine Wallace. Janine had just moved here from St. Louis, hoping to make it big in show business. Janine was optimistic after attending both the University of Missouri-Columbia and business school in Memphis, inspired by the big city of Los Angeles and to see what Hollywood offered. Janine was just a tad over twenty-one, the legal age for the afternoon happy hours the quartet still had at the Grove. Ashlee called Carole and asked if she'd meet to give Janine the low down on Hollywood. Carole obliged, saying a few blockbusters needed her attention but happy to meet the new member and add to the quartet. Janine said there was one drawback: her older brother, Keller. Janine embarrassingly noted he was gay but timid. Carole and Ashlee said that would be great as they had the perfect man to meet Keller, and of course, it is one Cole Forrester. Sadly, Cole was still in Austria and on his way back in just a matter of days. Ashlee thought to herself, Janine was working in the steno pool with her. She would secure Keller a job in accounting or wherever Keller felt comfortable. As soon as Janine and Keller got situated, Ashlee called her ex-studio competitor and talked with the head honcho managing her ongoing grievances. Dalton Mueller was his name, and not to be fucked with, but Ashlee had him in her back pocket. Anytime Ashlee needed anything, and I mean anything, Ashlee would get it. As you recall, Ashlee had these executives' brass balls blasted all over the place. Whatever Ashlee asked for, whether big or small, she wanted to extend the tickets from four to six attendees to future Academy Award ceremonies. Of course, Dalton would take care of it.

Ashlee found a medium 2-bedroom apartment where Carole

and Beau lived to share with the Wallace duet; Keller didn't mind sleeping on the couch, hoping very gay Cole Forrester would like him. LOL Coming from St. Louis, trying to free from "clingy" parents. The duo needed a fresh start. Ever so thankful to Ashlee and Carole's gracious friendship and fast-moving in securing them both employment within the highly competitive studio back-stabbing system and a place over their head was more than enough. How would they ever pay for their generosity?

The following two months were rapidly passing by. Ashlee had sent Cole a cable over to Austria to explain his anticipation for his return. Cole quizzed Ashlee, "Why?" Ashlee had a man for him to meet. Cole reluctantly asked her if she could hold till the Cole middle of June before his return. Post-production on the Great Race had ended. Unexpectedly, his parents, Stewart and Rebecca, showed up at his hotel, the Marietta in Obertauren. As usual, Cole bluntly exclaimed, "Why the FUCK are you here?" Rebecca, being coy, said, "Darling, we are here to see you."

Cole said, "This is FUCKING BULLSHIT, how did you even know where I was?" Stewart said, "Now, son, don't talk to your mother like this; you know it's not every day we get to see our son." Cole bounced back and said, "You haven't seen me in six years, and you just suddenly show up, what the FUCK!" Stewart said, "Calm down, son; if you must know, Mother has been asked to do some backup designs with designer Julie Harris for the new

AND THE OSCAR GOES TO…

Beatles movie HELP!" "They are due here in Austria in the next few weeks. Cole said, "OK! I was about to head back to Hollywood; my friends need me, especially dear Ashlee; she lost her mother and is still grieving." Cole abruptly moved out, trying to get out from underneath their thumb, too. Stewart and Rebecca never could understand Cole being gay, as he wanted to be on his own and prove he could make it. Cole promised his parents to stay for another day, but he had to get back to Hollywood and find out about his new sound effects assignment. Not to mention, especially after Ashlee mentioned meeting the Wallace duo of Janine and Keller, he was anxious to meet them and see if there would be sparks between him and Mr. Keller Wallace. Now, after all that, Beau and Carole were determined by the end of 1965 or early 1966 there were a few things on the agenda concerning our dear Ashlee and Cole,

1) Get Ashlee out of her funk (stop mourning Mom)
2) Concentrate more on work (not much happy hour)
3) Get Ashlee in a safe environment/relationship.
4) Include the Wallace duo and welcome them to the fold.
5) Help Ashlee find Cole a steady relationship (Keller Wallace) (evil grin)

Cole left Austria and his parents behind with nothing resolved on a new relationship in the future. It was apparent they weren't too concerned about making up lost time either; nothing ventured, nothing gained. Cole was ready to get back to his friends and Hollywood. After six years working in the Hollywood system, Cole finally found his niche in the sound effects department. Granted, it was a massive leap of faith, and Cole finally made it on his own, leaving behind the richness and snobbery of Beverly Hills.

Upon returning home to Los Angeles from New York and Salzburg, Cole was exhausted; all he wanted was a Dewars and soda to relax. Beau met Cole at the airport, hoping he was hungry because Carole had fixed two big dishes of her favorite lasagna and invited Ashlee. Beau told Cole to act surprised as Ashlee was bringing guests. Yes, you were right. Ashlee invited the Wallace duo to meet Cole. Err, correction there, and Cole will meet Keller and see if the two "girls" would "hit" it off. Time will tell. Beau said, "Oh, you are going to like Keller; he looks like a dead ringer for Tab Hunter." Cole remarked, "Hope he doesn't mind talking to a whiny, spoiled Beverly Hills brat!' "You will be fine, Cole, don't worry," Beau said. Beau ran Cole by his place to drop off his luggage and get a quick shower to freshen. As Beau waited, Cole yelled out, "Hey babe, you want to wash my back." Cole knew damn well he would never have Beau; it was worth a shot when Beau came in the bathroom to pee. I see where you are going on this, and it's in your mind, but nothing is happening! Get your evil minds out of the gutter, and Cole peered around the shower curtain, glancing at Beau's manhood. Beau said, "I am a married man now; we can't go down this road." "Besides, you are going to meet your future boyfriend tonight in Keller Wallace." Cole finished his shower, toweling off as he walked into the living area. Cole started flashing Beau his ass, and cock, of course, was not budging. "Cole, I am not playing. I have told you I am not interested in you. Can you please hurry?" Beau yelled to him as he was getting ready.

Waiting ever so patiently, Keller and Janine were waiting outside the office for Ashlee; Keller said, "So, sis, wonder how things will go with this Cole guy Ashlee wants to set me up with." Janine replied, "Bro, I don't know; I hear he is effeminate and a spoiled rich Beverly Hills brat." Janine further referred to Keller, saying Cole should be perfect, considering the last relationship Keller had in St. Louis was a whiny music teacher. As Ashlee said goodbye to Dalton, she closed his office door behind her and said, "Kids, are you ready to make some new friends? Let's get the fuck out of here! The trio ran down the sidewalk to the studio lot, and Keller said, "Ashlee dear, do we need to stop and get any refreshments?" Ashlee said, "That's so sweet. Maybe we can get some red and white wine for the pasta." Janine giggled like a little schoolgirl working by cooing, "Wine, I just love wine." It was Friday, and the weekend was here; time for everyone to let their hair down and have a wonderful time. The trio arrived early from Ashlee's meeting with Dalton, now waiting on the gay boy and Carole's husband. Time would tell when they arrive, especially after Beau rebuffed Cole's advances yet again. Will it ever get through his head that Beau is simply not interested, no matter what Cole does? He does not want to get naked with him. Yet again, being rejected, Cole needed a drink before they left for the feast. Beau told Cole several times he would not be jumping the fence for anyone because Carole was his one and only. The boys finally arrived, and as soon as they were walking in the door, Ashlee rushed up to Cole, asking about his trip overseas, making a complete fool out of herself. Cole rapidly excused himself to the kitchen where Carole was busy, sneaking in a quick peck on her cheek, "Hi you, doll face, how's tricks?" Carole said, "Calm down, go back in the living room and meet our new friends." Cole walked back into the room and said, "So, Ash, are you going to introduce me to your new friends from the Show Me State, or do I have to do it myself." Ash said, "Oh, excuse me, Cole, this is Keller and Janine Wallace from St. Louis, Missouri; I am so sorry, dear heart." As Cole walked up to them, he kissed Janine on the cheek and said, "Welcome to Hollywood, the pleasure is all mine," and from the corner of his eye, he winked over at Keller, stretching his hand out to shake it, "Nice meeting you both!"

The quartet was getting acquainted. Beau went into the kitchen to help Carole and apologized for their delay, trying to explain Cole's aggressive behavior. Carole laughed it off by telling Beau not to sweat it because she was concerned that matchmaking would be in the air tonight. As Carole and Beau were finishing

AND THE OSCAR GOES TO…

dinner preparations, they could hear conversations ranging from what brought them to Hollywood and how they liked the studio system. Janine chimed in by detailing it was rough putting up with some of the hardnosed executives, and Keller said he was getting his way around the sound effects department. Cole let a big whoop and said, "You are kidding me, right? You can't be in the same department as me!" Ashlee said, "I told you, Cole, Keller is in the same place as you; that's why I thought it would be nice for you to meet." Cole was feeling excited now by remarking whether there was room for two queens. Everyone roared with laughter as Carole announced dinner was ready.

With the meal going smoothly, the six were getting along famously; nobody noticed except for Cole and Keller. Keller was rubbing his leg up and down Cole's. Cole was getting woody and desperately trying to hide it with his napkin, but embarrassingly, nothing was working. During dinner discussion, Ashlee mentioned she had Oscar tickets in hopes Keller and Janine were fans because they would be included in the quartet's annual festivities.

The year ended well; Cole and Keller hit it off and started spending more time together. It was either at work, bidding for the same films, and after, instead of going to the Grove, Cole would fix dinner at his place. Ashlee and Carole included Janine in lunches when Beau was on location off the studio lot. Janine explained to the ladies that Keller and she were very appreciative of the attention given to them. Janine gushed that she already had a "crush" on someone. To their surprise, more so to Ashlee, Janine had the "hots" for one Dalton Mueller. Dalton Mueller was a snake, but Ashlee determined to let Janine find out for herself. Dalton was a married man but that didn't stop him from flirting through aggressive maneuvers with ladies in the offices. Dalton knew better than to do anything in front of Ashlee, fearful of being ratted to Janine. Dalton kept his wits about himself and tried desperately to keep his cock in the pants around the office.

Chapter Eight

T he award season looked quite competitive from the end of 1965 to the beginning of 1966, and epics were seen with glowing reviews from critics and fans alike. Peers were trying to figure out who would take the most nods; two of my mom's favorites were destined: Dr. Zhivago and The Sound of Music. Both were very lavish productions, and the direction of David Lean and Robert Wise was impeccable.

The nominations were announced on February 21st, and three of our sextet were on the edge of their seats, hoping the films they feverishly worked on would grab some nods. It's too bad Beau opted out of going to Russia to film Dr. Zhivago, but his lesser title, A Thousand Clowns, garnered four nods to Zhivago's ten, tied with The Sound of Music. Carole's work on A Patch of Blue garnered five, Cole's The Great Race got five as well, and his father's mentor, designer Julie Harris, got one for Darling. Looking like a battle of

Julie's as both Julie Christie and Julie Andrews were nominated. The ceremony will be held again at the Santa Monica Civic Auditorium with Bob Hope at the helm. It will finally be richly presented with an Honorary Oscar for his unique and distinguished service. It would also be the first time that the telecast was in color.

As April 18th drew closer, the ladies were trying to figure out where to get their gowns; Carole and Ashlee assured Janine they would have her dressed to the nines to show her off. As for the gentlemen, Beau and Cole kept it simple: getting Keller fit in a tuxedo, making both guys and gals swoon. Cole had other ideas; in just a few short months of meeting Keller, he wasn't about to let him out of his sight; he wanted Keller forever. Cole was smitten with Keller; obviously, the feelings were mutual. Cole didn't shy away from his feelings for Keller and even told the trio he was thinking of asking him to move in but was nervous. Janine was scared for her brother since it was a big city compared to St. Louis, and she did not want to see him get hurt. Ashlee had warned Janine of the snakes in the steno pool; sadly, Janine was naïve and didn't listen very well. Janine found herself in dire straits and falling so deep she couldn't get out. Janine found herself in the throes of an affair with Dalton Mueller. Always putting other feelings before her own, Janine was hurting inside because Dalton Mueller was using her as many others before Dalton was married and could not risk a divorce yet, falsely assuring all his mistresses before there would be marriage. Janine kept it a secret for now, pregnant and unsure about what to do with an unborn child. Janine had not even told Keller or her new confidant, Ashlee. Janine was fearful of what percussions she would do if told Keller, as he was very overprotective of his sister and often had a temper.

It was shop till you drop for Oscar gowns, the ladies making last-minute choices down Rodeo Drive, getting fitted and having cocktails, or at least Carole and Ashlee were. Carole noticed Janine was not drinking and mentioned it to Ashlee. Ashlee reassured Carole it was nothing but knew damn well something was wrong. Sitting in the dressing area with champagne and awaiting Janine's exit from a dressing room to show them her gown, Ashlee excused herself. Ashlee shouted out, "Janine dear, you need some help in there," Janine shouted back, "Sure, come on in, just can't seem to get this." As Ashlee walked into the area where Janine stood, she said, "Oh my God, girl, you got a little bump there that wasn't quite here a few weeks ago." Janine said, "Oh, don't mind me, it's all those chips we have been snacking on watching the late show." Ashlee knew better; Janine was indeed preggers. Janine pleaded with Ashlee not to tell the guys because Keller would kill Dalton if they had the chance. Breaking down in uncontrollable sobs, she was indeed with child, and it was Dalton Mueller's. Ashlee remarked to Janine that Dalton was not going to have anything to do with her if he found out she was pregnant. Ashlee asked with no hesitation, inquiring what Janine was going to do. Janine certainly could not afford a baby on her own, especially on the wages as the steno pool paid squat, and the benefits were terrible. Ashlee reassured Janine that she and Carole would help by getting her the necessary care and having an abortion. Janine promised she would tell Keller and especially Dalton when the time was right. When would be the right time, though?

The quartet grew into a sextet, and Beau asked if there was enough room for six. Keller added that he didn't mind taking his car and giving Cole and him some much-needed privacy. Cole could play with both stick shifts, and we know how much Cole loves thick shafts; he met his match in Keller. Cole bragged to Beau that he had nothing to worry about because Keller had him beat by the least quarter of an inch. Given those dimensions, Keller would be at least close to eight and three-quarters in cock compared to Beau. Cole wasn't a size queen by any means; enjoying it so much and could not wait for Keller to move in. Beau assembled the ladies in waiting for his Cadillac Coup de Ville as the two gay boys followed him in Keller's Mustang. The vehicles were piling in the stretch and screaming valets a sense of urgency to take seats as soon as they entered. From the outside, sounds were deafening as you heard the orchestra quietening, and Bob Hope was to deliver his monologue. The sextet ran to the open doors; Ashlee was fearful Janine would trip and fall, trying to see the celebrities through binoculars.

AND THE OSCAR GOES TO...

Hope, funny as always, poking fun at Julie Andrews playing a nun and singling out George Hamilton, who had the pleasure of squiring Lynda Bird Johnson, daughter of President Lyndon B. Johnson, to the ceremonies. All eyes seemed to focus on the new couple, gossip mongers united as reporters and paparazzi tried ambushing them. Alas, the Secret Service was not too far behind to avoid any confrontation. The evening was quite festive with the siblings; Janine and Keller were just in awe, gawking at all the glitz filling the auditorium and walking to their privileged seats. Janine was taken aback by the gowns, remarking they find dresses like those for next year's ceremonies. Beau mentioned to Carole that she should do her hair like the beauties Yvette Mimieux and Kim Novak presenting their respective awards for sound effects and cinematography. Cole and Keller were scouting hunky guys like George Hamilton, James Garner, James Coburn, Gregory Peck, and George Peppard.

The sextet were winners in their circle, as announced. Beau's A Thousand Clowns won, and Martin Balsam took the Best Supporting Actor. Carole's A Patch of Blue won Shelley Winters her second-Best Supporting Actress close to consecutive years. Cole was excited to see Best Sound Effects went to The Great Race. The most important Oscars went to Robert Wise, winning not one but two Best Picture and Best Director for The Sound of Music. Poor Julie Andrews missed winning her second-Best Actress award consecutively; instead of going to the other Julie, Julie Christie took the gold for Darling, and Best Actor went to Lee Marvin for Cat Ballou.

The usual routine follows Monday Oscar night, back to work. Travels were on the horizon for the men of the sextet. The men were selected to go abroad during the latter part of filming; Beau was heading to Taiwan and Hong for Sand Pebbles with handsome Steve McQueen, and the new couple, Cole and Keller, were headed to Belgium, France, Italy, and Monaco for Grand Prix, the race car drama with sexy James Garner.

There was no time but the present; Janine had to have a heart-to-heart with Keller as he finished his move-in with Cole before leaving on location. Keller could see something troubling her the last few weeks after the Oscar ceremony. Keller didn't want to pry, it was much-needed relief when Janine offered to fix dinner just for two while Ashlee was busy working late. Keller and Cole moved in together not long after the last Oscar ceremony. As they sat in silence eating at Janine's famous Mom's meatloaf, she said, "Keller, brother dear, there is something I need to discuss with you, and it's not pleasant." Keller nodded his head in unison, "Sis, you know there is nothing you can't tell me that will upset me. Just don't tell me you want to go back home to Missouri." Janine reassured Keller she would never leave him. Keller mentioned that if Janine wanted him to stay and forgo the location trip, he would. Janine said,

"Brother dear, I will be fine. I have Carole and Ashlee to help me." The ladies were an immense help. Out with it, here it comes. Janine just blurted out, "I guess you think I look like a pig, gaining so much weight since we moved here, but the truth of the matter is, I am three months pregnant, and I need to have an abortion quick!" Keller started to get slightly agitated by screaming, "Who is the bastard? I want to kill him?" Janine calmed her brother down, saying she ended the affair and relationship. Keller said, "I assume he is married just like the rest? Janine said it was Dalton Mueller. Keller told her as much after Cole told him what a slime ball he was to Ashlee and others in the steno pool; how could she let this get so carried away? Keller told his little sis he would be there for her till his last breath; as they embraced and kissed, Keller brushed Janine's soft hair out of her bloodshot eyes from crying. They promised there would be no more secrets between them.

As the trio of men headed abroad, Carole was ecstatic learning she was assigned not one but two jobs behind the scenes handing scripts to Liz and Dick, that's Elizabeth Taylor and Richard Burton to you. Carole also assisted makeup artist Gordon Bau in making them look much older and frumpier than ever in Mike Nichols' Who's Afraid of Virginia Woolf. Awaiting their flights, the trio were sitting in the lounge when Keller spoke up, "So fellas, what should I do about my sweet sister." Cole knew very well not to speak, so Beau replied, "Why Keller, what the hell are you talking about?" Looks like Carole kept Janine's secret from him. Being coy, Cole remarked to Keller, telling him just be there for her, overbearing and over 100 percent. Puzzled by this mumble jumble, Beau said, "Again, I ask you, what the fuck are you two talking about." Keller finally said, "Well, if you must know, my sister had an affair with one of the married studio honchos and got knocked up, and of course, she ended it and had an abortion while I was gone." Beau sat back down, feeling very defeated in his chair, to say, "Oh my God, bro, I am so very sorry!" Keller said, "Don't knock it; the guy is a big loser anyway!" Beau's flight left first, leaving them too soon as they kicked back, awaiting their international flight.

With the men out of the country, Carole and Ashlee took Janine under their wing, needing their loving care and support during these dark days. Despite the heavy nature of the film Carole was working on, she explained to Bau it was an emergency. Bau understood and told her to hurry back soon because Elizabeth Taylor was being very persistent, saying she enjoyed Carole's expertise. Days after Janine returned to work, she constantly heard some behind-the-back chatter in the breakroom, trying her best not to let her guard down and lash out. Being new on the block at the steno pool, she tried staying optimistic, finding herself often going to the ladies' room to have a good cry. Janine buried herself in her work and avoided Dalton whenever deemed possible; there were a few tense moments. Especially opportune moments when he would exit from his office, bringing correspondence needing to be sent. Finally, before getting too awkward, Janine went on her lunch break to discuss with Human Resources she needed a transfer. Luck would have it, there were openings in another studio. Human resources were hesitant to move her, being one of the newest team members, deeply concerned about why Janine wanted to make a move. Janine explained she felt deemed necessary as a conflict of interest.

Days turned weeks into months, and Janine pined for her brothers' return because of loneliness and craving for male companionship. After work, instead of going to Grove happy hour, Janine wanted to go home and read a book, watch television, or listen to music, a far cry from her beginnings in Hollywood. Carole and Ashlee were running out of ideas to get Janine out of this funk. Summer was coming up. Carole suggested the ladies take a drive to Palm Springs. Ashlee thought, too, that this would give Janine a unique perspective enjoy life more, and a change of scenery. Carole couldn't stop talking about the tension on the set of Virginia Woolf; she spilled dish on how Elizabeth Taylor and Richard Burton were playing true to life as a bickering couple despite being married for a brief time. Carole said Sandy Dennis was a laughing riot, as George Segal was aloof at times. Ashlee added she was on better terms with the executive suits by calling them on what happened behind closed doors, and Janine noted collaborating with her new team was a definite change of pace.

The men were having an exciting time on their respective sets, and Beau was missing Carole terribly despite the exotic views of Taiwan and Hong Kong for his work on Sand Pebbles. Beau said in letters to Carole that Steve McQueen, Candice Bergen, and Richard Crenna could not be more gracious to the crew. Cole and Keller were seeing plenty of eye candy doing sound effects on the racing scenes for the Grand Prix and getting acquainted with James Garner, Yves Montand, and the lovely Eva Marie Saint, who were equally kind to the crew. Principal photography was complete; minor lighting and sound effects were needed ensuring everything was ready for release to the studios and on to the anticipating filmgoers. The holiday season will soon be here. Any of these international locales are proving worthy of box office gold and Oscar nominations in the upcoming year.

The holiday season was melancholy gathering at Cole and Keller's, reminding Keller and Janine to give thanks to the quartet for making them so welcome. Janine tearfully thought if she kept her unborn child, and Keller expressed his love to Ashlee by opening her home and heart to them, coupled with matchmaking uniting him with Cole. Beau was thankful for another year, with Carole apologizing for being gone during summer. Carole shrugged it off, expressing absence made hearts grow fonder, giving the ladies time to build a sisterhood. Carole also was sorry for keeping things from

Beau concerning Janine. Carole explained it was a female thing and a delicate, sensitive subject; Beau would understand. Beau implied they should never keep anything from anyone again. Let's make a pact: we six are family now. Cole and Ashlee were reminded of their parents' love. It is more hurtful for Ashlee with her mom's passing, with Cole not acknowledging his hurt for the longing of his parents. Cole couldn't shake their awkward meeting on location a few years back. Beau was trying not to think about his parents in Memphis, but Carole never spoke of her parent's senseless tragedy. Janine and Keller briefly discussed their homesickness, their first year away in St. Louis, and a possible white Christmas, not happening in Hollywood. Only white Christmas was watching the movie and Holiday Inn on television. LOL.

Chapter Nine

Hollywood buzz was rapidly getting around the studios, and the ladies were running their mouths and listening attentively, seeing what others were saying as well. Most definitely, Who's Afraid of Virginia Woolf, Sand Pebbles, and Alfie, to name a few, were getting early buzz. The performances this year were strong with Michael Caine, Elizabeth Taylor, Richard Burton, and Sandy Dennis. Hedda and Louella were pitting a sibling rivalry to play out as in 1941, sisters Olivia De Havilland and Joan Fontaine were up for Best Actress, and some said it could play out for the Redgrave sisters, Lynn and Vanessa. Nominations came out February 20th, and nobody seemed more surprised than anyone that the domestic drama Who's Afraid of Virginia Woolf garnered thirteen nods, eight each for the Sand Pebbles and the historical drama A Man for All Seasons and five each for Alfie and Fantastic Voyage. The sextet became ecstatic learning. Work was recognized;

AND THE OSCAR GOES TO...

efforts of the men's assistance to Joseph MacDonald's color cinematography work on the Sand Pebbles and Gordon Daniel's sound effects for Grand Prix were nominated.

The Oscars were held on Monday, April 10, 1967, with Bob Hope as the host yet again and the venue being the same, the Santa Monica Civic Auditorium. The sextet did not seem too excited with the ceremonies as Hope tried seeking much-needed comedic relief from the audience to whom he would ridicule. The presentation slowly moved on as the envelopes were opened, with eight nominations; a Man for All Seasons took home six, one each for Best Picture and Best Director Fred Zinnemann and Best Actor to Paul Scofield. There is no sibling rivalry here; both sisters, Lynn and Vanessa Redgrave, lost to Elizabeth Taylor for Best Actress as her husband, Richard Burton, went home empty yet again, and Sandy Dennis took home Best Supporting Actress. Best Supporting Actor went to Walter Matthau for The Fortune Cookie. The film was just the beginning of a great friendship and on-screen partnership with Jack Lemmon. The two were the new Abbott and Costello by critical standards. Beau didn't seem fazed when his Cinematography (color) lost out to A Man for All Seasons, but the boys, Cole and Keller, were super ecstatic the Grand Prix won for Best Sound Effects. Keller was a good luck charm, winning Cole's heart alongside their collaboration with Gordon Daniel. It was when Elizabeth Taylor was notified about her Best Actress win in London. She was very frustrated that her husband, Richard Burton, didn't win Best Actor, and she refused press conferences for two weeks.

Oscar season did not have much fanfare, considering most of the English commoners took home the gold as the sextet dived back for the remainder of the year leading into 1968. Sadly, the issues made for an exceptionally good year for films depicting several topics like interracial relationships, racial injustice, civil rights activism, the penal system, real-life crime stories, romantic comedies, and drama about divorce. Performances were strong as locations began moving out of the studio to international as well as inside the United States, with some heading down south to Texas and Mississippi.

Beau left for Texas to do cinematography work with Burnett Guffey and actors Warren Beatty and Faye Dunaway in Bonnie and Clyde. Carole went to Mississippi as a script girl for In the Heat of the Night, only being joined by Keller and Cole for a few months in England doing sound effects work on the male ensemble war drama The Dirty Dozen. With the duo alone and four on location, Ashlee and Janine found plenty of time on their hands. What could these two get into? Any mischief or just being good little girls? This gave them time to bond and discuss the sexual politics of working in Hollywood. The quartet began wrapping on their respective locations when civil rights activism started to gain notoriety. Dr. Martin Luther King Jr. began preaching all over the South, including

Tennessee, Mississippi, and his home state of Georgia. The presidential race was heating up, too, and an early bird set his eyes on announcing his candidacy to the public for an early Christmas present. The Kennedy family was making a comeback. Robert F. Kennedy tried swaying the Hollywood community by campaigning early with promises of a return, but in the summer of 1968. The holiday season released several films with social issues combined with early Oscar buzz. The movie list includes Spencer Tracy and Katharine Hepburn's swan song, Guess Who's Coming to Dinner, Rod Steiger and Sidney Poitier in the racially charged In the Heat of the Night, Dustin Hoffman in The Graduate, Paul Newman in the prison drama Cool Hand Luke, Warren Beatty, and Faye Dunaway as bank robbers Bonnie and Clyde, along with the ensemble depicting war violence in the Dirty Dozen.

Chapter Ten

T he holidays started a blitz for released movies in 1968, trying to prove they were Oscar-worthy. 1968 was shaping up to be quite a momentous year; combining civil rights activism and presidential hopefuls started to affect the way people saw their movies with emotions ranging from letting it go to leaving with heavy hearts. Racial turmoil was nothing new for Martin Luther King, speaking here and there, but nothing could be more poignant than previous years in 1963 with his infamous I Have a Dream and his 1965 Selma, Alabama speeches. These were two speeches given by the great human being King, Jr., who proved to be a force to resonate in 1968 and years ahead. On the flip side, there was an election in November 1968 with Democratic candidate Robert F. Kennedy, brother of the late John F. Kennedy, determined more than ever. The United States was a divided country, with Kennedy being more optimistic about his friendship with Dr. Martin Luther King

Jr., coupling his name with an appeal to the poor, African Americans, Catholics, Hispanics, and younger voters. One will wonder if this will make him a shoo-in with the Democratic voters. Did Robert Kennedy have the same charisma as his brother? How would the Hollywood community react to him and let past gossip be kept out of their minds? Hopefully, politics and civil rights unrest are doing their best not to be put on the back burner in hopes of not interfering with the box office receipts and feelings of all moviegoers. The Oscar nominations were released on February 19th, and the ceremony was scheduled to be held on April 8th. With the anticipation of the Hollywood buzz, ten nominations were for both Bonnie and Clyde and Guess Who's Coming to Dinner, nine for Dr. Dolittle, Four for Cool Hand Luke and the Dirty Dozen. The Graduate, In the Heat of the Night, and Thoroughly Modern Millie received seven as well.

With seven weeks to the ceremony, the sextet did not let the political and civil rights mumble jumble affect their feelings except for Cole's snide comment concerning Hollywood's love for Kennedy. Cole felt it awkward that Kennedy trying to sway Hollywood's votes after the way he and his brother John treated Marilyn Monroe.

Tragedy struck the nation as the Oscar ceremonies, scheduled for April 8th, were being postponed two days to April 10th. Dr. Martin Luther King Jr. was assassinated by James Earl Ray at a

Memphis hotel. Prior to the two-day postponement, four African American stars, Louis Armstrong, Diahann Carroll, Sammy Davis Jr., and Sidney Poitier, announced they were not attending to mourn Dr. King. Jack Lemmon and Shirley Jones were announced as replacements for Poitier and Davis Jr., respectively. This year, no Governor's Ball, and of twenty nominated performers, only two did not attend; Katharine Hepburn was busy filming The Lion in The Winter, and the late Spencer Tracy, whose nomination was posthumous, passed away ten months before the ceremony was held. The mood was relatively subdued, and you could hear a pin drop. Celebrities assembled into the auditorium in a quiet yet rushing matter, leaving the sextet and other behind-the-scenes peons scurrying for their seats as well. Despite a sad time in United States history, everyone appeared in panic mode. Given the recent events concerning Dr. Martin Luther King Jr.'s assassination, you could read explicitly what was on the Hollywood community's mind. The ceremony began with solemn words from then Academy President Gregory Peck, stating that the nation should unite as King Jr's legacy would be beneficial to rest in everyone's hearts. After Peck introduced Bill Miller from Price Waterhouse confirming Master of Ceremonies was again indeed, Bob Hope, Hope took the podium dais in clarifying the Oscars were called Passover at his home to a raucous laughter roar from the celebrity audience.

A true movie fan shouldn't forget in past years, for now and

AND THE OSCAR GOES TO...

in the future, just to be one of five nominees, you are a winner, regardless of the voting. The racially charged In the Heat of The Night received seven nominations and took home five gold statues; Rod Steiger won Best Actor over a competitive field of gentlemen as well as Best Picture. The Best Actress award went to Katharine Hepburn for Guess Who's Coming To Dinner. Best Director to Mike Nichols for The Graduate, Bonnie and Clyde's Cinematography, and Estelle Parsons in her hysterical moving portrayal as Clyde's sister-in-law gave her Best Supporting Actress and Best Supporting Actor to George Kennedy for Cool Hand Luke. Kudos to Gregory Peck and Alfred Hitchcock, both recipients of special Oscars; it was Hitchcock who stole the ceremony with one of the shortest acceptance speeches in Oscar history, growling, "Thank you very much indeed." Given that this speech was one word longer than its predecessor, fourteen years before William Holden, upon receiving his Oscar for Stalag 17, it was a simple "Thank You, Thank You."

Beau's work on Bonnie and Clyde was a winner in Best Cinematography to Burnett Guffrey. Carole and Keller's work on In the Heat of The Night was a winner of Best Screenplay to Stirling Silliphant from a novel by John Ball. Cole and Keller assisted the Best Sound Effects winner to The Dirty Dozen and John Poyner. The Oscar season ended with the sadness of Dr. Martin Luther King Jr.'s death, but business as usual, with Hollywood already talking about new films making their mark for Oscar gold for years to come.

In early June, the arrival of presidential campaigns forged ahead in full swing, with Robert F. Kennedy setting sights on Los Angeles. Kennedy appeared in town hoping to gain support from the Hollywood community; he, his lovely wife, Ethel, and their entourage appeared before their constituents upon his win of the California primary to make his famous speech with those rich, famous words "And on to Chicago!" was short-lived. In the early morning, around 12:15 am, as Kennedy walked through the Ambassador Hotel's kitchen, Palestinian Sirhan Sirhan gunned down Kennedy in retaliation for his support of Israel following the 1967 Six-day War. Kennedy passed away 25 hours later. This sudden change in the political picture set off unrest throughout the world, seeing two Kennedy brothers die by bullet assassination within five years. Coupled with Dr. King's death, the nation was a complete mess because of uncertainty, clearing the Republicans and Nixon to victory. One wonders whether America was ready for Nixon after he became Vice President of Eisenhower.

Despite being a sad year politically, 1968 was a momentous year for moviegoers, being excited about the variety of movies to choose from. Science fiction with Stanley Kubrick's 2001: A Space Odyssey, musical Funny Girl starring an unknown girl from New York, the Great White Way sensation Barbra Streisand, later making her mark being more than just a Broadway star. Drama splashed with Charly, The Lion in The Winter, and The Subject of Roses, and everyone was swooning, anticipating Paul Newman's directorial debut starring his wife, Joanne Woodward, in Rachel, Rachel. Neil Simon brought Broadway comedy from a new duo since Abbott and Costello, Lemmon and Matthau, starring in the farce The Odd Couple. Mel Brooks brought down the house with The Producers, starring Gene Wilder and Zero Mostel.

Chapter Eleven

T he New Year began with Richard Nixon, elected 37th president. Political activists were mixed, wondering how this presidency would be any different with Lyndon B. Johnson returning to his Texas roots in Austin.

There are many accolades bestowed to our motion picture performers, whether it be Golden Globes or Critics' awards from New York and Los Angeles. Indeed, proving the academy members' vote to determine the final nominations for specific award categories, thinking, do they watch the films or go by word of mouth to what critics say and write? February 24th is nomination time this year, and no surprise that musicals dominated the field, as Oliver did, receiving eleven nods, eight for Funny Girl, and seven for the flop Julie Andrews in the Gertrude Lawrence biopic in Star! Drama swept in, handing seven nominations for The Lion in The Winter and fewer nods for the sci-fi thriller 2001: A Space Odyssey, Rachel,

Rachel, and Rosemary's Baby, about the devil impregnating an innocent New York housewife.

Most of the films worth notoriety were California-based. Cole and Keller worked in San Francisco on Bullitt, and Carole worked In Los Angeles on two films, Faces and Rosemary's Baby, ironically set in New York City. Oddly, Beau worked in San Diego on Ice Station Zebra, and their set resembled the storyline of Scotland's Holy Loch and Orkney Islands. Beau thought to himself, if Ice Station Zebra did send him internationally, how would Carole react? The reason was that the couple was still very sexually charged and enjoyed every minute practicing every position imaginable; being away from each other was causing strain, mixing growing pains, not much major concern.

Predicting the outcome nearing their reality, the ceremony was set for April 14th with a new venue to be held at the Dorothy Chandler Pavilion in Los Angeles and a twist, no host. Nobody was more nervous than the first-time nominee, Barbra Streisand. With winners being announced, Oliver! took home five of their eleven nods, one for Best Picture and Carol Reed for Best Director, beating favorite Paul Newman. The rest of the evenings' awards went to Cliff Robertson, Best Actor for Charly, Jack Albertson, Best Supporting Actor for The Subject Was Roses, Ruth Gordon, and Best Supporting Actress, Rosemary's Baby. To everyone's surprise, Best Actress resulted in a tie; Katharine Hepburn had won her consecutive awards, a first since Luise Rainer in 1936 for The Great

TIM J. CULBERTSON

Ziegfield and in 1937 for The Good Earth and Hepburn's co-star in many films, the great late Spencer Tracy went back-to-back in 1937 for Captains Courageous and in 1938 for Boys' Town tied with Barbra Streisand. It was Streisand's two words accepting her gold from John Wayne, exclaiming, "Hello Gorgeous!" bringing down the house. In a split second, given Streisand's birth to the Academy, this was the beginning of a wonderful relationship. A star had arrived! Sadly, the assistance of the quartet's labor of love as studio scripters, sound effects, and cinematographers on their respective films went empty-handed.

Sluggishly returning to work, Ashlee and Janine went to the steno pool in their respective areas as the creative quartet, checking the communal board of upcoming films for 1969-1970. Is it a risk for Carole and Beau to be apart yet again or look for something together? Upon hearing that principal production had already started, big names were looking for much-needed behind-the-scenes assistance. Here is a list of some films the quartet was looking at catching early 1970 Oscar buzz:

Anne of a Thousand Days	*Bob Carol, Ted & Alice*	*Easy Rider*
Butch Cassidy and the Sundance Kid	*Cactus Flower*	*Goodbye, Columbus*
Goodbye, Mr. Chips	*Hello Dolly!*	*Midnight Cowboy*
True Grit	*The Wild Bunch*	*They Shoot Horses, Don't They?*

AND THE OSCAR GOES TO...

After viewing the list, the quartet inquired concerning the locations. In an instant, Carole and Beau found work mixed with pleasure in Butch Cassidy and the Sundance Kid. If you remember, the lovebirds did not have a "real" honeymoon, and working together on this project with writer William Goldman and Cinematographer Conrad Hall, two legends, would be perfect. A bonus would be working with Robert Redford and Paul Newman as well. The location was not in Latin America as the real story was told, but it was in the beautiful scenic views of the southwestern part of the United States. This specific locale was the ghost town of Grafton, surrounded by Zion National Park, Snow Canyon State Park, and the city of St. George. Simply beautiful breath-taking adventures – a match made in heaven and quite perfect for a getaway!

The two gay boys, yes, Cole and Keller, were beyond excited upon hearing Hello, Dolly! was being developed to film with their new favorite, Barbra Streisand, following her Oscar-winning debut in Funny Girl. Hello, Dolly! was a gay man's dream come true under the direction of Gene Kelly and seeing Streisand every day. It was surreal! The boys were headed to the Big Apple, New York City, hoping for the city itself to show the boys to be in Yonkers; Gene Kelly decided to film it in the city of Garrison.

With the quartet away on location, Ashlee and Janine became beside themselves on what to do after work. At times, they found time to have happy hours with girls from the steno pool at the Grove, eat in fixing exotic dishes, eat out, or just watch TV to rehash daily work gossip. In 1969, there were only three networks for public viewing pleasure: ABC, CBS, and NBC. How boring! The networks offered lots of options: crime dramas, slap silly fun comedies, or even variety shows.

The film holiday season was here. Ashlee and Janine could not wait to swoon over Newman and Redford, seeing how their friends' work turned out as Carole was ready to see Hello, Dolly! with Cole and Keller becoming a big Streisand fan. Beau was looking forward to seeing Easy Rider and The Wild Bunch.

The year ended with Beau receiving word his father had passed away in Memphis. Despite their estrangement, Beau was devastated by trying not to show emotion. Carole offered to travel and see his family. Being stoic and trying not to be sarcastic, not being family these last few years, why repair the damage now?

Chapter Twelve

E arly in the year, Hollywood buzz began taking shape, with naysayers leaking that an X-rated film was making a public splash. Openly gay director John Schlesinger put together a haunting tale of male prostitution with Jon Voight and Dustin Hoffman in Midnight Cowboy. In the late sixties, this raw topic was depicted on screen with rich, powerful performances and being well received by critics and the public alike. As the buzz for Midnight Cowboy was on fire, others were trying to steal some of its thunder. Worth noting were Anne of The Thousand Days, an epic costume drama about Anne Boleyn, one of Henry VIII's wives; True Grit, a John Wayne western; Bob, Carol, Ted, and Alice, a comedic farce about wife swapping; and Easy Rider, a film about an executive and his midlife crisis fascination with motorcycles.

The nominations were announced on February 16th and were held on April 7th at the Dorothy Chandler Pavilion with no official host. This year's telecast would be the first to broadcast via satellite internationally and only live in North America, Brazil, and Mexico. As the announced nominations were released, there were no big surprises: ten for Anne of The Thousand Days, nine for They Shoot Horses, Don't They? Seven each for Butch Cassidy and The Sundance Kid, Hello, Dolly! and Midnight Cowboy.

Oscar Gold did not disappoint in spreading wealth to two stars of yesteryear and shining brightly for a couple of newsies to be welcomed to the party. John Wayne took Best Actor for True Grit, and Gig Young took Best Supporting Actor for the dance marathon drama They Shoot Horses, Don't They? British actress Maggie Smith took Best Actress gold for The Prime of Miss Jean Brodie, and Laugh-In television actress and comedienne Goldie Hawn took Best Supporting Actress for Cactus Flower. The critics' naysayers were spot on predicting the awarding of Midnight Cowboy Best Picture and Best Director. Indeed, it won the 1st X-rated film, but the rating changed to R in 1971 after the MPAA revised its criteria. The only other X-rated film to be nominated was, in 1971, A Clockwork Orange; for its quirkiness and excessive violence, it lowered its rating after excessive cuts were made.

Our sextet was on cloud nine. After a few years of their work not being recognized, this year was the icing on the cake, as two films they worked on were. Besides winning for Best Screenplay and Best Cinematography, Beau and Carole's film, Butch Cassidy and The Sundance Kid, won two others, including Best Song, one of the cutest songs ever, Raindrops Keep Falling on My Head, going to Burt Bacharach and Hal David. Cole and Keller's film, despite being labeled a miscast mish-mash wash, gave Streisand a pairing with Walter Matthau in Hello, Dolly! taking Best Sound, Art Direction, and well-deserved Costume Design.

A true highlight of the ceremony was between Bob Hope and Fred Astaire, presenters for Best Documentary. Hope asked Astaire why he never danced at the Oscars before. Astaire remarked he had given up dancing, which became a reality when Hope left the stage, not without the orchestra missing a beat, allowing Astaire to do an impromptu jazz style to a tap for the audience.

The offerings for 1970 started early production with far away distance war dramas like Patton and Tora! Tora! Tora and the satirical war comedy, M*A*S*H. The drama kept pace with the war saga with an all-star blockbuster called Airport based on the Arthur Hailey best seller Women in Love, Ryan's Daughter, Love Story, and I Never Sang for My Father. Location was calling our sextet, and believe it, for the first time in their friendship, Twentieth Century Fox leadership needed help in Spain on Patton. Director Franklin J. Schaffner and Producer Frank McCarthy enlisted help from the steno pool for expertise in travel itineraries, purchase orders, and foreign correspondence. Ashlee and Janine jumped at this excellent opportunity, especially hearing Carole was going to help with the script and makeup team, and as a bonus, the trio of men were going as well.

This should be fun; despite the grueling days of shooting on location, the big brass told our sextet a bonus for all their hard work, there was a three-week vacation upon completion of the film. It was going to be a surprise; they just must wait. Curiosity killed the cat, they say, but anticipation of ending this project could not come sooner than expected. Production ended in late May or early June and was very grueling. The ladies felt out of place surrounded by testosterone, especially from gruff George C. Scott. Sources say producers could have made a better choice for the lead, remarking Lee Marvin, Burt Lancaster, Robert Mitchum, John Wayne, and even Rod Steiger, who later said he regretted turning the role down. Charlton Heston turned down Karl Malden's role as Omar Bradley. Given the ones turned down, production would have gone smoother; it looks like makeup did a wonderful job on Scott; he looked the part of the real Patton. With production done, the sextet anxiously awaited what the studio had in store for all the behind-the-scenes workers. At the postproduction party, after most of the crew left for the States, the only ones left were behind the scenes, but Director Schaffner and Producer McCarthy decided to announce the surprise. In everyone's wildest dreams, upon hearing Schaffner's announcement, everyone was being flown to Barcelona with a weekend getaway to Sitges all-expenses paid. Having said that, the sextet was over the moon with excitement and was able to see all the sights Barcelona had to offer, and the resort lifestyle was too much. A dream comes true. Three weeks in Spain was going amazing, but working back in early August in California was a downer! Minor projects were to be a piece of cake as the sextet was certainly deadbeat, tired from the grueling shoot on Patton and decided to lay as low as possible for the next four months.

Chapter Thirteen

B ox office numbers were mixed; men headed to theatres to see war films as the ladies turned to sappy dramas. Everyone will be interested in how this new genre will appear soon and prove beneficial to the box office numbers, too. Who will flock to the theatres to see it? This new genre is the ensemble disaster film, this specific one based on Arthur Hailey's bestselling novel, Airport. Airport created four sequels and two comedic spoofs, Airplane and Airplane II, and delved into other disasters like Earthquake, The Poseidon Adventure, The Swarm, and The Towering Inferno. Dramas and comedies were on everyone's list as well. The tearjerker love story, based on the Erich Segal bestselling novel, packed movie theatres as well as the satirical comedy M*A*S*H to war dramas, Patton and Tora! Tora! Tora!

As the nominations were announced on February 23rd, noted that the Oscar telecast will be on NBC, the first time in eleven years as well for the third consecutive year, again no host, and held at the Dorothy Chandler Pavilion. Ten nominations went to Patton and Airport, seven for Love Story, five each for M*A*S*H and Tora! Tora! Tora! and Four to Five Easy Pieces, Scrooge, Women in Love, and Ryan's Daughter. In another strange of events, George C. Scott, who previously protested a nomination for The Hustler in 1961, later did the same for his role in Patton, describing the Oscars as a two-hour meat parade, citing it as a public display with contrived suspense for economic reasons. Worth noting for Best Actress were five ladies never nominated, and Helen Hayes was first nominated for Best Supporting Actress after prior her win in 1933 for Best Actress. Another note of trivia: the documentary Woodstock received three nominations, being a rarity.

The ceremony was under scrutiny, allowing George C. Scott to be a horse's ass concerning personal feelings toward the academy; voters did not seem to let it sway and bother them. April 15th, the show went on as normal without any controversy; there was no shocking surprise when Goldie Hawn announced Scott's name as Best Actor. The Oscar for Scott and Best Picture can now be found in the George C. Marshall Foundation Library at the Virginia Military Institute in Lexington, Virginia. Even after many years of toiling on this labor of love, producer Frank McCarthy started back in 1953 after Patton's widow passed away and asked the Pentagon and Patton's family for several items of access; it was not until 1959 that the US Army finally convinced them to co-operate. Patton was awarded seven of its ten nominations. Continuing with the ceremony, British actress Glenda Jackson won Best Actress for Women in Love; Best Supporting Actor went to the father of Hayley and Juliet Mills, John won for Ryan's Daughter, and as predicted, her stowaway role in Airport, Helen Hayes won Best Supporting Actress. Whew, what a night, but of course, tomorrow is another day, work to be done, and this, too, will pass.

A few films were pining for some early help overseas. The sextet declined a few offers to go abroad to do Nicholas and Alexandra in Spain and Yugoslavia, even if it meant a reunion of sorts with Patton director Franklin Schaffner. Another period piece, Mary, Queen of Scots, was filmed in several European countries, but the answer was still NO! One project dear to Cole and Keller's heart, hoping for something exotic, Diamonds Are Forever. Luck would not be on their side, and this Bond film was produced mostly in Las Vegas and California, with opening scenes in France, which did not require their help. You would think the boys jump at the opportunity to see Sean Connery with his shirt off, which is the sole reason for this project choice. Luck was on their side; they just drooled with their tongues on the floor every time Mr. Connery walked by. Beau and Carole's thumbs down to the foreign locales, option for their services to not one but two beautifully made films, dividing their time between the East Coast and down in the heart of

Texas. These two films, coupled with rich screenplays from novels and cinematography, were Summer of '42 and The Last Picture Show. Respectively written by Herman Lauchner and Larry McMurtry with locations of Nantucket Island off Cape Cod and Archer City, which is in North Central Texas near the Oklahoma border.

The quirky Stanley Kubrick was dallying with A Clockwork Orange, based on the novel of the same name by Anthony Burgess, depicting violent images as social satire on diverse topics bizarre beyond comprehension. In later years, despite its mixed reviews, A Clockwork Orange became a cult classic. Topol reprised his Broadway role, making an enormous splash in the musical Fiddler on The Roof. Gene Hackman, getting his start with a leading role as Detective Jimmy "Popeye" Doyle in the true-to-life crime drama The French Connection, was quite a ride for the public. Jack Nicholson, Candice Bergen, Ann-Margret, and Art Garfunkel tackled sexual issues with Mike Nichols' Carnal Knowledge. As previously mentioned, Peter Bogdanovich's love story to Texas in black and white, suggested by veteran Orson Welles with The Last Picture Show, and John Schlesinger bounced back with the love triangle, Sunday, Bloody Sunday hitting the big screen during the holiday season.

Carole and Beau relished dividing their time between Cape Cod and Texas with their respective movies. The hot and humid

Texas heat proved quite grueling, and the breezes of Massachusetts felt welcome. Just as luck would have it, coupled with constant back and forth between locations, brought allergy season and summer colds for the duo.

Now, it is time to kick back and enjoy the fall television season on the boob tube and upcoming films in discussion for Oscar buzz. You would think that after working on a movie set or studio office, the last thing these behind-the-scenes workers want to do is watch television or do anything related to the arts. Far from the contrary, most of their weekend viewing pleasure was the eye on CBS and shows All in The Family, Funny Face, The Mary Tyler Moore Show, the New Dick Van Dyke Show and Arnie.

Chapter Fourteen

W elcome to 1972. Filmgoers were busily exiting theatres with smiles from ear to ear, bringing on such a variety of films by looking at their faces. What exactly was on their minds? Was it the music in their ears from Topol, the rough and tough demeanor of Gene Hackman, or the tender grace of beauty of Jennifer O'Neill walking the sandy beaches of Cape Cod? Romance is always in the air when it comes to cinema; how can you not resist it?

Ashlee had been quiet as a church mouse lately. Janine caught on very quickly; Ashlee was seeing someone. Janine saw the writing on the wall but was fearful of jinxing it. Ashlee's "secret" was much older; he was Simon Tolliver. Simon was married and divorced thrice and was an old college chum of famed entertainment lawyer Greg Bautzer. Bautzer, though retired, did not let it stop visiting the steno pool from time to time and brought Simon a few times. Ashlee was smitten with sly Simon, and his pushing sixty-two did not matter. The cat slowly got out of the "bag," Janine called Carole and said we must intervene. Carole remarked that she thought Ashlee was a big girl and that she did not need interference. Carole was often reminded of the quiet times when Ashlee was over her head and thought it best, keeping her distance and mouth shut and suggesting that Janine do the same.

Ashlee was still "mum" about her off-again, on-again "fling" with Simon. Simon was single now; it was common knowledge he was available as Ashlee wanted it on the down low as possible. Even with skepticism, Ashlee feared the gossip despite the spectacle years before when she threatened the studio brass with her harassment claims. Ashlee did not want to be the butt of jokes or gossip about being another slut. She felt the need to be taken seriously as a woman who could manage a sincere yet complicated affair. Ashlee did not know the whole story. Of course, there were rumors around the steno pool, but she shrugged it off. Occasionally, she would find little notes on her desk, some not so nice. Only time would tell; Ashlee was determined to let nature run its course, and not all these undermining comments hurt her feelings. The lovers were having Sunday brunch at Coconut Grove with the rest of the gang when Simon announced to the sextet that nothing was going to stand in his way of expressing his love for Ashlee, yet he was incredibly determined to make things right between everyone. Simon asked

Ashlee if she would consider something more serious if the situation was different. There was a slight gap between ages, and Ashlee seemingly appeared not to care. Everyone was enjoying their brunch, feeling uncomfortable; Simon explained he needed to get to his apartment. It was falling on deaf ears as the sextet was laughing at Cole, telling one of his silly jokes. As the laughter got a bit louder, Keller, out of the corner of his eye, noticed Simon clutching his chest and screaming, "Can't you hear me? I need help!" Keller quieted down his friends and told Ashlee they needed to get Simon to the nearest hospital. Ashlee laughed at Keller, "Oh, he does this all the time; it's just a joke." Keller nudged Ashlee: he was not funny this time. Ashlee reached over and then all sudden started screaming at the top of her lungs, "Oh My God, Simon, do not pull this shit on me!"

Simon was gasping for breath and clutching his fists to a thud when suddenly he stopped struggling and fell out of his chair. Simon Tolliver was gone. The sextet just sat there at their table, dumbfounded and puzzled about what to do next. It was shocking as Simon's sudden heart attack (real) and death proved too much for Ashlee to bear. Seeing two people pass in the last few years, coupled with the anguish from the harassment claims, Ashlee was not in a good place. She asked the steno pool manager for a few weeks to clear her head and take some much-needed "Me time." Reluctant, the manager gave in to Ashlee's whims; she was a total basket case, delving into drinking and taking Seconal to help her sleep at night. Still rising early, thinking she had to work, Ashlee would waddle to the kitchen and make coffee for Janine. Janine was increasingly more worried than ever. When she got to work, Janine called Carole for advice. Carole said Ashlee spiraled when her mother passed, and again, with the work repercussions crumbling around, this too will pass.

It was a cool February morning when the 44th Oscar nominations were announced on the radio as Ashlee was drinking her third cup of coffee. Twenty-five nods were announced and as being rattled off, obviously looking as a three-ring circus was set for musical Fiddler On the Roof, crime drama The French Connection, and black and white The Last Picture Show would duke it with eight nominations, six went to Nicholas and Alexandria, five for Disney's Bedknobs and Broomsticks and Mary, Queen of Scots, four for another X rated (as predicted) film, A Clockwork Orange, Kotch, Summer Of '42, and Sunday, Bloody Sunday.

Spring was in the air, and Ashlee was getting her act together, stronger than ever. It was time to take everyone to the Oscars, so get ready. Ashlee returned to work by keeping her ears away from all gossip. There were a few trying to play on her insecurities, but Ashlee confronted the problem head-on and would not have it. One night over dinner, Keller remarked he had to hand it to Ashlee for sticking to her guns. Ashlee said, "Well, do you know what? You just must be strong for the ones you love, not the ones you love to hate." Cole added to the sentiment, saying Ashlee was here to stay and Hollywood would never be the same! April 10th, finally, Oscar night arrived! Beau was ecstatic, wanting to show off his new car, a Cadillac Eldorado convertible. A noticeable change for the Eldorado was the script versus the block letters depicting its name on the front fenders and trunk lid. Beau felt he had arrived, taking the whole gang in style.

Announcer Hank Simms welcomed everyone again to the Dorothy Chandler Pavilion, and the hosts were the quartet of Helen Hayes, Sammy Davis Jr., Jack Lemmon, and Alan King. The sextet was anxious to see if any movies they feverishly worked on would win Oscar gold. At first, after Fiddler on The Roof won for Cinematography and Sound, it looked like a musical was bound for a sweep, but crime paid for The French Connection. Gene Hackman took Best Actor, and William Friedkin took Best Director and Best Picture, winning the night with five awards. Best Actress went to Jane Fonda for her stirring turn as a prostitute, Bree Daniels in Klute. Peter Bogdanovich promised his cast they would not go home empty-handed during filming on The Last Picture Show. Lo and behold, Bogdanovich was true to his word when Supporting Awards went to both Ben Johnson and Cloris Leachman. It looked like the only redeeming quality for Carole's labor of love on Summer Of '42 was awarded for its beautiful Original Score by Michel Legrand.

1972 was election year again. Preliminary results showed Nixon appeared to be running for re-election, and Democrats wanted to stop him. Hollywood A-Listers were making it well known who they were campaigning for, a debacle it became, seeing lots of disaccords amongst the community.

As the stars were shining bright, the sextet was scouring the trades on what movies would bring them praise from the brass. There was a book written about the Mafia by an unknown author, Mario Puzo, that was garnering buzz and was being made into a blockbuster epic by Francis Ford Coppola. Irwin Allen was doing disaster duty with an all-star cast in The Poseidon Adventure, Bob Fosse was doing a musical with Liza Minnelli in Cabaret, Billie Holliday's life was being brought to screen life with Diana Ross, and many others. In a surprising twist, Carol Burnett took time off her CBS variety show to do a dramedy with Walter Matthau called Pete and Tillie, making Hollywood look at her as a serious actress. Cabaret's postproduction ended in western Germany, and Bob Fosse enlisted sound and cinematographers. The trio of men were itching to get out of California, giving ladies much-needed time alone. The Candidate with Robert Redford was looking for extra writers. Carole seized the opportunity to see Redford up close and personal even getting to see Natalie Wood, who appeared in a cameo as a favor to her friend. As productions wrapped on these films, as mentioned, Nixon was in full re-election mode. George McGovern forged to be his opponent, and in November 1972, Nixon crucified McGovern by a landslide. Political activists scrutinized the fact that Nixon had been in the political limelight. Was it time for a change?

Sleigh bells were ringing, and moviegoers were listening. Hollywood was making sure-fire hits with the Poseidon Adventure and the Godfather-packed houses. Musicals like Cabaret and Lady Sings the Blues with Diana Ross playing jazz legend Billie Holliday were making a comeback, and comedies like Heartbreak Kid and Butterflies are Free were giving a critical buzz to screen veterans Eddie Albert and Eileen Heckart.

Chapter Fifteen

A s 1973 started, an unknown secretary from Youngstown, Ohio, named Maureen McGovern, made a splash with the theme from The Poseidon Adventure. Studio brass from 20th Century Fox releasing the film started a record company and signed McGovern to a contract as "The Morning After" was rising to number #1 on the Billboard Top 100. It might be nothing, but McGovern did not sing the theme in the film, capitulating Maureen to stardom and achieving much success with Broadway and recordings. The public could not get the song out of their head as McGovern became an overnight sensation.

As usual, anticipation mounted on who would get the most nominations. Hollywood reporters were pining for a successful disaster film, scoring many nods from a Mafia family drama to a musical or a moving family drama about African Americans in the South. Who would have guessed the competition to be so fierce? So

AND THE OSCAR GOES TO…

here they are, an early Valentine's Day present from Hollywood on February 12th; nominations displayed a love for The Godfather and Cabaret with ten nominations apiece, fighting for Best Picture and Best Director, followed with nine nominations was The Poseidon Adventure, and dropping to five was Lady Sings the Blues. One bit of trivia: it was the first time in Oscar history two African American women were nominated for Best Actress to give Liza Minnelli a run for Oscar gold.

Nominations were not without controversy, especially in the music category; as a surprise, The Godfather received eleven nominations, but its original score nomination was declared ineligible, for the love theme was used in the Italian film Fortunella years previously. If that was not enough, Best Song hit a snag as the theme, and Freddy's Dead in Superfly was declared ineligible as well because it was performed instrumentally in the film versus with lyrics that were not sung. It was brought to the Board of Governors, and John Green, then governor, mentioned that both lyrics and music must be heard in the film to be recognized for nomination.

As the ceremonies grew closer, the men in our sextet went shopping for rental tuxedos to look like the Godfather trio of Pacino, Caan, and Duvall. What a motley trio they have become. They have been doing lots of work together lately. Cole joked with Keller that he once had a vibe for Beau, hoping he could turn him gay. Cole told Keller Beau to put up a gallant fight. Cole kept reminding himself how hot Beau was and more determined to see him naked every chance he got while they were on location working on Cabaret. Cole even tried to get Joel Grey and Michael York to nudge Beau, but he was not doing it. Keller shrugged Cole off by noting he was not interested in having another guy share their bed.

This year, the Oscars were held on Tuesday, March 27, 1973, where else, the Dorothy Chandler Pavilion and hosted by the quartet of Carol Burnett, Michael Caine, a shared nominee for Best Actor with Laurence Oliver for Sleuth, Charlton Heston, and Rock Hudson. This year's surprises did not disappoint many, and you would say shocked more like it. In as many years, a musical, Cabaret, famous for its much Broadway success helmed by Bob Fosse, won eight of its ten nominations, which included Best Director and Best Actress Liza Minnelli and Best Supporting Actor Joel Grey. Oddly, The Godfather took home Best Picture and Best Actor Marlon Brando, who sent Sacheen Littlefeather to decline his award for him. The Godfather, considered a favorite by critics, took home only three awards and was quite a disappointment indeed. Best Supporting Actress went to Eileen Heckart, a veteran of stage and screen, for her role as the domineering mother to Edward Albert in the Goldie Hawn comedy Butterflies Are Free.

As the sextet slowly drudged to the valet waiting on Beau's car, Carole mentioned how lovely Diana Ross and Cicely Tyson took in stride to Liza's triumph for Cabaret, and Ashlee was shocked at Brando for not accepting Best Actor. Overall, it was a crazy ride, with Carol Burnett going toe-to-toe with the other three men in true comedic fashion.

Welcome to the day after the Oscars, and you know what that means! The timing could not be perfect for the sextet to start looking at what post-production duties could be fulfilling to start the 46ᵗʰ Oscar season buzz. The roster of movies looked quite promising, with top A-List directors and stars, and 1973 appeared to be in full swing. The A-listers ranged from Barbra Streisand to Paul Newman to Robert Redford to Jack Lemmon and directors from Ingmar Bergman to William Friedkin to George Roy Hill to Bernardo Bertolucci. The movie genres ranged from horror movies depicting the devil possessing a child, teenage romance, star-crossed romance, and 1920s-era con artists to a musical about Jesus Christ or a road trip between father and daughter.

So much to choose from, and who and where to work would be the dilemma of the sestet: should they travel out of the United States or go international again? It was fun while it lasted as the two ladies played stenographers; the quartet stayed close at bay with various projects within the confines of Universal Studios, working on the Sting or off to New York City for Way We Were or even down to the nation's capital, Washington D.C. for the Exorcist. What fun would they have until the holiday season?

During the early part of April and early May on Universal's backlot, Carole and Beau reunited forces with George Roy Hill, Newman, and Redford for The Sting. As soon as it finished, they took off to Washington D.C. to join Cole and Keller for The Exorcist. Fresh off an exciting whirlwind journey in New York City, our gay lovebirds again worked with Barbra Streisand and her new leading man, Robert Redford, in The Way We Were, which was a dream come true.

Boredom settled in for our two stenographers as the others were out traveling from set to set. Making the best of both worlds, lifetime friendships with celebrities and crew was getting to be fun. It is always an extra plus for bragging rights, and over at the steno pool, you can expect the unexpected. Never know who you will meet. Celebrities in the flesh, their nice and not-so-nice agents, personal assistants, often their spouses, lovers, children, and whomever in the office. Who would ever think of an entourage of guard dogs showing up along with a bodyguard, their chauffeur, nurse, or doctor? You would be surprised. Literally, Ashlee remarked she had even seen a popular Jewish celebrity bring their rabbi.

As the holiday season was around the corner, the buzz was already getting out. It was so good to see Paul Newman make a comeback, especially with his friend Robert Redford. Equally sweet, the star-crossed romance with Streisand, Redford was becoming everyone's heartthrob, and soothing loving hearts was hearing Barbra singing the theme song over the opening credits of the film scaring everyone to death was The Exorcist set in the nation's capital about an actress on location and the devil possesses her daughter. Only time will tell what films will garner the most nominations and win Oscar gold in April 1974.

Chapter Sixteen

1974 rolled in a massive rush from studios releasing films capturing our hearts, shaping a monumental year for academy members to decide what lies ahead. As the saying goes, so many men, so little time, might as well be so many films to see, but never enough time. There is nothing better than watching on the big screen with your love, popcorn, a hot dog, and a beverage of your choice.

Nominations rolled out on February 19th. It is worth noting that there were ten nods for The Exorcist (horrifying) and The Sting and six for The Way We Were. A welcome first-time nominee to future Star Wars creator George Lucas. Alongside their friend, Francis Ford Coppola helped Lucas co-produce the nostalgic teen film American Graffiti. This film starred an array of total unknowns co-starring with famous television stars who then became famous in their own right in television and movies, these were Harrison Ford,

AND THE OSCAR GOES TO...

Richard Dreyfuss, and Suzanne Somers.

Our ladies at the steno pool were busily gathering documents, ensuring safe travel for foreign nominees Ingmar Bergman and Bernardo Bertolucci to attend the April 2nd ceremony. The other four were scurrying around looking for local odd jobs on the various studio lots to busy themselves, ensuring their attendance as well. Cole and Keller especially were looking forward to seeing Streisand and Redford. Carole and Beau had enjoyed working with Newman and Redford as well and hoped to sneak a peek at Joanne Woodward, Newman's wife, who made quite a stir in the drama Summer Wishes, Winter Dreams.

As the nominations were publicized, it was noted that Marlon Brando, who refused the Oscar the previous year, was nominated for an X-rated film, the Last Tango in Paris, and Tatum O'Neal was nominated for Best Supporting Actress in Paper Moon was the youngest ever at age 10 years and 148 days.

As Tuesday, April 2nd, inching to reality, studios were scurrying around to finish their day's work, allowing their staff to hurry home and change for the 46th annual Oscars. Cole and Keller were on the backlot for ABC and Garry Marshall's creation, Happy Days. Carole had been appointed assistant to make up for CBS's revamped New Perry Mason, and Beau was taking it easy, awaiting word for a cinematography gig.

As the sextet were hurrying with their attire, Cole and Keller were anxious to see if Streisand would sing the theme song to The Way We Were.

Earlier in the day, they heard Peggy Lee sing it; what was this old soul singing? I am sure Marvin Hamlisch was extremely angry. If you remember, back in those days, most of the performers who recorded the songs did not perform at the ceremony, even though it would have been great to see Streisand sing on national television.

It was held again at the same place, Dorothy Chandler Pavilion, and hosts this year were John Huston, David Niven, Burt Reynolds, and Diana Ross. The trio of our sextet were anxious to see how many wardrobe changes the Supremes diva would change into. The Oscar producers must have been hard-pressed to have other actors perform the nominated songs. As I said earlier, it is so much better to have the actual recording artist singing instead of who's who to perform. The only redeeming feature was the classy Peggy Lee warble The Way We Were. Here, I am hoping Hamlisch and Streisand were pleased. To pull all the stops, Connie Stevens sang Live and Let Die accompanied by dancers, and then Dyan Cannon sang the theme from A Touch of Class and the Straw Breaking the Camel's Back; out of nowhere, Telly Savalas sang the theme from Cinderella Liberty. Music enthusiasts are sure songwriter Paul Williams and recording artist Maureen McGovern, who released it as a single, weren't pleased.

Given the ten nominations The Sting and The Exorcist both received, it looked like a landslide in the making. The Sting took home Best Picture and Director, giving Julia Phillips the first female producer to win Oscar gold and only five more as The Exorcist and The Way We Were taking two apiece. Best Actor went to Jack Lemmon for Save the Tiger. British actress Glenda Jackson took Oscar number two as Best Actress in as many years for A Touch of Class. Youngster Tatum O'Neal stole the film and Oscar gold from Best Supporting Actress in Paper Moon, and septuagenarian a spry 71-year-old John Houseman took Best Supporting Actor in The Paper Chase. These two awards were the biggest age gap ever for two wins in a major category; as I mentioned before, O'Neal was 10 years old, and Houseman was 71 years old.

On the downside of the 1973 Oscars, ever as always

beautiful, Susan Hayward made her last appearance, presenting Charlton Heston the Best Actress Award. Subsequently, Hayward passed away from brain cancer in March 1975.

On a rarity note, three ex-wives of Eddie Fisher, Debbie Reynolds, Elizabeth Taylor, and Connie Stevens would grace the stage at least once during the ceremony. It is unknown if they saw each other.

The best was saved for last, though; posing as a journalist, an artist, and streaker, Robert Opel appeared onstage, flashing the peace sign with his hand. David Niven, one of the hosts, is preparing to introduce Elizabeth Taylor to present Best Picture, the last award of the evening. As host Niven, in his sly humorous response, said," Well ladies and gentlemen, that was bound to happen .... But isn't it fascinating to think that the only laugh that man will ever get in his life is by stripping off and showing his shortcomings?" There was talk that it was a stunt made easily by producer Jack Haley, Jr., as Opel cut through an expensive background curtain to make it to the stage. Sadly, Opel was murdered in an attempted robbery at his San Francisco studio in July 1979.

1974 was shaping to be quite a busy year for Hollywood; the "disaster" movies were back, the Corleone family reunited, Roman Polanski was directing again, and Mel Brooks was back, to name a few.

AND THE OSCAR GOES TO…

As the sextet was wrapping up from their television gigs and the streaker incident at the Oscars, preparations were being made for their new projects. Beau was working on The Towering Inferno. Cole and Keller found work on Earthquake. Carole was doing double duty as a script girl and makeup in Chinatown, with the possibility of going to Arizona and working for Martin Scorsese on Alice Doesn't Live Here Anymore.

Cole and Keller worked on Earthquake, an all-star cast disaster film starring big names like Charlton Heston, Ava Gardner, Genevieve Bujold, and Richard Roundtree, among others, and its bizarre yet odd casting, Lorne Greene playing Ava Gardner's father. This disaster film was set with the premise of a Los Angeles earthquake and its cast struggling for survival. It was directed and produced by Mark Robson and introduced a new sound feature called Sensurround. This new feature developed by Universal Studios and executive producer Jennings Lang was a bright, shining moment in Cole and Keller's careers working for sound editors. Sensurround was a series of large speakers made by Cerwin-Vega powered by BGW amplifiers that pumped sub-audible "infra bass "sound waves measuring 120 decibels, which is equal to a jet taking off to give the filmgoer a sense of feeling an earthquake.

Beau was working on The Towering Inferno, a joint venture from 20th Century Fox and Warner Brothers under the production helm of Irwin Allen. It was another all-star ensemble with A-listers of Paul Newman, Steve McQueen, Faye Dunaway, William Holden, and many others. The filmset in San Francisco, with the story surrounding a dedication ceremony of a glass tower. Beau was excited working with the cast, especially reuniting with Paul Newman and the hob nob opportunity with McQueen and Holden.

As Beau called San Francisco his home away from home, Carole joined him to work on the crime drama Chinatown starring Jack Nicholson, Faye Dunaway, and Roman Polanski directing. Proving it to be an intriguing shoot, scenes were shot depicting film noir turning back in time, giving a Raymond Chandler vibe. Carole never worked with Nicholson or Dunaway, more so interesting with Polanski, which proved quite challenging. Carole did her job staying to herself with a few exceptions, Dunaway making her feel at ease.

These were some of the films people were buzzing about early in the year, and as summer was approaching, post-production on the sequel to The Godfather was the place to go, but our sextet was not much in travel mode. Carole was approached after Chinatown wrapped. Would she be interested in going to Arizona and doing makeup for Ellen Burstyn in Alice Doesn't Live Here Anymore? Ellen remembered Carole on the Exorcist set, reluctant to go, agreed most so to meet Martin Scorsese.

Packing movie houses for the holidays, the sextet settled in on several movies. Some of them were two Mel Brooks comedies,

AND THE OSCAR GOES TO...

Blazing Saddles and Young Frankenstein, comedian Art Carney being dramatic in Harry and Tonto, an Agatha Christie star fest, Murder on the Orient Express, and a powerful film biography on comedian Lenny Bruce, Dustin Hoffman in Lenny.

Chapter Seventeen

I t was a proven fact that the blockbuster "disaster" films, helped by their astronomical numbers, the Towering Inferno knocking out the ballpark, and its disaster rival, Earthquake, were doing equally well. Now, it was time for the busy bees of Oscar buzz-circling beehives to decide not just who but what will be taking Oscar gold in April.

Nominations were announced on February 24th with little but no surprises; Godfather II and Chinatown both received eleven nominations, Towering Inferno received eight, and Lenny and Murder on the Orient Express both received six. Naysayers were already noting it appeared that the two crime dramas would duke it out to the end with the tower sneaking in to still its ride of thunder. Best Director looked like a race destined for the bettor's table. Would Francois Truffaut or actor-turn-director John Cassavetes steal the other well-deserved nominees of Coppola, Fosse, and

AND THE OSCAR GOES TO...

Polanski's thunder? With Godfather II's numerous nominations, one would wonder, since there were three for Best Supporting Actor, would they cancel each other and divide the members' votes, or would one prevail to win it all? In an odd twist, too, two-time Best Actress winner Ingrid Bergman was nominated for Best Supporting Actress in the ensemble mystery drama Agatha Christie's Murder on the Orient Express.

The ceremony was held on April 8th and presided over by Bob Hope (again), Frank Sinatra, Sammy Davis, Jr., and Shirley MacLaine (again) at the Dorothy Chandler Pavilion in the heart of Los Angeles. It was clear that Godfather II was going to have better luck than its predecessor. Sadly, the Academy members were more intent on gifting the production versus the acting, going home with six Oscar gold, which included Best Picture, Best Director, and Best Supporting Actor Robert DeNiro. Al Pacino and Dustin Hoffman seemed lost for words when comedian Art Carney took home Best Actor for Harry and Tonto. Best Actress went to Ellen Burstyn for Alice Doesn't Live Here Anymore, beating out dark horses Faye Dunaway, Gena Rowlands, Valerie Perrine, and Diahann Carroll. Best Supporting Actress went to Ingrid Bergman, being the second actress in history (at the time) to win three Oscars and second to win Best Actress and Best Supporting.

Poor Towering Inferno and Earthquake, touted as "disaster flicks," didn't win any major awards, but the technical aspects of both films garnered them some preferential treatment. Redeeming quality, our songstress, Maureen McGovern, had two of her recordings nominated for Best Song. Wherever Love Takes Me, the theme from Gold, and We May Never Love Like This Again from Towering Inferno, was in competition with a few others, and the theme from Towering Inferno took the gold home. As years passed, Ms. McGovern was forever identified as the "disaster theme" queen of pop until she eased into a new repertoire classic Gershwin and jazz, bringing her smashing success.

Our quartet of Cole, Keller, Beau, and Carole seemed pleased with their contributions to Earthquake, Towering Inferno, and Chinatown—all four earned praise from each of their directors, producers, screenwriters, and other higher personnel. Despite Godfather II gaining more gold, there was finally evidence their work was being well rewarded. It made them wonder if it was necessary to keep doing the same ol same ol, just like Ashlee and Janine pecking their way through the steno pool. Is there really any hope that our characters will do anything more substantial for the motion picture communities? Time will tell. Stay tuned.

As the 1975 film season started to roll in, the generated buzz around Hollywood about several films was setting the frenzy as the sextet was set in trying to land their feet.

As luck would have it, our sextet was going to be doing some traveling this season. The two ladies from the steno pool were summoned by Stanley Kubrick, who overheard their expertise on Patton was exemplary in inquiring if they would join the cast and crew on location. Kubrick was doing a period drama titled Barry Lyndon with Ryan O' Neal as the lead role. Principal production started in December 1973 and only took eight months to shoot in England, Ireland, and East and West Germany. Ashlee and Janine went abroad in early 1974, but Kubrick asked them to return for some post-production duties. The ladies said yes in hopes of catching up with O'Neal again, but this time, no sexy Ryan was seen. Drats! Damn, the bad luck! LOL.

As for our gay duo, they overheard Streisand was making a sequel to Funny Girl with Funny Lady and asked Ray Stark and director Herbert Ross to join them after studio bigwigs asked to cut 136 minutes. How could they say NO to Streisand, even as she appeared aloof at first because she disliked Stark's production? A bit of trivia: Ray Stark was Fanny Brice's one-time son-in-law, and Streisand was contracted for one more film with him. She often remarked it would take litigation for a sequel, but after reading his script, she gave in. James Caan was cast as Billy Rose after Robert Blake read first, and DeNiro and Pacino were mentioned briefly. Funny Lady didn't fare well at the box office, but it was fun that Cole and Keller got to "play" with Streisand again.

Screenwriter Bo Goldman and Cinematographer Haskell

Wexler were adapting Ken Kesey's 1962 novel, One Flew Over the Cuckoo's Nest, in January 1975 at Oregon State Hospital on location in Salem when studios asked Carole and Beau if they would like to go. Given the theme of mental psychiatry coupled with deep psychological roots, the lovebirds reluctantly agreed, given Carole's opportunity to collaborate with Jack Nicholson again. The production was only three months, a grueling shoot, given it was winter and, as mentioned before, the film's premise. Carole was over the moon reading the screenplay, remarking on reading the book in high school. Carole told producers Nicholson was perfect for the lead, who would play the lead nurse.

Contrary to belief, rumors swirled before Nicholson was offered the lead; big names like Hackman, Brando, Caan, and Burt Reynolds were all offered but turned down. For the female lead, Angela Lansbury, Geraldine Page, and even Colleen Dewhurst were offered. Casting director Fred Roos was an acquaintance of unknown actress Louise Fletcher, who eventually won director Milos Forman and executive producer Michael Douglas, Kirk's son, over after four to five meetings drawn out over a year. Originally a Broadway play in the early sixties, Kirk Douglas bought the rights and never could find a studio. Frustrated, I am sure, he sold the rights to his son, Michael. Michael recently quit the ABC-TV drama Streets of San Francisco, first cashing in on dad's name as a producer before as a leading man like Nicholson and other A-listers.

AND THE OSCAR GOES TO…

An interesting note for the film: During rehearsal, both Fletcher and Nicolson attended group therapy sessions and observed "shock" treatments. Some patients and staff were used as "extras" unbeknownst to the crew.

With these and many others being released in 1975, the sextet was quite content with its accomplishments thus far. Who would have known that these youngsters from all over the United States would make it to Hollywood? They have weathered many storms of sexual harassment, deaths in the family, love affairs gone awry, the difficulties of relationships, travels to parts unknown, etc.

Other films in 1975 generating buzz were Al Pacino in Dog Day Afternoon, JAWS based on the best seller by Peter Benchley, Shampoo, loosely based on Beverly Hills hairdresser Jon Peters, Nashville, the Robert Altman ensemble surrounding country and gospel music entertainers readying a concert for a Presidential candidate and Day of the Locust, a dark mystery surrounding Hollywood's early days.

Summer is in the air for our sextet, time to relax and readying for the fall and winter films, new television season, and time to spend reading and/or just pool time. The summer temperatures ranged between 70 and 75, balmy and nice enough to catch the much-needed sun. Weekends were eventful; at times, when not on location, Beau strongly suggested the sextet take a road trip to San

Francisco or Palm Springs. It was the lesser of two evils: you drive to the desert or the confines of being in a cooler temperature. Which would it be? Even a side trip to Las Vegas was in the cards; do anything just to get everyone out of their doldrums, making it easy for a change.

As fall turned the leaves, it was time for Ashlee and Janine to try love again. They were doing their best not to try to mix work with pleasure. Occasionally, after work, hit the Grove and check the "scenery" during happy hour to see if any hotshots from other film businesses hob-knobbing were. Not to say that Ashlee and Janine were sluts; they just starved for attention. Especially the writing on the wall; Cole and Keller are a couple, as were Beau and Carole, duh? You don't see them looking for other extracurricular activities, or do you?

This fall-October Saturday evening, after a long, tedious week, Ashlee and Janine decided the need to let their hair down and enjoy themselves a night in the town. Eat dinner, have drinks, dance if anyone asks, and who knows, take guys back to their apartment for some fun. It was easier said than done, given the fact baseball season was over, at least for the Dodgers anyway. The Grove was crawling with athletes from all sports, baseball, basketball, football, hockey, golf, you name it, jocks were on parade. Take your pick, ladies; it doesn't look like you wouldn't have any trouble getting laid tonight. Finishing their dinners and having nightcaps in their booth, two hotties walked over and asked if they could sit down. Ashlee remarked to them sure, have a sit. Conversations quickly turned to concern for two hot women alone on a Saturday night to what the others did for work. Back and forth, the ladies became quite flirtatious and coy with the two men. Giving in, the men finally told the ladies no, they weren't in the film business, but they were in sports. Janine inquired if the mystery men were agents. The men politely said no, they played a specific sport. Ashlee and Janine giggled, remarking that they didn't look like basketball or football, so they were golfers or baseball players. The two athletes finally broke the ice with no pun intended to say they played professional ice hockey for the Los Angeles Kings. Just slightly tipsy, Janine said, "Oh, I am from St. Louis. Do you ever play the Blues?" One of the guys remarked we sure do; we carry a big stick around those guys.

Janine giggled and remarked she likes guys with big sticks. Ashlee chimed in by remarking follow us back to our place and show us those big sticks. Jumping at the chance, these two-star athletes were off till tomorrow, and they wanted to get their cocks wet, so they went off in their cars, following each other to Ashlee and Janine's pad. Upon arrival,, Janine put a pot of coffee to sober the foursome up. Before they were on their second cup, the athletes noted just passing through to Ft. Worth as they were farm system players for the Texans. Janine drunkenly giggled and said, "I don't give a flying fuck hockey puck just as long you carry a big hockey stick." In a split second, Janine was already down in front of Ashlee and the other athlete, making a fool out of herself.

Ashlee yelled, "Oh my god, Janine, look how big it is!" Laughing in a roar, Janine looked down, noticing a huge penis was out of the zipper dangling in front of her mouth. Janine didn't waste any time servicing the hockey player to say, "Come on, big boy, take me to my room and have your way with me." Ashlee was laughing so hard, trying not to look too embarrassed. Turning to the other athlete, who was already fumbling his zipper and stroking his cock to say, "Well, my lady are you ready for my stick." Ashlee said with a big smile on her face, "Hell yeah, you don't have to ask me twice; come on with it!" And off they went, Ashlee pulling on his cock and leading him into her room. The next thing you know, you hear moans and groans coming from both rooms. Screaming in ecstasy, both ladies reached their plateau stage of orgasmic glee in unison as the two hockey players with the big sticks achieved their scoring goal, getting their rocks off. Whew, what a night. Sadly, no names were exchanged, nothing nil, nada, just a big kiss on the cheek and goodbye in the morning. Four consenting adults being slutty as possible. Oh, what fun they had. Ashlee and Janine would never be the same. Be quite possible, come Monday morning, the two sluts be walking bowlegged in the office. LOL

Well, here we are, near the end of 1975, reporters were

starting their bets on the who's who of next year's nominees. Would Streisand pick up one for the sequel to Funny Girl? Will Al Pacino catch Oscar gold for Dog Day Afternoon? Will the shark from Jaws take a bite out of the member's hand? Will George Burns be a sentimental favorite for the Sunshine Boys?

Chapter Eighteen

A s 1976 rolled in. Box office receipts were flying off the charts; as the slogan said, just when you think it was safe to get in the water, JAWS and the sharks were biting off the moviegoers' dollars as they went by the millions. It was fun seeing Warren Beatty be funny and sexy with Shampoo as the over-sexed hairdresser who couldn't commit Julie Christie. It was Debbie Reynolds' daughter, Carrie Fisher, who stole the movie as the flirtatious teenage sexpot daughter of co-star, Lee Grant trying to seduce Beatty to give him a taste of his own medicine. Who thought Fisher would become a big office draw in a few short years with Star WARS?

Nominations were announced on February 17th, giving the Academy members just a bit over a month to select their winners. Nine went to One Flew Over the Cuckoo's Nest, seven to Barry Lyndon, six to Dog Day Afternoon, five to Funny Lady, the

Hindenburg, and Nashville, and rounding out four went to JAWS, the Sunshine Boys, and Shampoo. It was announced the Academy decided to give the legendary screen actress Mary Pickford an honorary award. No real surprises of the who's who in nominees, except a few famous foreign filmmakers. Federico Fellini was nominated Best Director for Amarcord, and Czechoslovakian Milos Forman directed One Flew Over the Cuckoo's Nest. George Burns received a nod in the Best Supporting Actor category, and unknowns Louise Fletcher and Isabelle Adjani for Best Actress.

The month leading up to the ceremony had everyone rushing to theatres to see their favorites; naysayers were saying Jack Nicholson was proving to be the best to beat and if not him, Al Pacino could take him down, and a peculiar move in a one-man show was James Whitmore as former President Truman in Give em' Hell, Harry.

When the awards were presented on March 29th, ABC reclaimed their broadcast rights from NBC as a quintet of hosts were selected: Walter Matthau, Gene Kelly, Robert Shaw, George Segal, and Goldie Hawn. As the awards were presented, it looked as though JAWS might sweep the awards. Still, One Flew Over the Cuckoo's Nest prevailed and won five out of five major categories, which included Best Picture, Director, Adapted Screenplay, and Best Actor to Jack Nicholson and Best Actress Louise Fletcher. Lee Grant took gold for Best Supporting Actress in Shampoo as a sentimental favorite, and octogenarian George Burns won Best Supporting Actor in The Sunshine Boys.

After the ceremonies were held and back to work, our sextet went. Luckily, the quartet had already been working, just resting in between Oscar ceremonies and going back to their respective locations the next day. This was separation anxiety for Beau and Carole. Carole was heading to Philadelphia. At the beginning of the year, Carole was selected by United Artists to be a script girl for an unknown screenwriter and soon-to-be actor, Sylvester Stallone. Stallone had written a script in three and half days after watching a heavyweight championship match between Muhammad Ali and Chuck Wepner in 1975 and inspirations from other matches and Rocky Graziano's autobiography and film of the same name, Somebody Up There Likes Me. This movie is what's known as the blockbuster Rocky. Big names like Redford, Reynolds, Caan, and O'Neal were being thrown around as leads; United Artists agreed to a lower budget of a mere close to $1.5 million. Boy, United Artists was in for a major surprise, with Rocky becoming the highest-grossing film of 1976, making $225 million worldwide! Filming began in Philadelphia and utilized a new method called Steadicam when Garrett Brooks introduced it with films like Marathon Man and Bound For Glory. Steadicam was a unique technique utilizing smooth photography when someone was running. Rocky fans noticed him running through Philadelphia streets and up and down the Art Museum's steps, which are now known as Rocky steps, which is the implementation of this technique. This film became an all-time favorite franchise, producing many sequels and introducing a character named Apollo Creed and his son, who became famous in his own right and has spawned three sequels as well.

With Carole dividing her time between Philadelphia and Hollywood, Beau was in Arizona toiling in the fields of a musical with Cole and Keller. This was the first musical the boys were doing set around concerts and huge plus getting another opportunity with Ms. Barbra Streisand. The film, of course, is A Star Is Born, the third remake of this franchise. A Star Is Born was often referred to as a rough shoot, starting with crew shuffling a challenging time securing the perfect co-star for Streisand as names from Elvis Presley, Neil Diamond, and even Brando were thrown around. After these three had to pass, Kris Kristofferson landed the leading role as the washed-up, alcoholic, fading rock star. Another noted film in 1976 was Network, a satirical look at television news brought to the screen by film veterans. Paddy Chayefsky and Sidney Lumet starred Faye Dunaway, William Holden, and Peter Finch in his final role. Robert Redford and Dustin Hoffman brought Bob Woodward and Carl Bernstein's Watergate best-selling drama to the big screen in All the President's Men, packed with an A-list star cast from Jason Robards, Hal Holbrook, Jack Warden, and Martin Balsam portraying prominent figures in history. Taxi Driver, Marathon

Man, a biopic about Woody Guthrie based on his book Bound for Glory, The Seven Percent Solution, and the Stephen King bestseller thriller turned film chiller, Carrie, rounded up favorites.

As the four of the sextet were busily travelling from their respective locations awaiting release dates for their films, they were enjoying downtime with Ashlee and Janine. Whether it be pool time, happy hour Grove time, dining at various restaurants in Hollywood, barbecuing, or occasional weekend road trips to Laguna Beach, Long Beach, Las Vegas, and Palm Springs, making time fly.

As the fall television season started and films packed theatres, word of mouth passed, television and film halls steno pooled, and behind-the-scenes work reached staffing all the time. Television work was remote within studios as films were seeing lesser studio lot activity, moving travel nationwide to internationally extensive, making budgets to make a blockbuster more expensive. Do you know what that means? Box office receipts would have to almost double their gross to pay for the film being made, you reckon.

The holiday season was upon us; films before mentioned were making box office gold. Rocky and A Star Is Born were making millions. Star Is Born was making gold with record sales, as well! Who could resist when Streisand sings Caching? Caching!

Chapter Nineteen

H olidays were gone as a not-so-good for memories being made. In a million years, you would never know who decided to drive from St. Louis to Los Angeles. The Wallace family decided they were homesick for their kiddos. I am sure of it; Keller and Janine weren't going to be so happy about this. Once declaring their independence and living the high California life, they were adjusting quite nicely, and having the burden of parents showing up unannounced was just WRONG! I mean, WRONG! Keller left St. Louis with hopes of really finding his own persona and being who he was - a gay man in hopes of settling down with Mr. Right. At first, you could hear Janine scream out, "MOM! It is a period where I feel it has added to my maturity. Oh, how nice it is to see you!" Ashlee runs out of her room with a robe on, exclaiming, "What's going on?" Janine invites her parents in, sits them down, and crosses between excited and annoyed at the same time she introduces them to Ashlee. Ashlee scurries, saying she will put coffee on. Janine tried to contain herself, wondering what they were doing here. Geoff spoke up first as Rennie tried to chime in, explaining that they wanted to see their babies. Janine thought to herself they could have at least called first. Janine said she didn't know if Keller was home as his schedule was quite busy.

As Ashlee was busy making coffee looked to see if there were any pastries to share with their new unwelcome guests. Janine excused herself to call her brother. Ashlee tried being the best hostess with the moistest as Janine returned from her room. Oops, you just missed him; Cole and Keller were on location. Ashlee gave Janine a stare as if looks could kill, as if she knew Janine was lying through her teeth. Janine explained to her parents since moving to California, life was very taxing between Keller's travels and her busy office work. They rarely see each other, and it is three weeks to a month sometimes, Keller comes home for a weekend.

Geoff and Rennie related they wouldn't stay long in Los Angeles; just wanted to get out of St. Louis cold and feel some California sun. Janine understood completely as she wouldn't have much time to show them much of Hollywood as Monday was the beginning of a new work week.

The Wallace duo stayed two days without seeing their son (pout). Good for Keller, I suppose. Geoff was rocked with guilt as to how Keller could be gay. Was it that he pushed him so hard to try out for sports, or was it Keller's flair for the drama club in school? Rennie wondered why Janine was quiet about her love life; Janine remarked that she was busy with studio executives and often had the opportunity to travel. Rennie remarked she was indeed so proud of both her children having opportunities to meet famous people.

With the family visit behind her, Janine was letting her brother have it once she saw him. How dare he not answer his phone when damn well Keller was home. Earlier in the week, Keller just told her that he was busy working doing sound for CBS and the show The Incredible Hulk. Was it that Keller knew their parents were coming to Los Angeles? Was it Keller who didn't want to face his parents and meet Cole yet, or was it an impromptu intervention for Janine? Either way, both failed; luckily, they arrived on a Sunday, and Janine couldn't show them much of what Los Angeles and Hollywood had to offer. Next trip?

When nominations were announced on February 10th, nobody could be happier to be Sylvester Stallone. An unknown to Hollywood, who brought his script after numerous studios and rejections to United Artists and producers, Irwin Winkler and Robert Chartoff gave him this lifetime opportunity. Rocky scored ten nominations, which included yet another surprise: Stallone himself was nominated for Best Actor and Screenplay. This was nothing short of a Cinderella story. Especially critics and movie goers alike embraced Rocky with huge money at the box office as well as their hearts. Ten nominations were also rendered to Network; two specific notes were to Peter Finch for Best Actor, who was posthumously nominated who suddenly passed away in mid-January, and Beatrice Straight, holding the record for shortest screentime of five minutes and two seconds. Will they prevail? Eight nods went to All the President's Men. Another first was a woman for Best Director, the provocative Seven Beauties, Lina Wertmuller. Wertmuller was also nominated for Best Foreign Film and Best Screenplay Based on Material not previously published or produced.

As the weeks leading up to the ceremony, naysayers were buzzing about the who's who to win the coveted gold statues. The ceremony was held on March 28th, and Ellen Burstyn, Jane Fonda, Richard Pryor, and Warren Beatty hosted.

This ceremony was the first that the Academy allowed the actual recording artist of a song to sing their nomination. Turning gold for Barbra Streisand, becoming the first female songwriter to win. The Cinderella story continued for Rocky as it took home four statues, one for Best Picture and Best Director, and Network won four as well, taking home three of the main four acting awards: Peter Finch for Best Actor, Faye Dunaway for Best Actress and Beatrice Straight for Best Supporting Actress. Best Supporting Actor gold went to Jason Robards as Washington Post editor, Ben Bradlee in

AND THE OSCAR GOES TO…

All the President's Men, and took home Best Screenplay.

Overall, it was a good evening. The sextet was pleased with the results - were busily getting some television and film work here and there. Keller had been working with CBS, separately from Cole to gain some valued experience on The Incredible Hulk. Cole and Beau combined their sound and cinematography expertise working on a science fiction film, Close Encounters of the Third Kind, in various locales from right there in Burbank and spreading to others like Wyoming, Alabama, and India, which the boys didn't go there. Carole was lucky enough to go to New York City and work on not one, not two, but three films and just a tad on a fourth. Working as a script girl, she went set to set on Woody Allen's Annie Hall, Neil Simon's The Goodbye Girl, Joseph Brooks's You Light Up My Life, and Richard Brooks's Looking For Mr. Goodbar. It was the latter; Carole reunited with Diane Keaton, and Beau came to assist with his expertise with William A. Fraker, famed cinematographer.

Carole was beginning to enjoy time in the Big Apple, making contacts through work, seeing Broadway shows, sightseeing, and going to museums. She was doing it right. Missing Beau made matters worse, but over the top when he joined the Looking For Mr. Goodbar location.

Cole and Keller enjoyed time spent with Streisand on her musical journey and were fascinated by the new craze, action-

135 | P a g e

adventure mixed with comic book genre and science fiction. Keller was doing Incredible Hulk at CBS Television Studios, and Cole was working with Steven Spielberg and even dabbled a bit with George Lucas in Star Wars. Looks like things were on the upswing for our quartet of behind-the-scenes workers.

The steno pool duo weren't doing too shabby either; between going crazy with athletes on the weekends, their expertise was required. Director Fred Zinnemann inquired and asked them to join the location shoot of Julia in England and France. Ashlee and Janine were overjoyed with good fortune, meeting the likes of Jane Fonda, Vanessa Redgrave, Jason Robards Jr., and Maximillian Schell.

As the film season progressed, the famed producer turned director Herbert Ross filmed The Turning Point, a ballet drama concerning friendly rivals starring Shirley MacLaine and Anne Bancroft, garnering buzz. Noteworthy, Ross said to have gone to Monaco to woo Princess Grace out of retirement; she politely told him NO and supposedly asked Audrey Hepburn and Doris Day, too.

The holiday season was releasing blockbusters as box receipts were off the roof with science fiction, romantic comedies, and dramas, and theatres were packed. It's going to be interesting in February 1978 to see what movies would secure those Oscar nominations and try to capture Oscar gold.

Chapter Twenty

W ould there be love for the new genre of science fiction? Could it be the doldrums of ho-hum drama? Comedy? There was a Broadway play that had been turned into a film gathering buzz; could this be the swan song for Richard Burton in Equus? In comedy, we have George Burns playing God, and Neil Simon was bringing off-Broadway romance with the Goodbye Girl starring his wife, Marsha Mason.

Nominations were released on February 21st with a few surprises; sci-fi did break out with ten nominations for Star Wars and nine for Close Encounters of the Third Kind, and drama dominated eleven nominations for both Turning Point and Julia. Julia was based on a chapter from Lillian Hellman's 1973 Pentimento about her longtime relationship with a friend before World War II who fought against the Nazis. Comedy paved the way for five each for Goodbye Girl and Annie Hall, who received three solo nominations for Woody Allen. Allen made history by tying Orson Welles' 1941 Citizen Kane feat, which was nominated for Best Actor, Best Director, and Best Screenplay.

This year's ceremony would be the first to recognize winners in a separate category for Scientific and Technical Achievement. Presented and hosted by Kirk Douglas and Gregory Peck at the Beverly Hills Hilton on March 29th, five days prior to the April 3rd hosted by Bob Hope (again) telecast on ABC (again) and held (again) at the Dorothy Chandler Pavilion.

As the ceremony reached April 3rd, chaos was surrounding the Oscar festivities. Vanessa Redgrave, a nominee for Best Supporting Actress in Julia and a well-known political activist, had earlier produced and appeared in a 1977 film, The Palestinian, which depicted Palestine Liberation Organization (PLO) activities. Julia and its eleven Oscar nominations were already drawing much anger from the Jewish community for the film's anti-Israel slant. Making it worse, the Jewish Defense League chose to picket the ceremony, which was countered by protestors waving PLO flags. This was going to be an interesting ceremony, to say the least. Coupled with press and venue personnel, they were having a horrific time assisting guests into the auditorium and figuring out how this evening was going to play out.

As everyone assembled to their seats, heavy tension

surrounded the room as the ceremony began as normal. The president of the Academy, Howard W. Koch, welcomed guests, and Bette Davis and Gregory Peck explained the voting rules. So, here we go, the first of the awards, John Travolta, fresh from the previous year's nomination for Saturday Night Fever, presented the Best Supporting Actress award.

The field for this category featured a variety of nominees: an unknown ballerina, a precocious youngster, an alcoholic swinging sister of a sex addict, a mother who may or may not believe in UFOs, and an emotional friend with political motives in World War II. Of course, the winner was controversial, Vanessa Redgrave. Ms. Redgrave gave a stirring speech that was a mixture of boos and applause, given her speech content and the lengthy time at the dais. As the evening continued, we saw a shutout of no awards for the ballet drama Turning Point; Star Wars took six, Annie Hall won four, one for Best Actress Keaton and Woody Allen won Best Director, and its producer, Charles H. Joffe won for Best Picture. As usual, Allen was absent from the ceremonies, as he was back in New York City playing at Mike's Pub. Best Actor went to Richard Dreyfuss for the Goodbye Girl, and rumor has it, Richard Burton, who was in the running for Equus, was halfway out of his seat and down the aisle when Sylvester Stallone paused to say the last name after Richard was sure of a win. Sadly, that wasn't the case. Jason Robards won his second consecutive Best Supporting Actor for

Julia.

Despite the political overtures earlier in the evening, Paddy Chayefsky, presenting Best Screenplay, took a moment to reassure the audience this wasn't the platform for the acting community to express their views to either to or not taken as propaganda to say Thank You" would have been sufficient purely.

If there wasn't enough backlash, Debby Boone performed the Best Song nominee and winner, You Light Up My Life, with girl background singers said to have been from John Tracy Clinic for the Deaf to interpret the lyrics in sign language. Alliance of Deaf Artists later made protests; upon their findings, the girls indeed weren't deaf but were taught rudimentary signs for this specific performance.

It was a sentimental night as William Holden and Barbara Stanwyck presented the Oscar for Best Sound. Whew! Thought we would never get through all this drama. Hopefully, as years pass, there won't be much more drama. The Oscars are to be a fun occasion for celebrities to honor their friends for their work in their respective fields, not a place to exercise free speech as a political platform.

As the sextet heads back to work for the remainder of the year, it will be interesting if television and/or films dominate their time. Keller was really enjoying television work of late; being away from Cole was a bit of an issue. Was there a sense of worry as separation anxiety for the lovebirds? Keller was spending more time at CBS. Late in the previous year, Cole was dividing time between United Kingdom and New York City on Superman. Beau and Carole had been asked to go overseas, and New York City for The Deer Hunter opted to work together on the romantic comedy Same Time, Next Year.

Grease was the word, and the film season proved a blockbuster for Paramount as John Travolta was on a high ride. After leaving TV films and his television series Welcome Back, Kotter, Travolta lost his girlfriend, Diana Hyland, to cancer by throwing his grief into Saturday Night Fever. After screening other singers and actresses, Allan Carr had his Sandy for Travolta's Danny. Paramount and Allan Carr settled on music sensation Olivia Newton-John. They made a wise choice as it was chemistry, good friends for life, and box office gold.

Vietnam was on everyone's minds, too, as films like The Deer Hunter and Coming Home were released. Fun but light comedies made the rounds, such as Heaven Can Wait, Same Time, Next Year, and California Suite, and family drama was taking a heavy turn, with Woody Allen directing Interiors with an excellent ensemble cast.

As Superman wrapped up and Cole was home contemplating

his next gig, Keller was busier than ever over at CBS with various action-adventure series. You would think distance would have made the heart grow fonder for our two gay lovebirds. It was the opposite; distance only made them a bit more apart than together. Keller was really getting into this new, fast-paced genre tired by the time he came home from work. Cole was feeling alone. Beau and Carole were busy enjoying New York City after their work on the films being made there. Ashlee and Janine were busy at the steno pool, too, leaving Cole with time on his hands.

Wandering West Hollywood streets, Cole was drawn to male escorts strutting their stuff to bars, and porno arcades were plentiful of guys hanging around for one special trick. What was Cole to do? Would he submit to staying monogamous with Keller, don't tell, having idle time on his hands? Keller was very busy, long hours at the studio and Cole wasn't particularly looking for work right away. Cole had plenty of time to get in a few tricks before getting back home. Remember, it's the 70s, and times were changing, busier than ever.

As many films were in post-production and the start of the new television season, work was plentiful in both arenas. Beau and Carole were staying busy working on their films, shifting to and from New York to Hollywood.

Off and on in late 1977 to mid-1978, the steno pool was

minus two ladies. Yes, Ashlee and Janine, who are now labeled as the boobsey twins, are on their way to places unimaginable. Patton director Franklin Schaffner remembered their expertise and summoned the studio, asking for the ladies to join the crew on location for the Boys from Brazil. Based on the best-selling novel by Rosemary Baby's Ira Levin, set in South America and deemed impossible, Schaffner chose Lisbon, Portugal as a starting point. As shooting progressed, the crew bounced from London to Vienna and the Kolbrien Dam in Austria. Ashlee and Janine brushed up on their German speaking skills by wowing others in the process, coupled with lifetime friendships with ailing Sir Laurence Oliver, Gregory Peck, James Mason, Lilli Palmer, and famed acting coach Uta Hagen. This was a dream shoot that was too good to be true.

Fifty years of Oscar have passed, and many great films have been honored either by nomination or a win. Certainly, nobody was a loser, being a part of the recognition. Our sextet were learning their respective crafts, hob-knobbing with the very best, traveling to location after location, places unimaginable, and making lifetime friendships.

Chapter Twenty-One

Everybody was surprised by the so-called political backlash from Vanessa Redgrave's stunt. Better not invite Ms. Redgrave to any more Oscar parties. Jeez! It was looking as though an old but new genre was making a comeback of sorts to the big screen regarding separate times of history from the World War to Vietnam and some Nazi-Jewish backlash as well. Proving to be interesting to see if this will keep the audiences awake at the theatre and the academy members as well when previewing their future nominations.

Nominations were released on February 20th; The Deer Hunter and Heaven Can Wait lead the roster with nine. Coming Home received eight, six for the fact-based Turkish drug drama Midnight Express and five for Woody Allen's drama Interiors. Woody Allen wasn't the only one following in Orson Welles' Citizen Kane footsteps. Warren Beatty was nominated four times in all the same categories as Welles had in 1941 for acting, directing, producing, and screenwriting; time will see if history repeats itself. Co-directors Beatty and Buck Henry were the second in recent years to garner a Best Director nod, just as Robert Wise and Jerome Robbins had in 1961 for West Side Story.

The ceremony was to take place April 9th, as three days prior, on April 6th, hosted and presented by Gregory Peck and Christopher Reeve at the Beverly Hilton, the Technical Achievement Awards were presented.

Cole was super excited while Keller was busy at CBS; he was invited to the Technical Achievement Awards at the Beverly Hilton. Also, so as not to be rude about their personal issues, Cole arrived early to have some fun with one of the bellhops he casually cruised with at breakfast. The bellhop knew an empty room, and with no further delay, Cole scored some hot fun. Shame shame! Would Cole tell Keller what he had done, or would Keller have to figure it out for himself? Cole was also super excited he got to say hi to Christopher Reeve, who he worked with on Superman.

As rehearsals began, it was announced that Jack Haley Jr. was producing the show along with the first-time host, late-night king Johnny Carson. Haley added an extra segment to the music portion of the show, where the Academy's music branch protested. Haley told the branch that if it weren't to be seen on the telecast,

Carson and he would pull out. The branch gave in, and the segment aired as a salute to songs not nominated for Best Original Song, with Steve Lawrence and Sammy Davis Jr. performing a medley called "Oscar's Only Human."

Sentimentality proved sad for the Academy members as it was the last time they would see John Wayne and Jack Haley Sr., both of whom passed away months after the telecast. Wayne, who had been ill with cancer, was asked to present the Best Picture award, and Haley presented Best Costume Design alongside his Wizard of Oz costar, Ray Bolger.

The ceremony appeared to be running quite smoothly, showing no sign of controversy, and the entertainment was spot on. Predictions were true for Vietnam showing signs of rebirth when Deer Hunter took home Best Director and Best Picture. Robert DeNiro lost to Jon Voight for Best Actor in his powerhouse performance as disabled vet Luke Martin in Coming Home. To complete winning top lead acting honors, Voight's costar, Jane Fonda, took home Best Actress for her second win in recent years. The best supporting actress was Maggie Smith, who played an Oscar loser in Neil Simon's California Suite, and Christopher Walken in The Deer Hunter. This was two wins both for Fonda and Smith, Smith has the distinction of being part of a chosen few winning both Best Actress and Best Supporting Actress.

AND THE OSCAR GOES TO...

As the ceremony ended, the sextet was content on the way home, and Cole and Keller were in total silence. Cole nudged Keller to get him to say something; Keller yawned and remarked he was just tired from working so much. Cole tried to make him feel at ease by saying they needed a weekend getaway or hadn't had much time alone on vacation from work since they met. Keller remarked to Cole he was so right.

As the boobsey twins climbed out of the car, claiming a needed break was quite essential because of the excessive workload. They, too, expressed it; especially these overseas travels for them have been so excruciating, and despite the locations, they rarely had time to enjoy them. Not to mention, the grand gesture of generosity bestowed by Patton director Schaffner when he surprised them with that holiday in Sitges was super nice.

If the sextet were thinking of much-needed time off, they better hurry and get going. It looks like the 1979 film season is set to be plentiful, with great films coming on the screen near us. Heavy hitting dramas about divorce, unions in factories, musical loosely based on Bob Fosse's medical woes, musical might or might not be loosely based on Janis Joplin, nuclear meltdown, a river cruise from South Vietnam to Cambodia originally a novel based in Congo but set during the Vietnam War, coming of age comedy-drama based on American family, and legal system battles with the judicial system.

Apocalypse Now caught Cole's eye, having already started filming plagues in late '76 with many production issues and a location in Manila, Philippines. The majority of the crew was getting ill, and actors were dropping out during the pre-casting process. The thought of having to work with Francis Ford Coppola would look great on a resume, too. This was a location shoot, but it was not to be unless you want to return very ill or deceased. Next!

China Syndrome was about a nuclear meltdown, and its findings were shown vicariously through the eyes of a reporter, her crew, and a shift supervisor at a nuclear power plant near Los Angeles. It was a wonderful opportunity to collaborate with Jack Lemmon, Jane Fonda, and Michael Douglas.

All that Jazz and The Rose were loosely based extravaganzas on two icons, Bob Fosse and Janis Joplin, both equally opportunities to work with Roy Scheider and the divine Miss M, Bette Midler.

Two dramas with strong performances dealing with two different subjects were being touted as projects to be had. One was about divorce, and it was Kramer vs Kramer with Dustin Hoffman and rising star Meryl Streep. An odd piece of trivia, Aaron Spelling wouldn't allow Kate Jackson to rearrange her work schedule on ABC's Charlie's Angels, missing an excellent opportunity for stardom. The other was Norma Rae, with Sally Field about organizing unions in the factory workplace.

AND THE OSCAR GOES TO…

Keller had given up on television for a bit in hopes of saving his relationship and keeping working with Cole on The Rose. This would give the men an opportunity to rekindle their relationship in the throes of their passion: music and a fan of Bette Midler. Production had ended earlier in the year, but there were some post-production duties that needed some attention before its pending fall release.

Once again, New York City was calling for Beau and Carole. Kramer vs Kramer was the hot ticket now. Given the star power of Hoffman, where could you go wrong? Sadly, this was firsthand and indeed personal for the star. Having always thrown himself into his work and going through a divorce, Hoffman became disgruntled with film acting and disliked Hollywood, so it took a meeting with the producer and director. They flew to London on the Agatha location in hopes of rejuvenating his acting passion and family talking him into it after his declining. Hoffman was their 1st and only choice, as both Pacino and Voight turned it down. After Kate Jackson had to drop out, director Benton and producer Jaffe looked at Dunaway, Fonda, and MacGraw before settling on Meryl Streep. Streep had been cast as a minor supporting role, winning everyone over with an emotional audition as she was grieving the death of her partner, John Cazale, at the time. Hoffman said that, at the time, she sold herself by showing a "still fresh pain" in her performance. Never had a film about divorce displayed a must-see vulnerability of both sides given equal opportunity to shine.

As the holidays approached, several films on everyone's lips were released, with Christmas movies popping up on screens to get early dibs on what would be nominated in February 1980 for Oscar gold.

Chapter Twenty-Two

A s the year 1980 started, Hollywood seemed mixed with love given to Dustin Hoffman and a television actress who came out of nowhere to shine in movies. This person was everyone's darling, Sally Field. Bette Midler's stellar turn in The Rose spread huge buzz as well, wondering if it would turn Oscar gold or fade into the sunset and let some other rain on her parade. Dustin Hoffman was the golden boy now. Will there be someone else, perhaps Peter Sellers, to steal his thunder?

Nominations were released on February 25th, announced to be presented on April 14th, hosted by Johnny Carson (again), and the Technical Awards, three days earlier on April 11, with Cloris Leachman and William Shatner hosting.

Kramer vs Kramer and All That Jazz scored nine nominations apiece; Justin Henry became the youngest ever to be nominated at the age of eight for Best Supporting Actor. Francis

Ford Coppola's war saga Apocalypse Now garnered eight, and rounding up with four apiece were China Syndrome, Norma Rae, and The Rose.

During the time between the nominations and the ceremony, our sextet had begun work on the next year's film roster. Looks like Carole was back to and from Chicago doing script duties on the highly anticipated Robert Redford's directorial debut, Ordinary People. Cole and Keller got together again and started work on the sequel to Star Wars, the Empire Strikes Back. Beau was assisting in the cinematography of Coal Miner's Daughter, the film biopic on Loretta Lynn. The dynamic steno pool duo were staying close to California in hopes of asking for some much-needed time off to go on an extended girl's two-week journey well deserved with steno pool gals and hoping to persuade Carole to join after Ordinary People wrapped. As the ceremony started, there were tense moments in the auditorium. Nervous Academy members were on pins and needles, wondering if Bob Fosse could upset Francis Ford Coppola or if the dark horse would gallop in and take the big prize. Time will tell very soon.

Being There, a satirical look at American politics with an ensemble cast of Peter Sellers, Shirley MacLaine, and Melvyn Douglas, received another Best Supporting Actor after his last nomination for Hud in the sixties. Sally Field proved to the film community a TV comedienne could show dramatic chops, taking the Best Actress award from Bette Midler, Jill Clayburgh, and Jane Fonda, naming a few for Norma Rae. Of course, saving the best for last, Kramer vs Kramer slew the competition for Best Picture, Best Actor to Dustin Hoffman (a no-brainer!), and Meryl Streep took Best Supporting Actress.

As the ceremony ended, the sextet considered themselves the luckiest of the behind-the-scenes crew on the planet. What more can you ask for? An equally talented group of people who can travel around the USA and abroad for adventures to last a lifetime. Coupled with opportunities to tell, they had the pleasure of meeting and collaborating with some of the greatest motion picture stars on the planet.

As soon as Cole and Keller returned home from the ceremony, they repacked, returning to London finishing post-production on Empire Strikes Back. It was over budget, and production had begun principal photography months prior on Hardangerjokulen glacier in Finse, Norway. The boys made sure they packed extra warm clothes, as the Elstree studios stage lacked protection for chilly weather. Carrie Fisher had taken ill with flu and bronchitis, dropping her weight to eighty-five pounds while working twelve-hour days, causing at one time her to collapse on set from being allergic to steam, spray paint, and makeup. Most certainly, Fisher's well-known abuse of hallucinogens and painkillers made it even worse. Harrison Ford and Mark Hamill were either ill or injured several times.

Carole was readying a return to Chicago for post-production of Ordinary People and saw first-hand Robert Redford's masterpiece directing Mary Tyler Moore in the role of a lifetime mirroring her real life. Moore, fresh from leaving her goody two-shoe television image behind, appearing not afraid, showing the bitterness of a mother losing one son and avoiding the other, almost solidified and guaranteed her performance to be the one to beat.

Beau was heading back to Nashville, Kentucky, and Virginia to be near Sissy Spacek and Tommy Lee Jones in Cole Miner's Daughter. Beau came from a location with a better appreciation for country and Western music and a hard nose-to-nose with Carole. Predicting it was going to be too close to call between Spacek and Moore come the 1980 Oscars. We will have to wait and see.

As for our steno pool duo, they were staying close to California and just enjoying the downtime. They were asked by Roman Polanski upon hearing about their excellent job for Patton director Schaffner. Schaffner gave them glowing reviews and was hoping the two ladies would be for France, but sadly declined. What a loss. Polanski was directing Tess, set in Dorset, England. Polanski was in legal trouble in the United States on a conviction of sex with an underage girl and chose to live in Europe. Polanski chose several locations in France to shoot the film. Tess was set in Dorset,

England, but shot in various locations. Normandy (Cotentin, la Hague, Omonville-la-Rogue, Éculleville, Sainte-Croix-Hague, leVast, Bricquebec, Saint-Jacques-de-Néhou), Brittany (Locronan, le Leslay) and Nord-Pas-de-Calais (Condette) to name a few. Polanski fled to the UK before sentencing and would have been extradited. What a mess!

As the year ended and mentioned before, next year's Best Actress Oscar race proved quite competitive, with Mary Tyler Moore and Sissy Spacek fighting off Goldie Hawn in Private Benjamin. Robert DeNiro, playing real-time person Jake LaMotta in Raging Bull, had veterans Jack Lemmon and Peter O'Toole on his coattails. Best Picture had Ordinary People as the favorite. Raging Bull and Coal Miner's Daughter were gaining momentum. We will have to wait and see!

Chapter Twenty-Three

P redictions were constantly reminding the film community as well as the Academy of their jobs. After watching all these extraordinary performances, it was going to be a hard decision to settle on their nominations and, eventually, the winners. Everyone had their work cut out for them, deciding what to see and what to avoid—a fun time had by all. Just depending what genre appealed to you. You had sci-fi, historical drama, a real-time drama depicting two famous people, heavy family drama with a performance making your skin crawl, comedies; you name it! Hollywood studios depended on us patrons to pay ticket prices to pay performers' salaries.

Nominations were announced February 17th. The Elephant Man and Raging Bull received eight nominations apiece, Cole Miner's Daughter seven, Ordinary People, Fame, and Tess each received six, and Empire Strikes Back received four. It was

AND THE OSCAR GOES TO…

announced that a special Oscar would be presented to Henry Fonda for his body of work.

The Oscar ceremony was slated to be on March 30th, but due to the attempted assassination of President Reagan, the academy chose to postpone it until the next day, the 31st. Two weeks earlier, on March 15th, the Technical awards were presented (again) at the Beverly Hilton by Ed Asner and Fay Kanin. Johnny Carson hosted the ceremony and presented a segment, which was debated whether to air or not air by President Reagan, saluting the nominees and the Academy. Explaining the reason behind the previous day's event and why postponing. Reagan's segment was taped a month prior to the ceremony. The postponement was the first time since Martin Luther King Jr's assassination from an original date. The first award of the evening was presented by nominees Jack Lemmon and Mary Tyler Moore to her Ordinary People co-star, Timothy Hutton, who portrayed her son. Hutton recently lost his father, fellow actor Jim Hutton, a few weeks prior to the ceremony, thanking him in his acceptance speech, making him, at age twenty, the youngest male to win a Best Supporting Actor Oscar.

As the evening progressed, the musical Fame had two nominees for original song, a first-ever in the Best Original Song category claimed one beating out odds favorites Dolly Parton and Willie Nelson. Best Supporting Actress was given to Mary Steenburgen for Melvyn and Howard, Robert DeNiro won Best

Actor for Raging Bull, and as predicted, Robert Redford won Best Director, making him the only third actor to receive in a directorial debut for his moving Ordinary People. The film also won Best Picture; sadly, Mary Tyler Moore lost to Sissy Spacek for Best Actress. The final tally was evident: Ordinary People was king with four wins, three for Tess and two for Empire Strikes Back. One oddity is that Elephant Man, famous for the hideous makeup of John Hurt, was not highly recognized by the Academy, but next year, a new category was added. This gave Carol the ability to reclaim her craftsmanship in makeup.

Some of the films being released for the 1981 award season had already started and were filmed in locations afar, causing skyrocketing budgets and complaints between cast and crew. REDS started in 1979. Warren Beatty gathered his ensemble cast and crew from many locations; he was hoping the Soviet government would allow him to film in Moscow but declined. Beatty used Helsinki as his Russia and, being a perfectionist as a director, required some scenes and films have several takes, causing disgruntled cast members. Not to mention, his on-and-off romance with co-star and leading lady Diane Keaton was crumbling during filming, causing disaccord between the two. Cole and Keller were torn between a rock and a hard place, either work in England and Scotland for Chariots of Fire or France and other locales for Raiders of the Lost Ark. Steven Spielberg was having a rough time casting a leading man; the boys were waiting word to see who the lead was. Keller had been to Hawaii a few times shooting for CBS and met Tom Selleck, who was doing Magnum P.I.t. Selleck was the leading contender who backed out due to scheduling conflicts from CBS and Magnum P.I. Spielberg gave in selecting Harrison Ford. Keller told Cole how hot Selleck was! Of course, choosing the former locales of England and Scotland filming the scenes of the beach races, they saw more eye candy.

Carole and Beau were deciding if makeup or writing was her calling when Billy Williams summoned Beau to assist him with the Fondas and Katharine Hepburn in the family drama On Golden Pond in Maine and New Hampshire. Beau and Carole thoroughly enjoyed their time on the East Coast and hinted at leaving the Hollywood rat race and moving. Ashlee didn't like that idea; she really didn't want to see them move out East.

The sextet busy on their projects; everyone was in different locales, and distance was making strained friendships. Absence made the heart grow fonder as Carole and Ashlee wrote to each other constantly, making it harder explaining the relocation possibility.

The holidays were approaching, the sextet bracing for their last Christmas and New Year together, Carole and Beau came back from the East Coast with a hard dilemma. Will they move to the East Coast, rid of so-so California summers and Broadway? Will they stay in California, plentiful work, the rat race here or there? Would it be any better in New York? Moreover, if they move, they will probably only return for work and the Oscars.

Chapter Twenty-Four

C arole and Beau decided staying in California, not letting the
rat race get them down. Noticing film school graduates were
getting more and more jobs, leaving their age to be an issue. Cole
was almost fifty and getting looks from others. Cole wasn't about
let Keller know about his on-side dalliances in the men's room, on
location when they didn't work together, or the discretion of a star's
dressing room. Keller, pushing the big forty, was handsome as ever,
fearing nobody found him attractive except Cole. Keller was very
insecure, old-fashioned, and destined to stay with Cole no matter his
indiscretions. Keller confided to his little sis something was off,
determined to find out what was wrong in his relationship. Janine
reassured Keller, probably nothing because Cole grew up in
Hollywood; it was the norm to be unfaithful and try not to let it
bother him. Duh? Wake up, Keller! You decided to work in
television instead of movies and separate working close to Cole!

Hello! Janine had room to talk. Ashlee and Janine were queen sluts of the Grove ballroom.

The 54th Oscar nominations were released on February 11th, and it was announced that the technical awards would be presented and hosted by Lloyd Bridges and Academy President Fay Kanin on March 21st. The ceremony itself was scheduled the following week, March 28th, with Johnny Carson hosting for the third time in a row. Warren Beatty's Reds received the most nominations, with twelve, the second time in recent year, nominated for acting, directing, producing, and screenplay and the first person to receive it twice. The family drama On Golden Pond received ten, Raiders of the Lost Ark nine, Ragtime eight, and Chariots of Fire seven. Acting together for the first time, Katharine Hepburn and Henry Fonda were nominated in their leading roles, and Fonda's daughter, Jane, received a Best Supporting nod as well. It was announced that three honorary Oscars would be presented to Danny Kaye, Barbara Stanwyck, and Albert "Cubby" Broccoli. Broccoli is infamous for his work on the James Bond films. The ceremony was a "swan song" for Fonda in his last role, like when Hepburn previously paired with Tracy in Guess Who's Coming to Dinner. Critics thought when the ceremony started, On Golden Pond was a sentimental favorite given the screen presence of Hepburn and Fonda and the tender story on screen. Reds had the audience excited, but the story was long and served as backlash for the Beatty and Keaton breakup. Spielberg served another blockbuster, Raiders of the Lost Ark, thrilling audiences, young and old. Out of nowhere, the English drama Chariots of Fire, with a heartwarming story and thrilling score, glued you to your seat. Sentimentalists extended love to Hepburn and Fonda, taking leading Oscar gold, Maureen Stapleton took Best Supporting Actress for her stirring turn in Reds, and Sir John Gielgud took Best Supporting Actor as the comedic butler to Dudley Moore's Arthur. Best Picture went to Chariots of Fire, and sadly, after making Oscar history, Warren Beatty went home solo as Best Director.

The ceremony came to a poignant moment when Barbara Stanwyck was presented with her honorary Oscar. When Stanwyck delivered her tearful acceptance speech, referring to her co-star, William Holden, who previously thanked her last year when presented, for saving his career in 1939 by making Golden Boy. Stanwyck tearfully explained Holden, who passed away months prior to the presentation, by proclaiming, "I love him very much, and I miss him. He always wished I would get an Oscar. And so tonight, my golden boy, you got your wish."

In late 1980 and mid-1981, since they were all together in Spain working on Patton, the six went back and forth from Bihar, an eastern state of India, to work for former actor turned director Richard Attenborough making Gandhi. This trip was kept secret for fear that the India government was not happy publicizing the production of Gandhi, especially after almost 30 years of setbacks. Attenborough didn't want to jinx the film, as everything was quite tight-lipped.

After India, Cole and Keller were selected to assist with sound for Blake Edwards, who was directing his wife, Julie Andrews, James Garner, and Robert Preston in Victor/Victoria in England. Beau and Carole were headed to New York City, working together in make-up and cinematography for Dustin Hoffman in Sydney Pollack's Tootsie.

Spielberg was making a movie about an extraterrestrial sure to be certified box office gold. The Verdict had Paul Newman back on the silver screen as a washed-up alcoholic lawyer. Jack Lemmon and Sissy Spacek played father and daughter-in-law in a true-to-life drama about the disappearance of an American journalist in Argentina by renowned international filmmaker, Costa-Gravas in Missing.

Chapter Twenty-Five

T he 55th Oscars were preparing for its newest ceremonies, the critics predicting their nominations slated to be announced February 17th. There was word Paul Newman, an alcoholic lawyer, finally would walk home with Oscar gold in The Verdict, the Dustin Hoffman comedy Tootsie about an out-of-work actor finding work dressed as a woman or the historical drama Gandhi was selling tickets to pack theaters. Musicals were back in the air with Victor/Victoria with Julie Andrews and Robert Preston brought smiling faces to theatres; Peter O'Toole tried capturing recognition in My Favorite Year, and supporting stars in lead roles buzzed with Meryl Streep and Jessica Lange both made splashes in Sophie's Choice and a biopic about troubled actress Frances Farmer in Frances, respectively.

The historical drama Gandhi garnered eleven nominations, and the comedy Tootsie ten, E.T. nine, and Victor/Victoria seven were nominated for most Oscars. Unknown Ben Kingsley scored a Best Actor nod against predicted heavyweights O'Toole, Lemmon, Hoffman, and Newman. Best Actresses were Julie Andrews, Lange, Streep, and Spacek. As the supporting category was announced, history was mad. Louis Gossett Jr. became the first African American male for his stirring portrayal as a gunnery sergeant in the US Navy in An Officer and a Gentleman, and two actresses from Tootsie in the actress fold, Terri Garr and Jessica Lange, previously nominated for Best Actress.

The ceremonies were held on April 11th. It was announced Mickey Rooney would receive an honorary award, and the hosts would be Richard Pryor, Walter Matthau, Dudley Moore, and Liza Minnelli. With weeks away while the members voted, our sextet was off and on between gigs here and there. The steno ladies were laying low and sticking around Los Angeles, hoping for another international gig, but nothing seemed a fit. The remaining four divided time between Texas and Nebraska on two upcoming films with Jack Nicholson, Robert Duvall, Debra Winger, and Shirley MacLaine. These two films were catching early buzz on the street before this year's Oscars were even presented.

Gandhi was a no-brainer winner of the 55th annual Oscars, taking home eight of their eleven nominations, including Best Picture, Best Director, and Best Actor. Best Actress went to Meryl Streep, Jessica Lange took Best Supporting Actress, and Louis

Gossett Jr. took home Best Supporting Actor. Despite its lengthy running time to being a powerful film, Gandhi was well-received by critics and moviegoers around the world. Before the initial release of their respective films, critics were predicting Paul Newman or Peter O'Toole would finally win their long-overdue statues, but it wasn't in the cards. There were fresh faces Meryl Streep and Jessica Lange, proving to Hollywood they weren't prima donnas determined not to be pushed around. They were here to make a statement and stay!

Real-time true-to-life dramas were being brought to the silver screen; one generating buzz was Silkwood, starring Meryl Streep as nuclear power plant activist Karen Silkwood, and The Right Stuff, a drama about seven different military pilots selected to be astronauts for Project Mercury, the first United States human spaceflight. Barbra Streisand brought her labor of love to Yentl in her directorial debut, more so with determination as the first female director to win an Oscar, settling for box office gold and millions of record sales. Dramedies about a tumultuous mother-daughter relationship were explored in Terms of Endearment. College classmates' reunion scarred by the suicide and funeral of a friend was depicted in The Big Chill with an ensemble cast coupled with a groovy sixties soundtrack and a British film based on the play, the Dresser, describing the long-time tense friendship between an aging stage actor and his personal assistant.

In between Texas and Nebraska, where Cole and Keller were working on Terms of Endearment, they got the call to help Streisand with post-production on Yentl. Sadly, it was only a short trip enough to get the boys out of the United States and head to Roztyly, Czechoslovakia.

Beau and Carole were busily working in rural Texas outside of Big D on Tender Mercies, starring Robert Duvall as a recovering alcoholic country and western singer turning his life around in a relationship with a young widow and her son.

The third installment of the Star Wars saga, Revenge of Jedi, led the way as the highest-grossing film of the year as Yentl indeed proved gold for Streisand and the Big Chill brought box office dollars, not to mention the resurgence of sixties music brought groove back.

So much for ageism in Hollywood, the gang were fiercely working harder than ever.

168 | P a g e

Chapter Twenty-Six

H olidays came and went with no surprise; family visits for the sextet were highlighted by catching all the exciting movies. Cole and Keller were excited to see Revenge of the Jedi and Yentl. Beau and Carole were anxious to see their finished product, Tender Mercies. Gal friends Ashlee and Janine wanted to see the dramedy Terms of Endearment ready to bring the Kleenex. LOL

Every award season is full of accolades, whether it be in other art forms (music, Broadway, television, etc.); its expression has so much pomp and circumstance without trying to be biased or negative toward anyone. Lessons are learned; just be thankful you have been recognized by peers and continue your craft, pick yourself up, and make it better the next time. Case in point, award season isn't just for the Oscars; I am sure it's the highest achievement in every performer's mind. Once you win an Oscar, Tony, or Emmy, depending on your performance, is it wrong for you to try other things and compete against others who have been doing it their entire life? Is it ego, or just stretching into charted waters saying I am not here to take your place, I am just here to show I can do it too? Not to make it sound corny that I am better at some things as you are better at others. So, that is what competition is all about. Accolades given before any given award are sometimes but not always given as a predecessor to the official list for the grand prize.

This is going to be the year of the woman in Hollywood. Coupled with mesmerizing performances and first-time director Barbra Streisand, a key for Hollywood to recognize where it is due. Hollywood is no different than any workplace; equal opportunity for all, an equal amount of actors and actresses excel in everything, but when failure happens, dust yourself off and strive for success next time. With publicity honoring women this year, no exception, the Golden Globes honored Streisand as Best Director for her directorial debut in the drama musical Yentl. For all who don't know what the Golden Globes are, please allow me to explain. The Golden Globes are international journalists reporting on the American entertainment industry. The Hollywood Foreign Press honors performers and professionals for their work in movies and television.

Let's just hope EGO doesn't play the trump card, as nominations for the 56th Oscars were announced on February 16th. Eleven nominations were given to the dramedy Terms of

Endearment, eight for the space drama The Right Stuff, six for the Dresser, Silkwood and a foreign film, Franny and Alexander, five for Tender Mercies, the third part of the Star Wars saga, Revenge of the Jedi and Yentl. Sadly, Streisand was left off the Best Director nominees. Even as a big star Streisand is, this was a disappointment and a crushing blow below the belt. Yentl was a labor of love for Streisand.

Music was in the air for this Oscar season. Given the tremendous success of Yentl, the genres of dance and country-western poured into the hearts with Flashdance and Tender Mercies. Flashdance proved an enormous success, but Tender Mercies didn't fare well despite Robert Duvall's tour de force performance. Irene Cara, fresh from the movie Fame, proving to be quite a lyricist, being the first African American woman to be nominated for Best Song.

It was previously announced that Johnny Carson would host again on April 9th, and the technical awards would be on March 31st, with Joan Collins and Arnold Schwarzenegger hosting.

In early March, Cole suddenly fell ill at ABC studios working on sound for the Fall Guy starring Lee Majors. Cole began complaining of flu-like pneumonia symptoms. Not to alarm Keller, Cole was also losing weight and didn't confide in anyone, not even the ladies, and certainly didn't want him to know. Cole let a co-worker take him to the emergency room, where they did a series of blood samples and other routine tests. Cole sent the co-worker back to the studio with no word to anyone and was taking a cab to his and Keller's apartment after being released from the emergency room. Cole didn't seem to let anything bother him when the doctor started asking personal questions and other medical personnel poking and pricking in orifices where the sun didn't shine, drawing the line. The doctor told him they would get test results back in a few days. Cole told him he would return to normalcy, and mum was the word.

It really hasn't been very good sex-wise for Cole and Keller lately. Noticing Cole's distant, Keller asked Janine and Ashlee for advice; Janine told him not to worry, and Ashlee said Cole was being Cole. Getting older, still attractive, from time to time, Cole found himself with quick, easy trysts working at ABC and Keller at CBS. Cole sneaked to West Hollywood for lunch with the new ABC executive, Morton Freeman. Morton was new to California, fresh out of Harvard business school, and loved dad types. Cole was in his wheelhouse. Especially the one day, they crossed paths in the studio restroom with Cole at the urinal, entering tall, dark, and handsome Morton next to him, displaying an extremely enormous penis.

Cole couldn't help but notice, with no partitions between them, letting out a gasp to say, "Oh my God, what a lovely piece of meat!" As Morton blushed, he would relate, "Yours isn't too bad yourself, Daddy!" Next thing, one thing led to another. The two men were taking turns on each other in an oral session, and Cole remarked he'd love to have Morton inside him. Cole bent over the urinal wall as Morton entered him with no problem, still erect from their oral session, ready to finish the deed. Pulling their clothes up and walking to the sink to wash hands, Cole introduced himself as Morton did the same and gave his card to say, "Come see me at my offices some time." Cole was ecstatic with glee and nodded with an affirmative Yes, I will do that. It looks like Cole had met his match, and it had to be kept secret. Keller was so naïve sensing something was up but too timid to inquire about it. So, Keller kept himself silent at dinner and other matters.

Finally, Oscar night had the sextet readying for yet another ceremony. As the ladies were preparing their finishing touches of makeup, Janine said, anxious to see Shirley MacLaine on the radar to win Best Actress. Carole was anxious to see dapper Michael Caine and Tom Conti. As the giggles were getting louder, Keller yelled in the room, "Come on ladies, we need to hurry; I don't want to miss seeing Streisand!" Cole chuckled to Beau, telling him Keller was such a drama queen. The sextet arrived at the Dorothy Chandler Pavilion, and the valet drove away with the car. Cole grabbed his handkerchief out of his back pocket to wipe his bow, trying not to make a scene. Ashlee noticed out the corner of his eye and leaned over to whisper and offer support, "You ok sport?" Cole told her, "No worries, honey, I am fine; just let me be!"

Nothing too much out of the ordinary, the sextet nonchalantly gawking at the performers filling the venue and playfully posing for pictures like the ones doing the red carpet, was a sight for sore eyes. The performers were laughing and perhaps fantasizing about being in their shoes instead of the pomp and circumstance being famous. Everyone assembled; Quincy Jones conducted the orchestra, trying to hurry the attendees to start on time. They would have to wait for announcer Hank Simms to introduce Academy President Gene Allen, who, after his welcome speech, handed the ceremony over to host Johnny Carson. Carson gave his opening monologue and then introduced the evening's first set of presenters, Timothy Hutton and Mary Tyler Moore, handing out the first award, Best Supporting Actor.

As the night progressed, it was obvious Terms of Endearment was going to win five awards, leading the way to Best Director, James L. Brooks, and Best Picture as well as Jack Nicholson taking home Best Supporting Actor and the lady of the evening was, Shirley MacLaine, taking Best Actress. Linda Hunt took Best Supporting Actress, and Robert Duvall took Best Actor. In a rare oddity, Best Foreign Film nominee and winner Fanny and Alexander from Sweden, nominated four times, did a rare sweep of their other nominations, which included Best Art Direction, Cinematography, and Costume Design.

Cole was low and silent about what was bugging him.

AND THE OSCAR GOES TO...

Usually quiet, the vocal and flamboyant gay white male suddenly started being withdrawn. Keller noticed, taking sisterly advice, let it be and not let it bother him. Keller was wondering, especially when it came time for them to travel for location, Cole decided to stay behind and work in television. It was the reverse this time; Keller shrugged it off and could see the beginning eat at him. Just being away from Cole, Keller was hurting inside and, as usual, kept mum around the others as the couple started drifting apart. Beau was puzzled as he asked Carole if she knew anything. Carole remarked she hadn't heard Janine or Ashlee mention trouble in paradise. Word spread throughout the studio commissaries; the film community was being tight-lipped as being gay was just not talked about. Plentiful rumors of performers had been talked about for earlier years amongst it all; behind-the-scenes workers didn't matter because they really weren't considered important for a film's success. That surely shouldn't be the case; everyone involved in a film, either from the bottom of a key grip, sound, script person, makeup artist, costume designer, and not to mention, the performers. It's all a team effort to make the movie a success or failure. That's where we, as the public, deem a movie succeeds or a dud, either by critics' reviews or by going to the movie. Right?

Coupled with film school graduates slowly taking some jobs, longtime associates were starting to look for either 1)other jobs and/or 2)early retirement. As sad as it was, benefits were hard to keep upon retirement, and facing working elsewhere and starting all over again was going to be an uphill battle.

As next year's favorites were off and on in production and readying for release, five of the six were in Prague, and Kromeriz assisting Milos Forman in his epic, Amadeus which was based on the 1979 stage play of the same name adapted by playwright, Peter Shaffer. Forman heard nothing but great words about the sextet from Patton's director.

Cole stayed behind to work in television. Remaining secretive about his ailing him as well as the affair with younger ABC executive Morton Freeman. Keller didn't want to leave Cole behind for Prague. Cole assured him everything was fine. Keller, still puzzled and deep down with worry, decided to give up until their return determined once and for all.t. Keller was unsure if ready to find out what was troubling Cole; certainly not an earth-shattering shake-up, just not him but the other four as well. Cole wasn't prepared to explain the affair. It had been fun while it lasted, but the truth was unbeknownst to everyone. No holding back; the consequences are going to be hurtful, and you may as well let the chips fall as they may. Lately, the communication between the duo was total silence, and amongst the other four, everything appeared fake. When together as a group, there was always laughter and joking around like nothing was wrong. It was worse now with the overseas distance; Keller would call and write Cole from Prague.

Sadly, Cole wouldn't respond. It was as though Cole didn't care anymore; it wasn't that he didn't love Keller, just busy having hot sex, dinner, and drinks, not necessarily in that order, with Morton every opportunity he had. Morton had a private executive suite in the ABC building in downtown Los Angeles, which had an attached room to his primary office where he took his trysts, was very secluded. Morton provided more than Cole bargained for; he had been longing for a platonic relationship; the 24-7-365 days a year working and living together started to be boring, and life was stale. It didn't help much that Cole was older and more experienced than Keller. Keller was quite inexperienced and closeted when Janine and he moved to California from St. Louis. This is a very complicated relationship when you have two men who necessarily don't know how to express their feelings but still love each other very much.

With post-production on Amadeus wrapping up at the Hollywood studios, Keller and the rest of the gang were on their home from Prague. Given the silence at home, it was uncertain how things would be upon their arrival. On the long flight home, Keller stayed mostly to himself reading and tried not to worry about what was going to happen when he arrived. Believe it or not, Cole finally spoke to Keller and assured him that he would be home waiting for his arrival, and they would talk. Keller was on his way home; Cole paced the floor back and forth, trying not to wear out the carpet if he wasn't careful. Cole was nervous as hell trying to figure out how he was going to tell Keller about the affair and his ailments, which would be better to bring up first. Time wasn't really working in Cole's favor as Keller was due home very soon; the flight was long, and they needed to resolve the issues causing them so much pain and anguish.

Keller walked in the door, Cole sitting in the living area with a drink in his hand. Keller walked over to embrace Cole and kiss him on the lips; he moved, letting the kiss hit his cheek. Keller put his suitcase down and said, "Well, I thought you would be happy to see me!"

Cole replied, "Yes, I am happy, but it's not the same anymore. I do love you; we need to talk about more than just that." Keller countered back with a nod, implying what needed to be talked about and they were going to be okay.

Cole said, "I am not so sure after I tell you what I have to tell you."

Keller said, "I'm sure we can get past it and make it work; we just have to keep our faith." Cole said, "Well, there is no easy to say this, but I am not well." Keller noted the weight loss, distance between them with no affection, and sex were the two major things he could think of on the top of his head. Cole explained he was sorry about the no sex part; it's not that he doesn't love him anymore or was not attracted, but it was because he had been to doctors, and they found out what was wrong. As Cole was about to say what was wrong, he began to start to cry a bit and yelled out, "You probably aren't going to love me anymore, but I am HIV+." Keller was stunned to hear that; he ran over to console him, telling him everything was going to be okay. Keller explained to Cole that while the other five were in Prague, he had read some articles about AIDS and HIV.

Keller said, "Well, we will do everything we can and get you back to normal with all the drugs they have." Cole said, "That's fine, but you need to get tested because I have no idea who I contracted it from." Cole told Keller he had been sleeping with someone. Keller reiterated his inexperience and Cole's experience, saying that was it, right? Cole stated that he remembered telling Keller that, but this wasn't half of it as he had been seeing some other people, but lately, it's only been one in the last several months.

Keller said, "Oh my God, what have I done to make you not want me anymore." Cole stated it was just his inexperience and them being together so much he needed more. Keller stated again they could get through this if he just let him help. Cole said he didn't need any help. He would have to tell Morton about his HIV diagnosis he would end the affair. There was total silence for a few minutes as all you could hear in the room was uncontrollable sobbing from both men. Cole kept saying in between his tears how sorry he was, and Keller kept repeating he understood, saying that they would get

THROUGH THIS! Keller asked Cole how he was going to explain to the others. Cole reassured him in time and appreciated his help.

Upon returning from Prague and post-production on Amadeus, which kept Keller busy, Cole moved from ABC to NBC. Distancing himself away from Morton proved to be hard; to save his relationship with Keller, he had to face the music of going one last time to the ABC executive offices. On that day, Cole chose to drop Keller off at a clinic to get tested and stop at ABC. Morton was happy to see Cole and rushed to the door to embrace him; he pushed him away and stated, "I am not here for fun today, afraid there are urgent matters to discuss." Morton reminded me it had been a few weeks and no fun, and Cole told him yes, his boyfriend was home now and wanted it to work. Cole said, "As much it pains me to say we had lots of fun over the past several months, all things must come to an end. I hate to tell you this, but I have been diagnosed with the HIV that carries AIDS." Morton was quiet for a bit; the silence was a tad long. Cole said, "I had the most amazing sex with you, especially it's flattering that a young stud like you would think of someone older like me." Morton said he had always been attracted to older men; his college days were filled with sex. A four-year affair with the bi-married dean of residence life was only the beginning. Morton did acknowledge Cole; he wasn't the only one he had been bonking.

Cole was shocked and wasn't surprised to look at Morton,

who had all-American good looks. Morton started to apologize for stringing Cole and having him assume they were the only ones there. Cole finally summed it up, telling Morton. I am wondering, in between all my brief encounters at the adult arcades and with you, it's hard to tell who gave me this virus. Cole told Morton, "As I told Keller, you need to get tested." Telling Morton he was picking Keller up at a clinic and going to the grocery to stock up on a feast of steaks, ribs, and chicken. They were having a big barbeque to celebrate the five finishing the Amadeus production, and Cole was going to spill the beans to the others about his indiscretions and HIV diagnosis.

Back at the apartment, Cole picked Keller up at the clinic and stopped at the grocer; the couple was in the kitchen preparing the marinade for the meats and salads while listening to Streisand. Cole asked Keller how it went at the clinic. Keller explained they briefly counselled him after reading his sexual history and why he had the need for the test. Further explaining, Keller said the results would be back in two weeks, and the counselor reassured him that, given his history, he didn't think anything to worry about. Of course, it's the furthest from his mind; Keller was beginning to think if anything ever should happen to Cole, he would be beside himself. Cole, trying not to cry, remarked his sexual appetite was stronger and didn't deliberately intend to hurt or endanger him in any way. Keller thought to himself he didn't have to worry because it had been several months since Cole had a sexual encounter considered dangerous. Keller told Cole while he was at the studio overhead gossip on some things around in the gay community.

Dinner preparations rapidly progressed, and the phone rang. It was Ashlee, and she said that they might be running late as some of the international correspondence from Prague was not being properly delivered to the United States. Keller told her fine, get here before the food gets cold. LOL. Seriously, Cole was outside getting the charcoal and fire ready, now this. Jesus Christ, can't girls be on time? Gathering the silverware, glasses, and plates, Keller was staying busy making sure everything was perfect for tonight, beer and wine chilled alongside other alcohol for other drinks. Finally, around 6:30, everyone assembled at the Cole-Keller abode and settled around the bar as Keller mixed cocktails and Cole finished the meats on the grill. Carole and Beau offered to set the table as Janine and Ashlee finished mixing the salad to get the condiments for the baked potatoes. It was a team effort, and the six of us ate together for quite some time. Cole came in from the patio, sweating profusely from the barbecuing and nerves. Mulling over how he was going to break the sad news to his friends on the issues that were soon to be told over this prepared dinner by him and Keller.

Cole quietly excused himself from the kitchen and told everyone he was going to take a quick shower. Everything will still be hot to the touch and warm upon his return. As Cole stepped in to shower, Keller followed him to say take it slow, don't rush; everything will be just fine. Leaving the bathroom, as Keller walked out the door, he planted a big kiss on Cole's lips. Cole was shocked by this display of affection, especially after his indiscretions, "What do you think you are doing?" Keller told him nothing had changed. He still loved him, and nobody was taking him away. Cole reassured us with a kiss back and said, "Are you sure of yourself-NOTHING will stand in our way of happiness." Keller smiled with a nod and stated HURRY UP because I am hungry! Cole chuckled to say, "Keller, please stop with your Missouri jargon; you are Californian now; start talking like one!" Keller chuckled back, "Yes, Master!"

Keller returned to the friends to remind everyone Cole would be out shortly to help themselves to appetizers. There was some guacamole, salsa and chips, and fresh shrimp with cocktail sauce to keep them full, and please continue to make themselves at home. Keller walked over to the kitchen, checking the warmth of the meat and chicken. Ah, perfect. Everything was still warm to the touch per Cole's promise.

Cole made his grand entrance from the bathroom, saying hello to his friends and excusing himself for his tardiness over getting ready. As he said, slaving over the pit doing the barbeque was very excruciating, and he needed to cool off. "Everybody grab a plate and fill up because we got lots of great grub," Cole stated. It was going to be a long night; lots to talk about, and he wanted to hear about the overseas trip, but first, he needed everyone's undivided attention. Everyone was getting seated, Cole stood with a cold beer in his hand and said, "Before I start, I want to thank everyone from the bottom of my heart of hearts for coming tonight and how much I appreciate everyone's love and friendship. I know it's not been easy the last several months with all of you overseas and me staying behind. There is a logical explanation for everything, and I hope you will forgive me for what I am going to say. Of course, I know it's going to be hard, and if you choose not to be included in our circle, I truly understand." "Here goes, as you know, Keller and I have been at odds; it's not been a very good time for us. I have gone against the norm and have had some indiscretions I am not very proud of, realizing how much I need him more in my life than ever. Keller has chosen to forgive me, and I hope you will, too. I don't want a pity party; I am asking for your forgiveness and friendship because I am not well. Due to my indiscretions, as you might have been seeing in the news, there is a disease that is affecting the gay community called AIDS; it's a virus contracted through sexual contact and the immune system. It's not like gonorrhea or syphilis, venereal disease, or clap. I took a blood test, and it was positive."

As Cole finished his speech, you could hear a pin drop, and Keller rushed up to him, hugging and kissing him, reassuring his love for him. Keller t spoke up and told the quartet they could leave now if the need to and respect their privacy at this time. Next thing you know, you heard a few sniffles amongst the gals; Keller rushed over a box of Kleenex to them. Beau spoke up, "Well, I will tell you one thing: I know we are all far from perfect, and I respect your honesty. As you know, I wasn't very sexual when we first met, and you are going to need all of us to surround you with love, and I am here to say we are here for you—right ladies!" "Yes sir, we are here for you," Ashlee said, nudging Carole and Janine. Janine then said, "I know how much my brother loves you, and I love you. Just want what's best for both of you, and I will fight with you as long as it takes to have you here with us for a long time!" Carole nodded in unison to say, "Cole, I love you like a brother; you got this; nothing is going to come between us six; we are tight as thieves."

On that sad note, everyone finished their dinner as Cole started to chuckle, "You know I don't deserve all this, but I appreciate it so very much, and Keller does too, as we are going to need all your help." Everyone shouted in unison, "You have it!" The evening ended, everyone was busily assisting the boys with dishes and putting things away for leftovers, and everyone was stuffed and pooped to move. Cole said, "Why don't you five call in sick tomorrow, and we can sit and help me eat these leftovers!" It was getting near late news time, 10 pm! Cole told everyone it was either time to go or we were watching the news. Mentioning that Beau grabbed Carole and headed, laughing, towards the door as Janine and Ashlee laughed loud, yelling out, too, by screaming, "We are

TIM J. CULBERTSON

out of here NOW BITCHES!" Leaving single file, hugging and kissing everyone, Keller yelled from the couch, "Don't let the door hit you in your ass!" Cole shut the door behind Ashlee and joined Keller, nodding in unison, "Well, how do you think it went?" Keller said, "Cole darling, you deserve an Oscar for this performance; you really turned in a nomination." Cole reached over to give Keller a big kiss to thank him.

Cole was a rock in a hard place, finally doing the deed, telling his friends and his now former lover at ABC about his HIV diagnosis; it was time to go back to work at CBS. After coming clean like that, Cole really felt good about himself and was going to miss playing with the ABC brass. Fuck him, he was playing me like everyone else. Cole was making his promise to Keller, though, that he would not look twice at another guy as God as his witness.

Everyone was going to have to keep this current information about Cole secret as the clinic told him the virus wasn't being much-publicized yet, and there were a few cases in the United States. All the clinics were in the now, and with all the protocols promising, there wouldn't be much said about how it was. Cole felt defeated and wasn't in the mood to begin to look for work back at CBS or if NBC would have him. Fighting this virus meant not traveling anymore; Cole was fine with it. He would work on a studio backlot movie or an occasional television show; when Keller had to be away on location, he would grin and bear it. Keller did promise he would stay as close as needed.

Holidays were going to be somber this year with Cole not well and the rest of the gang wanting to help by staying close to Keller if need be. Cole didn't know how to react to all this attention, and Keller was determined to spoil him rotten as long as he could. Keller was encouraging Cole to talk to his parents, saying he didn't have anything to do with them because all they would want was to send him to Paris, where more advanced testing was about to begin in 1985.

Chapter Twenty-Seven

L eading the Oscar buzz was Amadeus, the Broadway sensation about Mozart; divorce drama Under the Volcano; real-life Vietnam drama, the Killing Fields; farm life issues in Places in the Heart and Country with Sally Field and Jessica Lange respectively leading the pack; and A Passage to India with Judy Davis and Dame Peggy Ashcroft. The nominations were announced on February 5th, and no shocking surprise: two films scored eleven nods, Amadeus and A Passage to India, followed by seven for The Killing Fields and Places in the Heart. In the music category, all five nominees for Best Original Song topped the Hot 100 on Billboard charts, and two African American artists walked off with Best Original Song and Original Score.

As HIV and AIDS rates increased, serious talk was being well documented among the entertainment community about whether the main cause of contracting the disease was through sexual contact, intravenous drug use, or possibly something else. Of course, the sextet was quiet, but you could hear the whispering amongst the commissaries about whether any "out" community members might be ill. Cole was doing his best not to work too much, even though he needed to keep his insurance and pay for the outrageous medical bills and medicine he was given. Unbeknownst to Keller, Cole stayed connected with Morton to check on him, especially after the bombshell he laid on Cole discussing their affair end. Morton was stubborn and hadn't gotten tested yet, despite his constant screwing every Tom, Dick and Harry. Cole was crushed and hurt by Morton's ignoring his calls and ignorance, plus a standoffish attitude towards his concern for him and his possibly being HIV+, too.

Cole finally realized he wasn't alone in his battle; at least he had the love of his friends. Cole told them he was in for the long haul and that he was going to take all the strength fighting the fight, stay around for a long time, and attend the Oscars with them.

As the ceremonies were upcoming, the sextet was looking for their next gigs, especially after spending most of the year in Prague with the Amadeus crew. Hoping to stay close in the States so they can keep an eye on Cole, assuring him taking meds, keeping up with doc appointments, and working when available by staying as comfortable as possible.

TIM J. CULBERTSON

The Oscars were held again at the Dorothy Chandler Pavilion in Los Angeles with Jack Lemmon as host on March 25, 1985. Amadeus was the clear winner of the 57th annual with eight wins, which included F. Murray Abraham taking Best Actor from his co-stars, Tom Hulce, Albert Finney, Jeff Bridges, and Sam Waterston, Best Picture and Best Director. Sally Field won her second-Best Actress in recent years against some fierce competitors in Spacek, Lange, Vanessa Redgrave, and newcomer Judy Davis. To compliment A Passage to India, Best Supporting Actress went to Dame Peggy Ashcroft, and in The Killing Fields, Haing S. Noir took Best Supporting Actor. In a deserving musical win, recording artists Prince and Stevie Wonder took home Best Original Score and Best Original Song, respectively.

Sir Laurence Oliver was so ecstatic to announce Amadeus as Best Picture he didn't even announce the other nominees. He ripped the envelope with glee; the film's producer, Saul Zaentz, was nice enough in his acceptance speech to acknowledge them. With the Oscars ending, new gigs were in the offing for our sextet. Cole got work with CBS, settling in doing Cagney and Lacey, comedies Kate and Allie and Newhart, keeping him busy. Keller selected work with Robert Zemeckis and Bob Gale in Michael J. Fox's Back to the Future comedy on the Universal Studios lot and the surrounding Los Angeles suburbs, keeping him close.

Sadly, the remainder of the sextet, including our steno pool chicks of Ashlee and Janine, were being asked to accompany Beau and Carole to Africa. Yes, you read it right: the quartet headed to work with Robert Redford and Meryl Streep in various African locations of Nairobi and Langata and some scenes in Surrey, England, which doubled for Denmark. At first, they didn't want to leave Keller caring for Cole alone; the boys assured them it would be fine. The location shoot proved grueling; in the last two and a half years, most of the sextet have been here, there, and everywhere. It was nice to go work in nice exotic places, but at this point in their lives when friendship was important and needed most, who could say NO to these past few adventures? Everyone was absent, apart from the two lovebirds; nothing could be sweeter than working well on their differences and being able to be in their near-perfect happy place. Cole seemed to be doing well going to the doctor and taking his meds, and in between, working, taking time to start a workout exercise routine.

While the others were overseas, an increasing amount of HIV cases through Los Angeles and the gay mecca San Francisco spread as Cole was getting super paranoid; he didn't want his condition to be made public yet. Bombshell news broke in an obscure way; it finally hit the nail on the head, and the national public was told Rock Hudson was indeed gay and suffering from AIDS. Unbeknownst to the world, Hudson had been diagnosed with HIV on June 5, 1984, three years after the emergence of the first cluster of symptomatic patients in the United States and one year after scientists initially concluded HIV caused AIDS. Over the next several months, Hudson kept his illness a secret. He kept working occasionally and traveling, hopefully to France and other countries, seeking treatment for a possible cure or treatment slowing the disease's progression. The world was further shocked when Hudson appeared with longtime friends and co-star Doris Day to promote her Christian cable show, Doris Day and Friends. Appearing gaunt and did very little speaking during the conference on July 16, 1985, claiming he was tired. Apparently, the world, seeing his appearance, speculated something was wrong. Two days later, Hudson traveled to Paris for another round of treatment, but on July 21st, he collapsed in his Ritz Hotel room. Upon this, his publicist and long-time friend, Dale Olson, reported to the press Hudson had inoperable liver cancer and was undergoing further testing. On July 25th, Hudson permitted his French publicist, Yanou Collart, to confirm the worst: he indeed had AIDS and would be returning home to the United States on July 30th. Upon arriving in Los Angeles, Hudson was so weak he was airlifted to UCLA Medical Center for further treatment and released to private home hospice care in late August, where he eventually passed away on October 2, 1985, in his sleep at the age of 59 at his Beverly Hills home he called "the Castle." Hudson was noted to be one of the earliest celebrities to be diagnosed with the disease. Hudson told his friends no funeral was to be held and cremated hours after his passing, with ashes scattered between Wilmington, Los Angeles, and Catalina Island.

Sadly, there were 5,523 HIV cases reported in 1985, having come a long way since then, but of this writing, more research but still no cure. Another of Hudson's longtime friends and co-stars, Elizabeth Taylor, before her passing along with many other Hollywood big names, pushed for more research and funding to raise millions of dollars by contributing their own monies through amfAR, an organization formed by Taylor and Hudson's physician, Michael S. Gottlieb and a New York-based group dedicating their efforts as non-profit for AIDS-HIV prevention and research. Before his death, Hudson had gotten the ball rolling with its first direct contribution of $250,000. Ironic to fate, Hudson was great friends with President Reagan and his wife, Nancy, through their Hollywood days till he passed, but Reagan chose making no public statement concerning his condition. However, noted in July, Reagan did talk to Hudson while hospitalized in France and issued a condolence statement once he passed.

As the quartet of Beau, Carole, Ashlee, and Janine ended another adventure of a lifetime to work with Streep and Redford on locales in Out of Africa, it was home for the holidays. Upon their arrival, Keller met them at the airport with his droopy dog's sad eyes. Janine, at first, was to notice it by remarking to her brother, "What's eating you, bro?" Keller shrugged his shoulders to say, "I don't know. I can't put my finger on it. Cole hasn't been eating much the last week, and he is losing more weight. He doesn't want to see the doctors." Before Keller could get his sentence out of his mouth, you could hear Ashlee and Carole in the back of the car sobbing uncontrollably. Beau. in the middle of the two ladies, put his arms to console them.

This was the holidays; everyone needed to be cheerful and thankful for what they had, as well as the six to be as tight as friends could be. The quartet promised Keller they would do everything in their power to cheer Cole on in his battle to beat this, wherever and whenever was needed. The sextet was getting excited about the upcoming holiday season, movies coming out, and gaining Oscar buzz and momentum for next year's nominations. The quartet was already teasing the boys that their Out of Africa was going to sweep 'em all next year, but they had their sights on The Color Purple, Murphy's Romance with Sally Field and James Garner, Prizzi's Honor, and Witness.

Chapter Twenty-Eight

T he new year started with the earlier buzz's momentum, but out of nowhere, a new star arrived! More famous for singing and never dreaming of having an acting career, Cher beaconed on the radar. This movie season was highlighted by a real-life portrayal of Florence "Rusty" Dennis, mother of Rocky Dennis, a young man with craniodiaphyseal dysplasia whose life was depicted in the emotionally filled movie directed by Peter Bogdanovich called Mask. Cher was the critics' darling at this point, even taking the Best Actress award at the Cannes Film Festival. Here's hoping this momentum could garner her a Best Actress nomination to sway the others gaining on her trail like Geraldine Page, Bancroft, Goldberg, and a slew of other possibilities. A tear-jerker, Mask had fierce competition tugging at heartstrings; The Color Purple, based on a best seller by Alice Walker, appeared on screen from Spielberg hoping for Oscar gold, too. Nepotism appeared on the silver screen, and famous actor/director John Huston and his daughter Huston put together a comedy-drama about hit men with Jack Nicholson in Prizzi's Honor, which generated praise as well.

The nominations were announced on February 4[th,] and in a major surprise, two well-deserved multiple nominations for Out of Africa and The Color Purple both received eleven. Next close was Prizzi's Honor, with eight as John Huston became the oldest ever to be nominated for Best Director at the ripe age of 79. Sadly, all the earlier hype for Cher would not be nominated for her stunning portrayal in Mask and odd trivia; after the eleven nods The Color Purple received, Spielberg missed a Best Director nomination. Still, later, before the Oscars were presented, he received a Directors Guild of America nomination and a win. As weeks passed, with the ceremony scheduled for March 24th, it was previously announced Paul Newman and Buddy Rogers from Wings, the 1[St] Best Picture Oscar winner would be honored for their extraordinary contribution to the motion picture industry. It's a shame that after an extraordinary lifetime in films, Newman was nominated numerous times for excellent pictures, but it just wasn't quite his turn and the fierce competitors. You can read into Oscar history concerning numerous worthy performances; we as fans must realize you can't win 'em all others who win either the award or ones with the honorary accolades, leaving ones who never win out in the cold. Either to receive either honorary or nothing at all, you would think nominations speak volumes as a win too, or for history repeating, you win one, then receive the honorary or the reverse.

On March 16th, eight days prior to the ceremony, daytime actor MacDonald Carey presented the technical awards at the Beverly Hilton and now to the annual presentations. On March 24th, the hosts assembled their guests at the same ol same place and selected for this year were Alan Alda, Jane Fonda, who previously hosted in 1977 for the 49th ceremony, and Robin Williams. This was the first time for both Alda and Williams to serve on the dais. As the awards were being presented, sad to say Spielberg's drama, The Color Purple, after so much rave publicity, was shut out by Sydney Pollack's Out of Africa; it was the second time in Oscar history that a film of such magnitude as the Turning Point did in 1977. Out of Africa scored seven out of eleven, which included Best Picture and Best Director as William Hurt won Best Actor for Kiss of the Spider Woman, slewing his competitors, Ford, Nicholson, Garner, and Voight. Veteran stage actress Geraldine Page won Best Actress single-handedly over Goldberg, Lange, Streep, and Bancroft. Angelica Huston won Best Supporting Actress over Amy Madigan, Meg Tilly, Margaret Avery, and talk show hostess Oprah Winfrey, and Don Ameche won in his sentimental Ron Howard's Cocoon against Eric Roberts, Robert Loggia, William Hickey, and Klaus Maria Brandauer. It is worth noting that Argentina's The Official Story was the first time a Latin American film ever nominated won

Best Foreign Film, and all lead acting nominees were born in the United States.

Oscar season for another year ended, and Cole couldn't return to the CBS studios; Keller took the next day off to take him to the nearest HIV clinic in West Hollywood. Janine volunteered to help Keller as Ashlee went back to the steno pool. Carole and Beau opted to check the common bulletin board concerning film projects for the remainder of 1986. The compilation was this:

A Room With a View	Platoon	Top Gun	Aliens	Round Midnight
Salvador	Crimes of the Heart	Hoosiers	Blue Velvet	Hannah and Her Sisters

Cole appeared very delicate, especially Keller, Beau, and Carole, who looked for gigs in California or other parts of the United States. Keller and Carole didn't mind missing the movie work; they could work on television, and if need be, Beau travelled nearby to stay close. Due to the extensive work of cinematography, Beau would have to work where the work was; the more the experience, the better. Janine and Keller were getting Cole ready for the doctor's appointment. Ashlee was busy with the steno pool, going digital, and replacing electric typewriters and word processor equipment. Carole and Beau were at lunch at the commissary discussing Cole's situation; out of the blue, colleagues from sound and make-up walked by. Steve Vaughan and Tracey Barrett were known to be busybodies; the duo was as tight-lipped as possible. Given the past several months, Hollywood still reeling from Rock Hudson's death as the newest duo on scene had been with the sextet on location before, pushed the envelope concerning Cole and Keller. Beau just told them the guys were laying low from all their overseas travels and returning to television and minding their own fucking business.

Well, it was doctor's time. Janine and Keller paced the floor while Cole was examined at the clinic. Knowing it wasn't doing any good worrying, sitting down thumbing through magazines and HIV literature on the wall. Keller had had enough; he went to the window inquiring how much longer. The receptionist reassured Keller be a bit longer since HIV was new, and the medical professionals were taking every precaution in their work with patients. No sooner did Keller sit down than Cole walked out, announcing feeling like a pin cushion by the bloodwork done. Keller tried comforting Cole, telling him to go home and relax. Janine kept quiet as the two talked when Cole yelled to the back seat, "Jeez, Janine, you don't have to be so quiet on my part!" Janine said, "No worries, I'd rather you let us know what we can do to make you comfortable."

Cole remarked they did blood work and discussed what meds he needed for him to be stronger. AZT would be the first step. Keller said, "What is AZT?" Cole said the docs claim it reduces the infection but needs to watch the side effects of headaches, fever, and nausea, possibly leading to major ones such as liver problems, muscle damage, and high blood lactate levels if not taken properly. It works as an inhibitor as an enzyme reversal transcriptase that the HIV uses to make DNA and decreases replication of the virus. Cole added that he will take it twice a day and monitor his blood once a month to check his T cell count and, eventually, as more drugs are available. The latest news certainly was hard to swallow. Keller asked Cole if they could start having sex again; Cole wasn't sure he was ready to talk about that yet. You know what that means, guess Keller will either look elsewhere for safe sex or masturbate all the time.

Well, everyone assembled over at Janine and Ashlee's after the doctor's visit. Beau and Carole came over after checking the bulletin board and are now waiting for Ashlee to get home. Carole told everyone about their commissary visit with the busybodies, Vaughan and Barrett, acknowledging didn't say a word but knew damn well they were hot for the scoop. Ashlee flew in about 4:30 on her broom, and soon she walked in, noticing everyone exclaiming, "Bitches, what a day, Janine, glad you weren't there!" Ashlee was referring to learning computers was going to be a nightmare. Wise up, Ashlee, it's the way of the world; technology rules! Carole mentioned after she and Beau ran in with the busybodies, she went to CBS to inquire about makeup and writing assignments. They told her to wait till the end of May as reruns will start and the fall season will begin. Carole went to hug the trio, telling them everything in her power was to help them. The trio nodded, feeling the love was greatly appreciated. Beau announced there was post-production cinematography to do on Penny Marshall's comedy starring Nicolas Cage and Kathleen Turner in Peggy Sue Got Married, and Paramount was doing the finishing touches on Star Trek IV: The Voyage Home, will be there to help when needed as well. After all this was agreed upon, you couldn't hear a pin drop for the total silence, and then, a little sob came from Ashlee… "Where is the goddamn Kleenex?"

Steady work was on the main burner; Cole kept low, and the meds given to him to resist HIV were causing minor side effects. He also experienced lack of energy and did not sleep well. Keller and Janine were constantly reminding him to take the meds and start exercising, walking several blocks instead of sitting around the house feeling sorry for himself. Depression was the worst thing for early HIV patients, not knowing how to deal with what was ahead. Even with medical professionals trying to guide the patients, have a cheerful outlook, do what they say, and keep up with regular doctor visits, etc., you should be able to lead a long-lasting life with HIV.

With lots of movies and new TV seasons, everyone was staying busy with their gigs. Beau was doing his expertise at its best with the Start Trek movie, learning some new techniques with the special effects team at Paramount. Carole joined CBS and did work for Murder, She Wrote, and Falcon Crest. Keller was doing odd gigs, staying closer to the apartment.

In their spare time, everyone was taking turns hosting dinners and an occasional night on the town, trying new restaurants, going to the movies, etc. Ashlee, despite getting the usual tickets every year to the Oscars, Janine started to get premiere tickets. A new way of hob-knobbing with the celebs, don't you know, those can be fun. Sadly, it's tiring for Cole, resorting to settling for going to the movie and missing all the publicity. There are full moons on occasion, where Cole feels well enough to fit in with the rest of the gang and partake. These special times brought a smile to his face and theirs too, allowing him to enjoy himself as well out of his comfort zone.

Chapter Twenty-Nine

C ritics were predicting war-themed movies like Platoon and Clint Eastwood's Heartbreak Ridge or the play-turned-film Children of a Lesser God, the English film A Room with a View being Oscar-bound. Could it be the science fiction thrillers Aliens and Star Trek IV: The Voyage Home, or possibly the dramedies Crimes of the Heart, Woody Allen's Hannah and Her Sisters, and Peggy Sue Got Married? Tom Cruise was a new heartthrob in Top Gun and alongside as Paul Newman's pool opponent in his possible swan song, The Color of Money, reprising his pool shark, Eddie Felson character.

The nominees were announced on February 11th at the Samuel Goldwyn Theatre in Beverly Hills with last year's supporting winners, Angelica Hutson and Don Ameche, along with Oscar-winning director and current Academy president Robert Wise. It was no surprise Oliver Stone's Platoon and A Room With a View scored eight nominees a piece, Ridley Scott's sci-fi thriller, Aliens, Woody Allen's Hannah and Her Sisters, and Roland Joffe's The Mission scored seven respectively, and five went to the play turned film, Children of a Lesser God. It was the first time in Oscar history that a deaf actress, Marlee Matlin, was nominated for a lead acting role, and the fourth time an actor performing a role in two different films was Paul Newman in The Color of Money. If Newman wins, he and his wife, Joanne Woodward, will be the second married couple to win acting honors. With six weeks leading up to the March 30th ceremony, it was announced veteran actor Ralph Bellamy would receive an honorary Oscar, and the hosts would be Goldie Hawn, Chevy Chase, and Paul Hogan. This would be the first hosting stint for both Chase and Hogan but the second time since 1976 for Hawn.

Eight days prior, on March 22nd, Catherine Hicks presented the annual technical awards. As the ceremony began, the buzz on the street was torn between Stone, Allen, and Merchant Ivory. The supporting roles for Allen were helping his film's momentum as Michael Caine and Diane Wiest were early winners. Putting along, Paul Newman, the sentimental favorite, won Best Actor and sweetheart of the night, Matlin. Taking the gold away from two previous winners in Spacek and Fonda and two newbies, Kathleen Turner and Sigourney Weaver. Now, it was redemption time. Would Woody Allen repeat his Annie Hall drama, or will Olver Stone take him down? The result was Stone won four for Platoon, Allen, and Merchant-Ivory teams won three for their films, respectively, and two went to Aliens. It was a reunion for former co-stars of the 60's film The Hustler, Piper Laurie, second-time supporting actress nominee for Children of a Lesser God, and Paul Newman, a Best Actor winner.

Cole declined Ashlee's invite for this year's ceremony, battling minor flu-like symptoms. Keller decided to stay home with him as the quartet promised a report upon their return. Keller fixed a nice dinner for two, watching the Oscars in the comfort of their apartment. Veal Piccata served over linguine, sautéed squash, and carrots with French bread hit the spot and champagne.

After the ceremony, as promised, the quartet showed up to tell who on the red carpet was in the auditorium and in the musical performances. Realizing it is late and duty calls, the ladies go back to the busy world of automation. One thing is for sure: going to computers has made work and their lives easier. Carole and Beau will be busy checking the boards to see what might be coming their way as Keller is going to stay home another day with Cole, and they told the quartet he might run him by the clinic.

The morning after the Oscars was always the worst: a champagne hangover. LOL. Janine was not feeling it today. As she stumbled to the shower, glancing herself in the mirror and leading out a shrieking scant, "Why me, Lord, help me, Jesus!" Ashlee laughed from the kitchen. The coffee was ready! The two ladies were readying for work, and Janine was thinking, should she call Keller or just let it be? The rest of the quartet were busy starting their day. Carole told Beau she was positive about what movies were available and hoping New York might be calling their names. Carole was itching for some Broadway. Luck might be in their favor, but deep down, hoping Cole feels better soon so the sextet can take a trip.

Keller woke first, trying to be quiet to let Cole sleep in a bit, sneaking into the kitchen to put coffee on and ready bagels and cream cheese for his Prince Charming. Suddenly, you heard a scream coming from Cole's room, "OH FUCK ME!" Cole and Keller had been keeping separate rooms since his diagnosis and needed space. Keller hurried into the room, "what's wrong, Baby Cakes?" Cole sat up in bed. He was soaking wet in sweat. Cole told Keller, "I was afraid this day would come, and I don't want you to worry anymore, but think it's time we look for better healthcare." Cole tried to explain he had been having night sweats but didn't want to worry Keller. Keller said, "What are you thinking?" Working in Hollywood just doesn't give you the best of the best in healthcare, and the bills will be pouring in. Especially with these new trials with HIV, it's hard to pay for medicine and hospitalization. Keller led Cole to the bathroom and told him to take a shower, brush his teeth, and do the same. We need to get you to the clinic. While Cole was in the shower, Keller called Janine at the steno pool, telling her their plans. Janine then buzzed Ashlee over at her desk, saying she was going to help Keller. Ashlee went over to the steno pool lead's office and said, "We have a family emergency here and need to go. Lead Katharine Jansen told them to go ahead and keep them posted. Before the ladies ran out to the parking lot, running by the bulletin board in hopes of seeing Carole and Beau, a big crowd. They didn't want to yell in to pull them out, so they let it be. Ashlee remarked they better hurry, and Janine agreed, jumping in Ashlee's car and sped away to Keller and Cole's. Upon arrival, Janine found Keller in the doorway, hugging her and thanking God she was there with him. Ashlee ran up to the door and saw Cole slumped over in his chair, "Come on bitch, need get you to the doctor." Keller helped Ashlee on each side of Cole walking him to the car, and speeding away, they fled. Arriving at the clinic, the quartet walked in; the receptionist led them straight to the examination room where Cole's doctor was waiting. Keller asked if he could stay, and the doctor said sure as the ladies went back to the waiting area. As they walked by the receptionist, Janine said, "Hey, I appreciate from the bottom of my heart what you did. I notice you have more on your plate. You didn't have to do that." The receptionist nodded to say, "No, no worries, sweetheart, I am starting to see it all, and it looks like your friend really needs it." As the ladies were impatient amongst the others in the waiting area, Keller sat in the corner of the exam room; the doctor examined Cole and asked questions. Apparently, Cole was sluggish in his answers, and Keller jumped in to say he found Cole all wet with sweat that morning. The doctor explained that was common as Cole's lymph nodes were slightly enlarged, and a fever of 102. The doctor continued his examination, feeling the need for Keller, and the ladies take him to UCLA Medical Center with a sense of urgency. Keller and Cole walked out and grabbed the ladies. Janine walked by again and said thanks. The receptionist told them they were in good hands. Upon arriving at the medical center, Keller gave Ashlee his keys and asked if she would stop by the apartment and get Cole some clean clothes. Ashlee nodded to say, "Sure, sugar." Janine said she was staying with the boys. Ashlee understood and hurried out of the hospital and sped to the boys' place. While Keller got Cole admitted and in his room, Janine called the office to explain their abrupt leaving further. Katharine said no worries, and she took all the time she needed. She understood. Unbeknownst to them, Katharine's gay brother was HIV+, too. Janine only had a little bit of change left, calling the communal area housing the bulletins to have Carole and Beau paged. Seconds being on hold turned into minutes. As Janine was just about to give up, Carole came to the phone. Janine, fighting back tears, told Carole they should come to the medical center. Cole had been admitted to the hospital. Carole said she would grab Beau, and they would be on their way. After completing Cole's admission paperwork, he walked over to him and inquired about wanting to put his parents down for emergency contact. Cole told him quietly HELL NO, put you and Janine. Keller smiled as he hugged Cole and kissed him on the forehead. As Keller returned the paperwork to the admissions desk, a nurse took Cole back to a room. You must remember, these two are just a couple, not legally married, but the nurse wasn't stupid and wasn't being rude or making a scene. The clerk could tell Keller was uncomfortable leaving Cole in a room alone. She will do whatever he and their friends do to go back there. Keller couldn't have been more grateful for what was starting off to look like a great day for them to be able to watch over him in close proximity.

Whisking Cole off, Keller and Janine waited for the rest of their peeps. Not taking long, Ashlee gathered clothes and followed Carole and Beau. Keller went to the admissions desk. The coast was clear, and they could see him. Of course, this was way beyond the call of duty and against protocol. People could lose their jobs over this. A doctor checked Cole's vitals, and quiet as church mice, he sedated him. The news on Cole appeared grim; he had an allergic reaction, taking too much AZ. Now stable but critical. The staff will monitor him every two hours and feed him food through IV, hoping to boost his immune system. The next twenty-four will be crucial in Cole's recovery.

The five appeared stunned by the news. Keller and Janine held each other in a tight embrace as Carole, Beau, and Ashlee held hands, fighting back tears. The doctor inquired who allowed them in the room. It was against protocol. Given Cole's grave condition, he needed love and support to rest comfortably. Carole brought it to Keller's attention, saying to call Cole's parents, he would wait and ask him again if and when he woke up. Quietly, Janine, Ashlee, and Beau went outside the room to give Carole and Keller alone time with Cole. Beau didn't see the need to upset Carole. Beau overheard some sad news. Ashlee loved gossip, especially if it wasn't about her. LOL. Janine remarked she wanted to be strong for Keller and Cole. Ashlee nudged Janine to take a chill pill and begged Beau to spill the beans by saying, "Come on now, you started it, and you might as well finish it!" Beau heard Morton Freeman, Cole's ex-fling, passed away the week prior to the Oscars at Cedars Sinai. Upon hearing this, Ashlee's heart sank, and hearing Janine's uncontrollable sobbing outside the room, Keller came out into the hallway and said, "Sis, for Cris's sake, can you tone it down a tad? Cole needs to sleep." Janine insisted nothing was wrong, just upset to see Cole lying there so helpless. Days passed into weeks, and Cole, still in grave condition, was eating and getting some meat on his bones. Keller stood by the whole time except for grabbing a quick bite of lousy cafeteria food or when Carole sneaked in food. Cole could talk but was very raspy. Four weeks turned into a month.

AND THE OSCAR GOES TO...

Keller asked Cole's medical team if there was anything they could do to release him because Keller needed to return to work and have money come in for rent, utilities, and Cole's medical bills. The hospital agreed to a payment plan. Keller asked Cole to make a last-ditch effort to contact his parents or even ask his own parents for help. Cole was adamant my parents didn't need to know. Keller and Janine thought of asking their parents. Worth a try! Couldn't hurt!

International flavor buzzed in lots of work. Beau looked at the Last Emperor or Empire of the Sun. Carole already said she was staying close to California and/or going to New York to look at projects such as Wall Street, Fatal Attraction, and Moonstruck.

The steno ladies allowed Janine to help Keller when Cole was released on Labor Day weekend. In October, Janine took Columbus Day weekend and flew to St. Louis and hoped to convince their parents pay extra money to help Cole with his medical bills. It didn't take much convincing. The parents were retired from Anheuser-Busch and Ralston Purina, respectively. Mom and Dad immediately said yes! Rennie and Geoff were shocked in disbelief. Cole let himself go and was relieved to know he was quickly on the mend, and anytime they needed to pay some bills, don't hesitate to ask. They would cut a check.

Janine arrived with a first check for $75,000. Cole was speechless. Between the three of them, Janine was crying the loudest, blubbering and blowing her nose zillions of times. Cole, in his best stationery, will write them a thank you note tomorrow. $75,000 was just a dent in the damage. Medical costs were over the top, and after being in the hospital for six months. Keller was ecstatic as well; couldn't get over their generosity.

As the trio were relishing this new lease on life, the other three, or at least the two travelers, were off to do post-production in New York City. Beau was intrigued working with Oliver Stone and Michael Douglas on Wall Street, and Carole was ecstatic about Cher on Moonstruck, Glenn Close, and Michael Douglas in Fatal Attraction and their joint effort with Holly Hunter, William Hurt, and Albert Brooks in Broadcast News.

Cole was feeling better, far from being cured, and wasn't heading back to work. He produced a plan. Cole's medical team treated him with AZT and other HIV drug cocktails to slow the disease. Cole continued staying in contact with the Wallace parents, loving him almost as much as Keller and Janine did. Cole had written them several nice "thank you" letters for the money paying his medical bills. Cole explained his estrangement from his wealthy parents and his appreciation and love for their children. Mom Wallace felt good about this, a kinship with Cole like another son. Cole was a godsend; it unified a newfound love between parents and children as Mom completely understood the need to stay busy, especially during the holiday movie season. So, shh, don't tell anyone. Cole had a surprise for the brother and sister duo. Mom and Dad Wallace were going to be in Hollywood for the holidays. With some of the received monies Cole wanted to pay back for their sincerest generosity, he was having the holiday dinners of Thanksgiving, Christmas, and possibly New Year catered, as well as their flights to and from St. Louis.

As Halloween ended with a wild, crazy night at Coconut Grove, the sextet had the best fun r since their friendship began. Certainly, it was time to get out and have a fun time. Keller and he were starting to see a significant improvement in their relationship as well. The ladies, Janine and Ashlee, were slowing down their so-called slutty behavior as well and found a few men knocking on their doors and ringing their telephones. Working in the steno pool was advantageous to the ladies as guys from all walks of life revolved in and out of the door. Specifically, these two guys had names and attainable positions within the ranks of the Hollywood ladder; you wouldn't think twice how these two would bat an eye at our two ladies. Enter Tyler Taylor and Kane Kellogg.

Tyler and Kane, best friends since their college days at Harvard Business School, graduated at the top of their class in the MBA program. Tyler, a third cousin of actor Robert Taylor and Kane, an heir apparent to the Kellogg cereal company. These two were the real deal not bashful about showing their affection for Janine and Carole. Ever since meeting them at the Grove one happy hour in October, the gentlemen hadn't left their site. It was quite interesting to see how far these romances were going to fit in this show business world. Upon graduation from Harvard, been in Hollywood for about four years, doing odd jobs throughout the system as an intern. As luck would have it, when the men met our two at the Grove, they all four thought it was funny what ties they had. Tyler promised Ashlee he would not let his last name interfere or come out as pompous or swayed to be aloof, as Kane did to Janine. He only promised he would keep cereal on her table. Now, having two new men on the scene, the group attending the Oscars grew to eight. Ashlee did tell the men, joining the elite of the elite she had lifetime tickets to the Oscars. Tyler possessed a drive to show his family destined to make a name in Hollywood without using his cousin's name. Janine told the men, hoping they didn't mind being included in a mix of four other fans, especially her gay brother and his lover. Tyler and Kane remarked that it would be a delight to meet the others. We are inseparable as two peas in a pod and have been friends forever. Nothing can break us apart. Upon hearing that, Ashlee began to wonder if this was strange. There must be some hidden agenda here. Janine told her to drop it for the time being and wait to see how their true colors would play out.

Janine and Ashlee had everyone over for crockpot chili and drinks and got Tyler and Kane re-acquainted with the others as Carole and Beau returned from a few months in New York City.

AND THE OSCAR GOES TO...

This was the first meeting for Carole, Beau, Tyler, and Kane. Of course, being nosy, Carole mentions its interrogation time and wants to know their intentions with Janine and Ashlee. LOL. Before the new boys on the block could get a word out, Cole said he had a huge announcement to make. Cole said, "Before I make my announcement, first, I want to thank all my angels here in the group who have been helping since last spring when I got sick. I am here for the long haul and intend to stay here till the Lord brings me home. Thanks to my lover, his sister, and their parents, as well as Carole, Beau, and Ashlee. You are indeed my family, and I love you very very much. Second, let's welcome the new boys, Tyler and Kane. Fasten your seat belts, fellas. This is going to be a bumpy ride. Welcome, and best of luck with keeping up with Janine and Ashlee." "They, or should I say, we are a wild and crazy bunch. You will have fun. Finally, there is a surprise for the holidays this year. Instead of us six having our festive dinners, we will have four more at the table, counting our two new members, and thanks to some of the extra money we have from my bills, I am happy to let you know, but Mom and Dad Wallace are coming to visit, and we are having our dinners catered." "Surprise, surprise!" As soon as Cole said that last surprise, you could hear a pin drop and the OH MY GOD coming out of Keller and Janine's mouths! If you could see the dumbfounded look on their faces. LOL. And now, back to your regular program. Welcome to Tyler and Kane, who is already in progress! LOL. Having dropped the big bombshell, Tyler and Kane nodded in unison to inquire how they were going to top this. Anyway, both gentlemen were very eloquent and sincere in their opening remarks, staring Carole down to reassure her they didn't have anything to worry about for the long haul as they were enjoying every minute with Janine and Ashlee. The men took turns briefly explaining their roots to seek fame and fortune as well as the ladies to spend the rest of their lives with. As the men finished, you could hear hoots and hollers from the peanut gallery and Cole yelling out, "Let's eat fuckers, this boy is hungry. It's unanimous: the boys can stay! Looking happy, she hugged the new dynamic duo; Carole still had a peculiar look on her face.

One thing noted the new dynamic duo, despite the "silver spoons" in their mouths, they decided to live simple in Hollywood, finding a nice two-bedroom apartment off Wilshire. Bet your top dollar. Carole will keep an eye on them without raising an evil eyebrow amongst the other group members. As the newly established octet was eating, Cole inquired if some good holiday movies were being released to take Mom and Dad Wallace to. Beau explained the international flair in a few, as the new duo mentioned. Their expertise was in International Finance and Law within the studio system. Nodding, Beau was anxious to discuss this further. Carole chimed in, saying lots were coming from New York. As Cole expressed a cool attitude, he mentioned to Keller that he had forgotten Mom and Dad were staying with them, and he had a sofa bed coming soon to accommodate them. As soon as Keller and Janine heard this, Ashlee looked over to Janine with a sigh of relief.

Recently, Keller and Beau were both trying to get rid of their luxury rides and traded them for a Jeep Cherokee, and the dynamic duo was doing the simple route by both having Acura Integras as Ashlee and Janine ventured and bought their cars. Long time coming, huh? Carole decided to join in on the bandwagon, and the three ladies decided on the Ford Escort GT.

Now, everyone was set with their own means of transportation except Cole. Keller and Janine taking turns running him back and forth to the clinics if needed. Keller felt need the roomier of the two this way, especially now with Mom and Dad coming in a few days. Aren't they beautiful rides?

Mumsy and Daddy have arrived! Cole, Keller, and Janine drove to LAX on Keller's new ride to pick up the loving duo. Who would believe this shit? They arrive at the terminal, pushing children to the side, heading straight to Cole for a kiss, hug, and showing love all over him. "Gosh, what do I deserve this," Cole remarked. Dad pulled back and reached in to hug the children and kiss them while Mom was still slobbering all over Cole and in between, hearing a few sobs. Janine said, "Well, since you are going to be here for an extended stay, I guess we'll get your luggage." Cole mentioned to Mom Wallace he and Keller had his room all set up for them, or they could try the new sofa bed they had just purchased. Cole added he was so appreciative for all they have done for them and didn't mean to be a charity case. Dad Wallace spoke up to reiterate, "Well, son, anyone who enters our child's life and needs love, we are to help whenever we can." "Now, if we can just get pretty little Janine married off to give us some grandbabies, we are all set!" Janine started laughing by replying, "Well, Daddy, I hate to burst your bubble, but my ovaries aren't ovulating to bust out any babies!" Mom Wallace sighed and nudged Janine to say don't be talking nasty like that. Cole remarked from the front seat, "You will be pleased with who she has in her life. He is a good fella!" Janine thought to herself, wondering what Cole was talking about. She hasn't told the gay duo half of what had been going on lately with her, Ashlee, Tyler, and Kane. Could there be some Peyton Place gossip behind the scenes, like Bob, Carol, Ted, and Alice's goings-on LOL? More on this later.

Before they get to Cole and Keller's apartment, Cole mentions he is the munchies and wants Mom and Dad Wallace to experience the burger experience, second best to the belly bomber of St. Louis White Castle or Steak and Shake. Janine, rolling in laughter and fighting back tears, "Now, Cole, how dare you punish my parents by taking them to In N Out!" Keller couldn't stop laughing either and said, "Mom and Dad, you are in for a treat, as these burgers have been in California since 1948." Woohoo!

After lunch, the trio took Mom and Dad Wallace to settle in at Cole and Keller's apartment to unpack and relax before dinner. Hoping the parents brought dress clothes because they were taking them to Coconut Grove to meet Tyler, Kane, Beau, and Carole. Keller yelled out take their time unpacking and have a quick nap. Dinner reservations weren't till 7:00. As Dad Geoff rested in the bedroom, closing the door behind her, Rennie walked into the kitchen and inquired where a glass was. She needed to take aspirin, having a headache. Cole reached into the cabinet and gave it to Rennie. "Here you go, Rennie dear!" Rennie scoffed, "Cole, we are family now. You can call me Mom, ok!" Cole nodded with appreciation by hugging Rennie close, acknowledging how much their money had meant to them and reminding her he was almost paid off thanks to their generosity. Cole did say, "This is one of the reasons I wanted to surprise Keller and Janine with you two here for the holidays. I just don't know how much time I am going to have, and I didn't want to leave this earth without meeting you and Geoff." Rennie added that she was so appreciative that Keller had met someone and got those thoughts off his mind. With all these early preventive medicines, hopefully, you will be around for a tad longer.

Lucky for the duo, Keller was outside talking to Janine about dinner reservations, out of earshot. Rennie reminded Cole again that he was family and that money was no problem. The children went to Washington University and the University of Missouri-Columbia on scholarships, so the money was sitting there. They were glad to help where needed. "It's a shame you are estranged from your parents, though," Rennie said. Cole said, "They weren't too happy about me being gay, and I didn't make it a point to flaunt it." Cole added he had to be his own person and make it on his own, thinking he had done quite well despite getting HIV and it was my own fault. I have paid dearly for losing Keller once and don't intend to lose him again; he has a great, forgiving heart, which I will forever be grateful for as long as I have on this earth. Rennie nodded. Keller and Janine are both very caring, and they get it from Geoff and her.

The duo was ending their discussion. Keller and Janine walked into the kitchen where, talking and remarking, hoping they didn't interrupt anything important. Cole said, "No, just getting acquainted with Mom while Dad is napping." Janine stated she was running late to meet Carole and Ashlee at the beauty parlor to get their hair lightened and cut. "See everyone at seven sharp, don't be late, and make sure Dad doesn't nap too long. He can't be cranky to meet the fellas, ok Ma," Janine said.

Janine darted out the door. Keller mentioned to his Mom that during their stay, they would be going to the movies, so be ready. As Dad Geoff was snoozing loudly, this was giving me the perfect opportunity to discuss something close to my heart. Rennie mentioned she was so happy to be here to meet the group and get away from the cold in Missouri and equally added Dad Geoff was too. Time was getting close to 6ish, coupled with the boys and Rennie having their showers, and Geoff putt put when you heard Rennie yell out, "Geoff, can you please hurry up!" Cole and Keller roared in laughter, with Keller remarking, "That's my Mama!" Cole said, "I can't believe my stars!" Keller told Cole that's not the only bad word she says. The ladies better watch it tonight. She might spew out the C word!" Cole was laughing so hard he was wiping back tears. It was 6:30, and Geoff was finally ready for them to leave for the restaurant. Cole called Ashlee to say they were on their way. Ashlee stated they would be, too, as soon as Tyler and Kane arrived. No sooner had Cole placed the phone in the cradle than it rang. It was Beau. They were on their way, too. Cole remarked they had better move quickly because the rest of the gang was leaving, too. Okey Dokey. The groups drove from their respective places. Everyone arrived at 6:50, with ten minutes to spare for outside hugs, handshakes, and introductions. Everyone dressed to the nines, Keller went to the hostess to remind Wallace of a party of ten. As she led the way, ladies first down the runway, LOL. Tyler and Kane raced to seat Mom Rennie in hopes of scoring points. You could hear Rennie say, "OK, bastards, back off. I may be older than dirt, but you don't have to seat me!" Dad Geoff scoffed, "I don't see any of you handsome men helping me to my chair!"

As the server came over to pass the menus to the table, Cole couldn't resist mentioning he was smoking hot. Janine and Keller were on both sides of him, slapping him. Laughing loudly, Cole screeched out, "You can't blame me for looking!" Rennie could see how protective Janine was over Cole, and she screamed, "Oh, Janine, let him have fun. Will you?"

The men were enjoying their special entrees of lamb, veal, prime rib, and other goodies. It was now time for dessert and after-dinner drinks. Rennie and Geoff remarked this was one of the best meals ever had, counting some of the best places in St. Louis. The evening was ongoing till 10 pm, as the new boys, Kane and Tyler, were saying the pleasure was all theirs to meet Janine and Keller's parents, and the same was true for Rennie meeting Beau and Carole. One big happy group with their bellies full and being reiterated,

Mom and Dad will be here for several weeks, including the holidays, with Cole catering the family dinners.

As soon as Keller, Cole, Rennie, and Geoff arrived back at their place, Geoff was already scoffing. It was time for bed as it had been a long travel day. Rennie scoffed back. He had napped all day; he couldn't be tired. Cole began to think Geoff didn't want to talk to him. Keller reminded him that he had no explanation for his dad. It takes a while to warm up to everyone. Cole mentioned while Keller was working the next day, he gave them a sightseeing tour of Hollywood and maybe take in a movie. Keller nodded. That would be nice. Keller and Geoff went ahead to bed. Rennie asked Cole if he minded staying up a bit and talking more. Cole said, "Sure, Mom, what's up." Rennie inquired to Cole about what the doctors were actually saying to him about his HIV diagnosis. Cole explained to her since it's in the initial stages, he could live a full life if he kept up with meds, appointments, and blood tests and utilized all information readily available to reassure her he would stay with Keller forever. Cole reiterated that he was so sorry if he put Keller in any danger through his indiscretions and very much appreciated her and Geoff's financial assistance. "I will do everything in my power to pay you back some way!" Rennie remarked there was no need. They have plenty for the children to have after they are gone. We are family and here to help; just keep loving Keller and Rennie, and I will be ok.

AND THE OSCAR GOES TO...

The next morning, Keller hitched a ride with Janine to the studios; he was going to look for work with CBS. He left his care for Cole. Cole was going to take Rennie and Geoff on a drive through Hollywood and Beverly Hills, lunch at Neiman Marcus, and see if Geoff would be interested in seeing The Untouchables as it had been out awhile or if Rennie were interested in Moonstruck. Cole took the parents to see both, and they were home in time to see Keller home from work.

The Holidays

The Wallace family was reunited for the first time since the children moved west, and including the rest of the gang was a delight – Turkey, dressing, sweet potatoes, cranberry sauce, pecan pie, yummy yum food in the tummy. The whole group was thankful for lots of things, great health for Mom and Dad, Cole slowly on the mend, the ladies finding love, and everyone working steadily in the movie and television industry. Christmas and New Year approached while the gang worked; Cole brought much enjoyment to Mom and Dad Wallace by keeping his appointments, taking them to lunch, the movies, and more Los Angeles-Hollywood sites. The whole trip was quite entertaining, especially for Rennie, who developed a deep connection with Cole. Geoff, on the other hand, was going with the flow, connecting with his children and their friends. Geoff was a quiet soul, letting Rennie do what she pleased, even if it meant taking Cole under her wing. The New Year rang in, and it was time for Mom and Dad Wallace's return home to St. Louis. They had one last supper with the gang. Cole had catered a big ol' country home cooking to send them off in fine fashion – lots of food to be had, honey-baked ham, black-eyed peas, cornbread, sliced tomatoes, etc.

Everyone got in their respective vehicles to drive out to the airport to say their goodbyes to Mom and Dad. As they hugged and kissed everyone, Rennie told Keller to be sure and take care of Cole and if he needed anything, don't hesitate to call. Geoff hugged and shook hands with Tyler and Kane, telling them to take care of Janine and Ashlee. The two men assured him they would. As they hugged the last two, Carole and Beau, Rennie remarked thanks for being the best friends to Keller, Janine, and now Cole. Keep them safe, and if they ever need anything, just call. Carole nodded, in unison, they would.

Chapter Thirty

T he holidays have come and gone; the group survived Mom and Dad Wallace's trip out West to see the kids, get to know their friends, and bring joy to their hearts. Things were smooth sailing as love returned in the air for the octet. Cole was getting stronger every day, gaining weight, had a great appetite, and was seriously thinking about work, but maybe in offices. Cole reassured Keller if he needed to travel for work, he would be fine as sweethearts Janine and Ashlee offered to take him when necessary for doctor appointments.

Before the nominations were due February 18th, Valentine's Day was the biggest ever; the octet decided to go back to the Grove. Damn, weren't they just there for Thanksgiving? Since Janine and Ashlee had love in their tummies for Kane and Tyler, there wasn't any sense in going there looking. But occasionally, the four would go for a cocktail or two after work before returning to their apartments for hot sex - not to go wild.

As the nominations were lurking around the corner, Keller, Beau, and Carole were gathering around the communal hall, glancing through the new projects that were readily available for the New Year.

Rain Man	The Accused	The Accidental Tourist
A Cry in the Dark	A Fish Called Wanda	Mississippi Burning
Gorillas in the Mist	Dangerous Liaisons	

New York, anyone, New York, anyone. Appearing in New York is a state of mind for Carole, who wanted to work with Mike Nichols again on Working Girl. Beau and Keller were eyeing each other overseas. Keller was thinking heavily about going down under to Australia to work with Meryl Streep in A Cry in the Dark, and Beau was serious about Africa working with Sigourney Weaver in Gorillas in the Mist. Beau and Keller were trying to convince Carole and Cole it was ok to travel overseas. Cole thought it would be wonderful for Keller to see Australia. Unfortunately, he wouldn't be able to go due to his initial HIV treatment. Drats! Carole was okay with Beau in Africa but fearful of airborne illness returning with him. Beau and Keller were headed to opposite parts of the world for post-production duties on two great movies. Keller promised he be back soon, and Beau said he would join Carole in New York upon his return because Sigourney Weaver had to finish some unfinished post-production on Working Girl, too. SPOILER ALERT: If you watch closely in Working Girl, Weaver's character Katharine returns from a business trip with a stuffed gorilla underneath her arm. Carole is on her way to work with Mike Nichols again in New York City.

Valentine's Day was celebrated by all at the Grove for dinner and drinks to celebrate their love for each other, and there was a bon voyage for Beau and Keller to their respective destinations and Carole heading to New York. Dinner ended on a high note; the four couples embraced and parted ways, Cole and Keller to their apartment, Beau and Carole to theirs, and the remaining four, Ashlee, Janine, Tyler, and Kane, were headed over to the boys' apartment. There was a Valentine's surprise in store. This was going to be the ladies' first visit to their bachelor pad. Leading the ladies to their pad, Tyler and Kane were super excited to show them what they had in store. The gentlemen asked the ladies, more bubbly; of course, who couldn't resist it? Kane said, "How would you two feel about a game of switcheroo tonight?" Ashlee was startled at first because she was close to ten years older. Would she be up to the challenge? Next thing you know, Tyler and Kane had all four undressed and ready for fun. Tyler said, "We promised you gals another surprise; there isn't any sense hiding it much longer as much we love you; we love each other too; we are bi-sexual." Would you mind spicing it up tonight and letting us express our love in front of you? "Nothing too explicit, just foreplay with kissing and oral; if you want to jump in, feel free to do so." Janine said, "I thought it would be exciting watching this, and it is going to be fun." Next thing you know, the men were hot, expressing carnal desires, and Janine joined in with tongues kissing each other, leaving Ashlee to what the hell? All four were doing everything you could think between two men or two women, leaving it to your imagination.

Nomination time was here! February 18th rolled in after Valentine's Day, and as Beau and Keller prepared for their respective trips, there were no worries, as they would be back in late March or early April for the ceremony slated for April 11th. It appears there was historical drama looking for Oscar gold this year. Nine went to Bernardo Bertolucci's epic, the Last Emperor, the story of Puyi, the final emperor of China, and six went to Empire of the Sun, Spielberg's coming-of-age drama about the wealthy son of a British family in Shanghai who becomes a Japanese prisoner of war in World War II. It will be interesting to see which will prevail come Oscar night. Comedies and dramas proved high stakes for Moonstruck and Broadcast News, with Cher duking it out with Holly Hunter and Fatal Attraction, Untouchables, Anna and Ironweed. A bit of trivia: all nominees for Best Director were born outside of the United States, and sentimental favorite Ann Sothern received a Supporting Actress nod for The Whales of August, stealing from legends Bette Davis and Lillian Gish.

AND THE OSCAR GOES TO…

Ashlee was speechless and exhausted after the tryst Valentine's night between the quartets. Make sure that never happens again! LOL. Ashlee couldn't keep quiet; she told Cole to make him promise not to tell the others what happened. Cole was a silly old queen, full of gossip, sure everyone would know before the year was out.

Weeks leading up to the ceremony, three of the octet away, Ashlee and Janine alternated taking Cole to the clinic for his blood tests, pharmacy, and whatever he needed to be done; they were there. Tyler and Kane were supportive of this. Often, the five would get together for dinners; Cole would cook for them. Whipping up his famous meatloaf, chicken Dijonnaise, and steak Diane, Cole was getting to be a regular Julia Child.

Carole was back from New York City and told everyone there was so much fun on the Working Girl set. Mike Nichols assembled the perfect cast for this ensemble comedy; Carole didn't realize how funny Weaver and Ford were. Weaver wasn't on set much as she was back and forth from Africa doing post-production work for Gorillas in the Mist.

Keller and Beau were due home before March 25th. Keller had been invited to attend the Technical Awards, and Shirley Jones hosted it. Keller invited Kane to get to know him better, as he was looking after Janine's best interests. Kane acknowledged the invitation with a yes; Tyler and Beau would tag, too.

Keller was glad to be home and talk about Cole's latest treatments. Cole reassured him everything was fine, still experiencing night sweats and low-grade fevers. AZT assisted in reducing the infections. Keller asked Cole if he started to sleep in the same bed again; he said yes. If the sweats start, I don't want you to think I wet the bed.

Beau arrived early on the 25th from Africa suffering from severe jetlag, hopeful to wear off before the 27th. The technical awards were held later that evening, and Beau was ready for a few cocktails with Keller and the others. The four would be attending their first Technical award presentation and meet Shirley Partridge, the one and only Shirley Jones, a Best Supporting Actress winner herself in 1961, co-starring with Burt Lancaster in Elmer Gantry. With the Technical awards done, the Oscar nominees anxiously awaited two weeks before the actual ceremony. Critics and entertainment reporters were starting to weigh in on the nominees and their predictions. Will Cher win Oscar gold? Will William Hurt duplicate the previous year's win?

The octet assembled in two cars and headed to the Shrine Auditorium on April 11th; the 60th Academy Awards were soon to begin, with Chevy Chase selected t as host for the second time. Cars were parked, ladies dressed to appease the men, drinks at the cash bar rushing to their seats, catching glimpses of celebrities stopping to say hi to their fans. Cole had a long nap today, refreshed, and looking forward to seeing Cher and Sean Connery, too. The Scottish star caught a glimpse of Cole and cordially waved, making him feel good. The evening seemed to be going smoothly, being a first for Tyler and Kane, despite the namesake, namesake, you would think, Tyler had been before. Tyler mentioned his third cousin, Robert, would always have some lucky lady on his arm, preventing any relatives from attending. It was Tyler's time to shine, so here is to all the other Taylor relatives: eat your heart out!

Moonstruck received gold first as Olympia Dukakis won Best Supporting Actress as Cher's mom in Moonstruck, Sean Connery won Best Supporting Actor for the Untouchables, and with the evening coasting, The Little Emperor was headed for a clean sweep, nine for nine becoming the second picture in Oscar history to win all their nominations since 1959's Gigi. Nearing the end, Cher won Best Actress, and Michael Douglas won Best Actor for Wall Street, making him the only actor who previously won as a producer in 1976.

Cole, Keller, Beau, and Carole raced home; the two had to re-pack and head out again for their post-production work in the Outback of Australia and Africa. Carole finished in New York and worked with Dustin Hoffman and Tom Cruise in Rain Man in Cincinnati, Northern Kentucky, and Las Vegas.

Keller's absence was taking a toll on Cole. Depression was settling in, keeping himself occupied; the travel office at a studio asked him to help once or twice a week. Janine, having a deadline at the office, took Cole to his latest appointment to say she couldn't wait. Was there a way he could take a bus or cab back? He said sure, giving a thumbs up. Oddly, a rare occurrence happened at this appointment that nobody saw coming. In the deep corner of the clinic, Cole noticed a guy sitting alone. Cole went over and, out of curiosity, introduced himself. Cole stretched his hand, shaking the other's hand; he recognized him working with him on Lee Major's ABC series, The Fall Guy. It was Bradley Morris. Cole thought he was gay when working together but never approached the subject. The two new old friends talked over old until Cole was called back to do his labs; he gave Bradley his number. Cole told Bradley he was partnered, and making new friends wasn't out of the question. He added he wasn't working due to his illness and offered to grab lunch sometime. Bradley told him to give him a call.

Spring turned into Summer; everyone was home from their post-production duties, contemplating what was next. Beau decided he had enough work. Carole and Keller were staying busy with television work. Keller was taking a rest as well; Cole's friend Bradley called and asked if they'd be interested in volunteering at the Los Angeles Food Pantry. Cole thought it would be a great idea to give back to the Los Angeles community for all they do for HIV patients. Keller loved listening to Bradley and Keller talk about their fond memories of working with Lee Majors and the cast of The Fall Guy. Often, Keller excused himself, turning melancholy. Discussing their status and where they were in the stages of illness. It often became very emotional.

HIV cases increased, and the FDA approved new medicines, steadily gaining support from politicians approving legislation and funding. More and more were being infected. HIV wasn't labelled a gay disease anymore, and people weren't infected solely through sexual contact; it was from blood transfusions as well. Despite the haunting stigma of HIV and AIDS coupled with the rising numbers, there was still no reason for all the bigotry and hatred in the world. With last year's holiday memories behind them, Cole asked his friends to volunteer at the pantry. The group didn't bat an eye and immediately said yes. Assembling in the pantry's dining hall feeding the HIV members, pantry director Alexis Van Slyke asked to have a word with Cole and Keller. Alexis led them to her office, shutting the door behind them and inviting them to sit. Alexis said, "As you notice Bradley's absence today, no easy way as it pains me to tell you, Bradley passed away in his sleep late last night!" Keller comforted Cole as he sobbed, "No, it can't be true!" Cole said, "I just talked to him yesterday afternoon; it can't be true!" Keller thanked Alexis, saying they could volunteer but fear Cole might be a distraction.

"Would it be ok if they come back another day?" Cole and Keller nodded in agreement. Walking out of the office and into the dining hall, Keller told Janine and others they were welcome to stay and help; he had to take Cole home. Janine said, "Sure, what's wrong big brother?" Keller told her he would explain later. Keller asked if he was hungry for In N Out Burger to cheer him up. He nodded yes, that would be nice!

The duo made it home as the phone was ringing, fumbling with the key; Cole pushed Keller aside, running to the kitchen wall. Keller pulled the key out of the lock; Cole yelled out, "Hey honey, it's Carole; she wants to know if they come over about 4?" Keller nodded yes by asking Cole if he was comfortable seeing people. Cole told Carole how about 5? I need a nap. The lovebirds showed up with fried chicken, potato salad, and slaw from Kentucky Fried Chicken; this should put a smile on Cole's face when he wakes up; he won't have to cook and not be too hungry after their burgers earlier.

The holiday week started slow; Cole called the pantry to see if there was anything concerning a service for Bradley. Alexis said it was planned for Thursday after Thanksgiving. Cole said it was perfect and that he would head over the following Monday seeing if there was anything he could do to help. Volunteering gave him a sense of pride, giving back to others and spreading his story to give others hope and inspiration. After the memorial, Alexis pulled Cole aside and wondered if he would be interested in being a part-time counselor at the pantry. Cole didn't even bother to ask Keller; he immediately said HELL YES! Working at the pantry was giving Cole a new lease on life. Losing Bradley Morris really hit hard and made him think twice about life and realize it's not taken for granted. Cole knew for sure he wasn't the only one Morton Freeman was sleeping with. Cole didn't know how much time he had left; it was NOW taking one day at a time; life can be taken away in an instant. You never know what tomorrow will bring. Cole chose to concentrate on staying healthy, focusing on his clients at the pantry, loving his friends, and keeping the faith to stay in love with Keller until and when the Lord calls him home.

Chapter Thirty-One

Movies coming out certainly sure cure all that ails everyone this year. Tom Hanks made a splash with ABC's Bosom Buddies with a Penny Marshall film called BIG was getting rave reviews; Dustin Hoffman and Tom Cruise played brothers in Rain Man; Mike Nichols directed again a film with a satire on corporate America with Working Girl, Sigourney Weaver played real-life wildlife activist, Dian Fossey in Gorillas in the Mist, Jodie Foster and Kelly McGillis played in the Accused about a rape victim and her female lawyer and Glenn Close, John Malkovich, and Michelle Pfieffer in the period drama, Dangerous Liaisons. These generated more buzz first of 1989 upon the nomination deadline and the actual ceremony in February and March, respectively. Nominations for the 61st Academy Awards were announced on February 15th. No brainer, Barry Levinson's masterpiece Rain Man was nominated for eight, Dangerous Liaisons and Mississippi Burning seven a piece,

AND THE OSCAR GOES TO...

Mike Nichols' return to directing's Working Girl received six, and child actress Jodie Foster surprised the academy with a Best Actress nod for the Accused. Beautiful Sigourney Weaver was nominated for two different acting categories and movies, Working Girl and Gorillas in the Mist.

Prior to the March 29th ceremony, it was announced there would be no host this year, per producer Allan Carr. Angie Dickinson hosted and presented the Technical Awards on March 19th. Entertainment oddsmakers slowly began their due diligence, predicting the winners as the nominees started their press junkets to promote their performances and films.

A few nights before the Oscar bash, the octet met up for dinner one night at the Grove when the lead discussion at the table was about everyone feeling older lately and going to the ceremony was getting stale. Maybe it was time they started watching the Oscars together at a certain home with appetizers and champagne or separately; what was the verdict? Tyler and Kane had the newest and largest apartment among the other six. Depending on Cole, Keller thought their place was too small for eight, and Ashlee and Janine spent more and more time with Tyler and Kane at their place instead of their own. Carole and Beau were busy working a lot, either on location in town or in other parts of the United States, and/or Beau was out of the country. Everyone started another discussion thread about who was going to win. Of course, the ladies were rooting for Working Girl, loving the satirical look at women in the executive-style working environment as the men seemed divided between Mississippi Burning and the evilness of Glenn Close in Dangerous Liaisons.

Given this, the last Oscar ceremony our octet would see in person, we decided to pull out all the stops with the glitz and glamour of old Hollywood. The ladies took a weekend shopping till they dropped up and down Rodeo Drive in hopes of finding the perfect dress to express their allegiance to all the years they worked in Hollywood.

Cole decided to pull out all the stops in celebrating the Oscars by fixing an Italian feast on Monday, March 27th, with champagne, lasagna, fettuccine alfredo, salad, and warm Italian bread and take it to Tyler and Kane's for a pre-Oscar party. Odd timing, the ceremony was held on a Wednesday this year, giving the octet plenty of time to eat and stuff themselves.

Gleefully, the octet assembled at the Shrine Auditorium one last time, pulling their vehicles to the valet and ogling the stars walking the red carpet; they couldn't resist yelling out their favorites. Out of the corners of their eyes, they noticed Kevin Kline, Sigourney Weaver, Dustin Hoffman, Geena Davis, and Jodie Foster.

With the switcheroo of no host, this was going to be an odd ceremony with no jokes. All seriousness aside, I am sure there will be something to make light of it all. Given an openly gay producer in Carr, this specific ceremony drew mixed reviews by the Hollywood community; a few noticeable changes, as fore mentioned, with no host, relied on presenters having some connection as couples, co-stars, and companions alike. One notable change was that instead of the presenters saying, "The winner is," for the first time, it was, "And the Oscar goes to." Despite mixed reviews, this was the most watched telecast of the Oscars with over forty-two million viewers, a record held until 1998, which surpassed over fifty-seven million. Critics weren't as kind either; the performances were "over the top" with a mixture of old Hollywood combined with new Hollywood. Sadly, this was the last public appearance of Lucille Ball, who, with Bob Hope, was introduced by Walter Matthau to introduce a performance segment. She passed away less than a month later.

Worth noting the five Best Picture nominees were announced in February, the United States box office had amounted to $186 million, which was an average of $37.7 million per film, and Rain Man grossed $97 million. Out of the top fifty-selling films of 1988, fifty-two nominations only went to thirteen films. As predicted, the winners four went to Rain Man, no brainer Best Actor went to Dustin Hoffman, Best Picture, Director, and Screenplay. Best Actress went to Jodie Foster for her stunner performance as a rape victim in The Accused. Best Supporting Actress went to Geena

Davis in The Accidental Tourist, and Best Supporting Actor went to Kevin Kline in A Fish Called Wanda. It was sad seeing Sigourney Weaver go home empty-handed after being nominated for both Best Actress and Best Supporting Actress.

During the talk on the drive back home, Cole couldn't stop how "over the top" Allan Carr mixed old with new, and Carole agreed, seeing the oldies linked in a set to resemble the Coconut Grove nightclub and then to the younger set doing their routine.

After the spectacle of the award ceremony, it was now time to focus on work for our octet. Looks like the circumstances of love being in the air for Ashlee and Janine, happy as larks with Tyler and Kane; the foursome was content being in their offices, staying grounded to Hollywood. Janine was more than happy to assist Keller anytime he needed her with Cole. Keller was staying put, working with CBS odd jobs here and there; at least it was paying the bills, and Cole was still assisting at the pantry. Being there meant so much; Cole was giving so much back to the LGBTQA+ community, and they were giving him so much love in return. Beau and Carole were still going here and there and everywhere in between, but work wasn't as easy for them. A much younger set had their eyes on jobs requiring travel. Occasionally, if a gig in New York City would show up, Carole was ready to jump at the opportunities she was missing her Broadway fix.

AND THE OSCAR GOES TO...

The studio brass explained age was just a number to the octet but could see the writing was clearly on the wall; it was probably a few more years before getting booted to the curb. Ashlee was doing her best to try to stay as attractive as ever to keep the early forties handsome Tyler from looking elsewhere.

There still was this little secret between the four of them switching it up on that Valentine's Day, happening a few more times, but nobody knew. Ashlee and Janine had grown quite closer after these hair-raising experiences, especially after seeing Kane and Tyler going after each other. Watching the two men having sex was just what the doctor ordered for all to be secure and comfortable in their own skin. What happened next didn't seem out of the ordinary. After dinner one night at the men's apartment, the doorbell rang. The men were busily gathering up the leftover food and plates; Kane asked Janine to get the door. Janine opened the door, and a man and woman stood there. Startled at first, Janine said, "May I help you?" The man in his mid-forties and the woman in her early thirties passed by Janine and Ashlee nonchalantly to say, "We are here, Kane!" As the men were finishing the dinner dishes, Tyler remarked, "Ladies, may we present Zach and Kylie? They work in my and Kane's department." Zach presented himself as sort of arrogant; he was tall, about 6'4, 180, with chestnut brown hair, tanned and blue eyes, and Kylie appeared shy, 5' 7, 150 blonde hair, blue eyes, and sporting a nice rack of boobs. LOL! Kane entered from the kitchen, toweling his hands and reaching to give the newest duo a big hug. Zach remarked, "What lovely ladies you two are; you must be Janine and Ashlee; we have heard so much about you two," with a sly wink. Having said that, Janine followed Kane back into the kitchen, cornering him to softly say, "What is this? You think we need some extra help in the bedroom, huh?" "Kinda kinky, you think," Kane said. Kane motioned Janine to go in there and show the new duo what she had. In a split second, Janine walked in one hot mess, entering the room; Zach was undressed and stroking Tyler, and Kylie was about to disrobe. Next thing you know, everyone was totally naked, and it was a love feast. After all the moans and groans coming from the wild sextet, it all got quiet for about an hour or so; everyone was gasping for air as the orgasmic aura surrounded them in a frenzy of lust.

After what was an explosive box office year, Carole and Beau were busily attending the meetings at the hall, glancing over the communal bulletin boards. Keller decided, even at Cole's urging, that he was feeling better than ever, wanting to stay close in California and continue the honor of his contract with CBS. Several films vying for Oscar Gold's next work would have their work cut out for them.

AND THE OSCAR GOES TO...

Crimes and Misdemeanors	Field of Dreams	Glory	My Left Foot	Born on the 4ᵗʰ of July
Crimes and Misdemeanors	*Field of Dreams*	*Glory*	*My Left Foot*	*Born on the 4ᵗʰ of July*
The Fabulous Baker Boys	Driving Miss Daisy	Henry V		Dead Poet's Society

After viewing the list, it was a no-brainer: Carole was heading to New York to work with Woody Allen. Beau was dividing his time between Massachusetts and Georgia to work on Glory, returning to Georgia for Driving Miss Daisy and a few weeks prior to 1989 in Dallas for Oliver Stone's Born on the Fourth of July. Keller went to CBS and started work on the revamped Twilight Zone on the soundstage of Television City. It was an interesting gig to keep Keller here in California and close to Cole.

With Beau and Carole traveling most of the year, Cole was staying busy with the pantry and Keller at CBS, and nobody seemed to notice the absence of Janine and Ashlee. Where were they anyway? Apparently, the duo were just as busy with the newfound sexual escapades with Tyler, Kane, Zach, and Kylie. Ashlee felt a rebirth of her sexuality; being post-menopausal, how could she keep up with the rest? This new free-spirited bisexuality was hard to explain; Ashlee knew damn well to keep her mouth shut around Cole, knowing he would tattle to the others.

Cole, finding his new call of volunteering at the pantry and a counselor, didn't have a feel for Hollywood anymore; it wasn't in his veins. This new purpose in life continued to make him smile more and feel better about himself every day. Keller was delighted; Cole was the least of his worries unsure what it was. Focusing on a new worry, Janine was up to something and determined if it took the holidays or after he would find out.

Chapter Thirty-Two

A new decade is here; the 90s are here! Hollywood proved itself to be more uplifting in sentimentality by the films produced in 1989. Who would ever think there would not be a correlation between the emotionality shown on screen and the liberation of women becoming freer with their bodies? Calling this hogwash from a sociological aspect, and if true, this supposed revolution was becoming a social development to free all humanity from their hangups. One factor was causing distress, perhaps, at a time when everyone was doing everyone. The late 80s impact of HIV was really showing the decrease of sexually transmitted diseases of earlier venereal diseases like syphilis and gonorrhea; HIV was clearly not just a gay disease. At first, HIV was said to have been at first being labeled as an unprotected sexual disease, but medical professionals were not ruling out other transmission methods.

TIM J. CULBERTSON

It has taken Hollywood and television studios years to tackle homosexuality as an issue to be shown on the silver and small screens, having been swept under the carpet for years. It was a touchy subject to be taboo, implied, perhaps, but never discussed openly. Even in 2024, is it an "open book." Everyone has their opinions and is entitled to them. One would think homosexuality is fully exploited, but I was not sure it was the right term when Rock Hudson passed away from AIDS. As Bob Dylan sang in 1964, The Times They are a-Changin'.

As mentioned, the subject was implied in films over many years; it took network television forever to tackle the subject as well, depicted in their made-for-television films or introducing a gay character in a scripted series. Those were the dark ages; we might as well let bygones be bygones and let it rest. People change. Things change. Change is the key word; just need to learn to deal and live with it. Easier said than done, right?

As the new decade started, there was much speculation these so-called "feel good' movies were going to inspire all the Academy voters in a frenzy of a who's who to a what's going to score the most nominations in the upcoming Oscar race. Would this feel-good fever continue for years to come as new genres begin to bring box office gold in hopes of gaining newfound respect from old Academy members? Time will tell!

AND THE OSCAR GOES TO...

Entertainment news agencies were slow on the draw, but plenty of performances were shining in the limelight. Robin Williams was making a big splash doing drama after his television comedic coupled with movie comedies in Peter Weir's Dead Poets Society, veteran stage actress Jessica Tandy was making moves in Driving Miss Daisy, English actor-director Kenneth Branagh was dashing in Henry V, and who could forget, Kevin Costner in the baseball time travel film, Fields of Dreams and Woody Allen was making a return. So, come Valentine's Day 1990, who would get their nominations hoping to turn into gold?

Valentine's Day showered flowers of love for Driving Miss Daisy, becoming the first off-Broadway play to be honored with nine nominations, and it was the first in a few years lauded so much praise without a Best Director nomination. Other films included Oliver Stone's Return to Vietnam, eight nominations, including the Best Actor nomination to Tom Cruise for Born on the Fourth of July; the Civil War drama Glory and the English drama My Left Foot received five; The Fabulous Baker Brothers received, four, Field of Dreams three and Henry V received Best Actor and Director nominations as well. An odd piece of trivia: Jessica Tandy, popular as a stage actress, was the original Blanche DuBois in A Streetcar Named Desire on Broadway; when it was made into a film, Hollywood wanted a big-name star when studios picked Vivien Leigh.

On March 3rd, the technical awards were hosted and presented by Diane Ladd and Richard Dysart. Party planners were pulling out the stops for the next three weeks in anticipation of the winners to be announced. Ashlee was feeling down; it was the first time in many years that her friends wouldn't be attending the ceremony. Maybe, just maybe, she could squeeze in one more ceremony; if not, it would be cool if Janine and her could host a little cocktail party. I'm not so sure; after the few sexual encounters with Zach and Kylie, it was fun, but it needed to stop. After their few encounters, Kylie was seen in the studio steno pool, and Ashlee scurried to the restroom when she appeared in the offices. As for Janine, she found herself in quite an odd predicament as well. She ran into Zach in the hallway one day while talking with Tyler and Kane. Wandering minds made it wonder what those three men could be plotting, either another sextet encounter or perhaps a three-way amongst the gentlemen. Janine walked by, offering a sexy hello and noticing from the corner of her eye that Zach was rubbing his crotch and licking his lips.

Predictions were mixed as the March 26th ceremony was getting closer to a reality. Golden Globes and the annual New York and Los Angeles Film Critics Awards were setting the tone. It's always been perhaps just a guessing game such awards are given, adding more fuel to the fires and anticipation for that moment of being recognized by their peers.

AND THE OSCAR GOES TO...

The octet and possibly a group of ten were gathered at Ashlee and Janine's, lounging wherever they could find a seat, either on the floor or up at the countertop near the dining room. Ashlee and Janine promised everyone a bit of intimate flair fed by chips, dips, champagne, beer, wine, and other alcoholic beverages. Keller noticed a few nervous twitches in his sister, and Ashlee nudged them as they were in the kitchen preparing the food trays. Keller inquired, "What's up with you two? You sure seem to be a tad on edge tonight?" Janine chuckled, "Nothing, bro; we are just anxious to see who is going to win tonight." Ashlee reiterated in unison why Keller would ever think something was up. Keller noted every time the new duo, Zach and Kylie, walked by with their mischievous smiles on the way to the bathroom.

As the Oscar telecast was about to start, there was a big *shhhh* coming from the peanut gallery. Cole told everyone to be quiet he wanted to hear Billy Crystal's monologue. Everyone quieted down to a whisper, and out of the corner of Kane's eye, he stretched back, rubbing Janine's back. Kylie smiled with her shit-ass grin. Zach gave Kane an odd smirk as well as walking by, getting another beer out of the fridge and giving him a soft pat on his crotch. Nobody seemed to notice, but Keller noticed it, softly whispering it to Cole; it didn't faze him because he was more concerned about the Oscars. That was a first, Cole not being nosy but glued to the television.

Before Cole and Keller left to join everyone, Cole typed a ballot with the nominees for the major categories and a place for everyone to vote for their favorites. Upon their arrival, Cole announced wanted everyone to vote, and then after the telecast was over, they would compare their votes,

As you know, watching these award shows at home can be brutal. You time your bathroom breaks or just go whenever it hits you, but when you are guests, it is best not to make obvious you are up to shenanigans. Looks like the new kid Zach was up to something, or was it Tyler? Or Kane? Kylie? Who cares? Let them have fun.

Karl Malden, then president of the Academy, gave his welcoming speech to the audience and handed it off to first-time host Billy Crystal. Nothing short of hilarious, Crystal had the live audience eating out of the palm of his hands; it's a wonder how come he had never been asked by the Academy before. Cole and Keller remarked on how funny he was in the ABC comedy SOAP and, his stint on Saturday Night Live, and finally making it on the big screen. Especially, this year he co-starred in the romantic comedy When Harry Met Sally with Meg Ryan, fresh off being on the CBS soap As the World Turns, directed by their good friend Rob Reiner.

As the ceremonies got underway, everyone was having a wonderful time eating and drinking. It was there in person; you can't have your cake and eat it too, I suppose. It had been a nice ride, able to see the Oscars in person, and there was the slightest opportunity working in Hollywood; you would be able to say hello to a special star. Hoping they will remember you. It was always great to reminisce about such memories, as the six certainly will spin tales for their new group members in years to come. Those were the days.

The first award of the night, often tradition, had the previous year's winner of the Best Supporting Actress present the Best Supporting Actor award, certainly no exception to the norm tonight. Geena Davis presented Denzel Washington the award, which appeared a no-brainer, given the other nominees, possible spoilers could have been Martin Landau in Crimes and Misdemeanors and Dan Aykroyd in Driving Miss Daisy playing Jessica Tandy's son and Patti Lupone's husband, respectively. Not so sure you would think that the Academy nominated Brando in a supporting category. If you remember, Brando burned them by refusing his Best Actor award years previous; if someone burns you, they will burn you again. Not sure what that was all about. Go figure!

Keeping with tradition, Kevin Kline appeared several minutes later to present Best Supporting Actress to Brenda Fricker for My Left Foot, a stunning performance playing Daniel Day Lewis's mother in a true-to-life story of a young Irish man who with cerebral palsy and only control of his left foot after growing up in a poor class working family became an accomplished writer and artist.

Fricker's stunning performance spoiled newcomer Julia Robert's role in the screen adaptation of the off-Broadway play Steel Magnolias and recurring co-star in some of Woody Allen's masterpieces, Dianne Wiest in Ron Howard's comedy Parenthood.

As the telecast dragged on, Zach was getting restless, keeping a roving eye on Keller being up in Janine's face almost every time she got up. It wasn't his concern; if anyone had to say something, it was Kane. Kane finally had enough and walked into the kitchen as Janine and Keller were talking. Zach saw this joining the three and offering some assistance; Keller was trying to relate; mind your own fucking business, as Janine told Zach, "It's ok, it's just family business we need to discuss; go back and enjoy yourself with the others, the major categories should be presented shortly." Zach stuck his head in business; nowhere it didn't belong. Keller excused himself and told Janine they would talk later. Janine quietly nodded towards the living area to watch the rest of the Oscar telecast.

Before the major awards were to be presented, Beau appeared very happy celebrating Glory's win for Denzel Washington and Cinematography. Telling his stories from the set was a long, fun shoot; getting acquainted with not Washington but Matthew Broderick was a pleasure, seeing him out of his comedic comfort zone.

AND THE OSCAR GOES TO...

Dustin Hoffman was on location doing a film, so veteran film star Gregory Peck presented Jessica Tandy the Best Actress award for Driving Miss Daisy, who was a shoo-in; none of the other females appeared close except maybe Pfeiffer for The Fabulous Baker Boys. In between Best Actor, famed directors, and collaborators, Lucas and Spielberg awarded famed Asian director Akira Kurosawa with the well-deserved honorary award for his lifetime achievement. DeNiro and Scorsese presented Oliver Stone, Best Director for Born on the Fourth of July, besting out Branagh, who was nominated for Henry V twice, once as director and actor, and Bruce Beresford, the Australian director who didn't even get a nod after Driving Miss Daisy received nine nominations. Jodie Foster walked to the stage, presenting Best Actor to Daniel Day-Lewis, who was clearly upset that evening over favorites Morgan Freeman, Tom Cruise, and Robin Williams. Beatty and Nicholson ended the ceremony with the win for Best Picture to Driving Miss Daisy, beating all the other nominees.

Another Oscar ceremony filled with feel-good emotions ran rampant in the apartment after Cole tallied up his distributed ballots. Carole was the clear winner; she picked four of the six that were missing Best Actor, chose Tom Cruise, and chose Julia Roberts for Best Supporting Actress. It was clear not everyone was feeling good about the night. You could hear a pin drop, with everyone saying goodnight, as burning animosity between Zach and Keller displayed somewhat civility as everyone filed out if looks could kill. Cole offered to stay, help, and clean. The ladies were taking the day off and replied how sweet it was; they were going to sleep in and tackle chores. Everyone was leaving with hugs and kisses; Zach, the last to leave, offered to spend the night pining for Janine right underneath Kane's nose. She told him quietly NO. As the two hostesses shut the door, Ashlee looked at Janine and boldly stated, "What the fuck was that??" Janine said, "Please, no questions, let's sleep it off, and I'll explain in the morning." Ashlee remained calm, hugging Janine goodnight and shutting their bedroom doors.

The next morning after the Oscars were always the worst, returning to work. The ladies called out in hopes of cleaning the two hot messes brewing in the apartment. Janine preferred staying in bed if not having to face Ashlee's brewing temper. Both ladies tossed and turned all night, trying to figure out what could be said to smooth it out. Beau and Carol slept in, clearing their hangovers, and hit the common building, checking any leads for some post-production help was needed. Tyler and Kane reported to work first thing, suffering much from the alcohol effects. With Zach and Kylie rushing back and stopping by Tyler and Kane's offices, he offered his apologies. Kane offered unsolicited advice to Zach for making an ass of himself; it wouldn't be tolerated anymore. Tyler put his two cents in by saying the escapades need to stop now. Zach said, "I got you men right where I want you; it is far from over. Just wait and see!" Keller decided to take the day off, give it to noon, and call Janine to check in.

Back at Ashlee and Janine's, it was about 830. Ashlee woke up first, took a quick shower, and put on a pot of coffee. Ashlee, hoping the French Roast aroma would awaken Janine, started cleaning quietly. The time is now 9:45, and still no Janine. Janine's phone rang at about 9:20. Ashlee didn't mean to eavesdrop from what she heard: big brother, I'm sorry for dragging you in. Apparently, Janine was talking to Keller. At about 10, Janine slowly walked to the kitchen and got a coffee cup; Ashlee said, "French Roast, your favorite." Janine noted, "Thanks, Ashlee, and before we get into everything, I just want to apologize. Zach was out of line; sorry, I egged him on." Hard it is to believe those words, and Ashlee said, "Honey, I can see Zach playing us to get to Tyler and Kane; we are pawns." Janine reiterated it was true Keller was furious watching it go that far. Ashlee remarked she noticed a confrontation between Zach, Keller and Kane come almost to blows. Be interesting to see if any apologies were forthcoming.

With everyone either at work or home nursing hangovers, the oblivious Beau and Carole to the shenanigans were at the communal hall checking the bulletin boards and viewing possibilities for work. The list read:

GHOST	*REVERSAL OF FORTUNE*	*MISERY*	*AVALON*	*DICK TRACY*
PRETTY WOMAN	*GOODFELLAS*	*HOME ALONE*	*TOTAL RECALL*	*MR. AND MRS. BRIDGE*
THE GODFATHER PART III		*AWAKENINGS*		

THE HUNT FOR RED OCTOBER

Beau commented to Carole that they needed another Godfather because they thought it might be fun working with Costner. Carole was looking forward to working with Garry Marshall, Gere, and Roberts on Pretty Woman in Los Angeles.

Trying not to remember the night before, Janine was frazzled after another call from Keller, saying he had stopped by to see Zach, Tyler, and Kane. The three pieces of shit were nowhere to be found. While talking to Keller, Ashlee's phone rang. Ashlee said it was Tyler, and the three were at their apartment for an early lunch. Ashlee heard giggling; she inquired, "OK, what's going on over there?" Tyler said, "Sweet Ashlee, no worries, we are having a little fun." Ashlee's assumptions were right, and the three were playing them, err, shall I say, the four counting bimbo Kylie. The party continued as Kylie got naked, and the guys were taking lines of cocaine between her boobs. "Well, I hope you are having fun," and hung up on him. Janine came out of her room to say, "What's going on, Ashlee?" Ashlee said, "Nada, it looks like the three lads decided to take a lunch break for some fun." Zach's agenda all along was getting to Kane and Tyler. Janine grew more worried and called Keller to tell him what Ashlee said. Keller said, "Listen, sis, Hollywood is a bad town; we just need to stay clear of them. I didn't want to interfere or hurt your feelings; they are bad news." No sooner had she ended the conversation than her phone rang again; it was Kane. Kane was in the other room while Kylie was servicing him. Janine said, "Oh, hello, Kane. We're just talking about you two," Janine said. In between the cocaine and alcohol, she heard a woman's voice; it was Kylie saying, "Fuck those bitches, come on back to the party!" Kane pushed Kylie away, "Janine, let me explain. Zach found out about our past and is blackmailing us; you have to believe me." Janine screamed in the phone," I don't believe you four enjoy yourselves and rot in hell," as she slammed the phone down, not realizing those were going to be the last words she said to Kane. In between the ladies continuing their clean up, both phones rang off the hook till about 2:30, when they stopped. Janine hugged Ashlee and said, "Looks like we are done here; let's shower and see if the boys want to go for a drive; we need to get out of the apartment." "

It was now 4 o'clock, and leaving their apartment, both phones rang. "Fuck it, we are out of here, let's go meet the boys!" Little did they know, it was both Cole and Keller saying there was something important to tell them. Ashlee stopped and went inside, paying for gas; the attendant mentioned not to go by Santa Monica pier; there had been an accident. Ashlee remarked they were heading back near Sunset Boulevard to get Cole and Keller. When Ashlee got in the car telling Janine what she had heard inside, Janine said she had heard about an accident on the radio. Ashlee said, "On our way, let's get the boys." Upon pulling to the curb in front of Cole and Keller's, the girls noticed the boys were outside waiting for them. Approaching the sidewalk and walking to the apartment, Janine said, "Why so glum?" Exchanging hugs, Cole said, "Before we leave, let's go inside for a quick minute." Keller was quieter than in earlier conversations, letting Cole talk. Cole mentioned a gay cop friend called at about 3:30; there was an accident. Ashlee nodded. They had heard about it when she was getting gas. Cole stopped her to say, "Shit, Ashlee let me finish, preliminary reports are confirming Zach, Tyler, Kane, and Kylie were in Zach's car, and it ran off the pier." Cole went on to mention that the police were over at Tyler and Kane's, checking the apartment. Apparently, the landlord heard loud music and told them to turn it down; they did so as they were leaving to pile in Zach's Mazda MX-5, cranking up the music. Landlord yelled out, "I'm calling the police; you are messed up." Zach yelled back, "Oh shut up, you old man, we will do whatever we damn well please!" The car sped away as a few police cars pulled up; one followed Zach, and the other cops asked to look around the place. The landlord let them in to look around. It wasn't a pretty sight. The cops found cocaine, Ecstasy, and LSD. As the other cop followed Zach, he hit the gas pedal faster, heading for the pier, and before the cops could stop him, Zach plunged the car into the ocean. The other cop inside called first responders as one stood outside the patrol car shaking his head. Within minutes, the first responders arrived, pulling the wreckage from the pier. All four instantly perished from drug intoxication and drowning, but there would be autopsies performed, and toxicology reports would take perhaps a few weeks.

Trying to soak all this in, the girls uncontrollably started to cry and console each other. Keller excused himself to call their cop friend; he was on his way over now. Thirty minutes came and gone; the cop friend arrived. The cop introduced himself as Lt. Carl Asner and offered his condolences, but he needed to ask a few questions. The co asked if there were any arguments today or before that caused this. In between wiping tears, Ashlee mentioned things had been tense the night before and a bit earlier today. The cop asked again if the girls were aware of Tyler and Kane doing drugs, as there was paraphernalia found in the apartment. Janine mentioned they weren't aware, except that Zach had been blackmailing the other men. It apparently was looking as though Zach had a motive to get drugged, take the drive to the pier, and kill everyone. Cole excused himself and called Carole and Beau and asked them to come over. The duo came over to console the girls, who continued to be interrogated by Cole and Keller's friend. Officer Asner thanked them for their time, apologized again for the loss, asked too many questions, and said he would be in touch. To make the evening lighter, Carole suggested dinner, and if Cole didn't mind, she would whip a quick pasta dish for the six to eat. Cole said it would be great and showed Carole where things were. The sextet ate in total silence; Carole found a bit of chicken, whipped up some chicken alfredo, and announced she was heading to Kansas City to work with the Newmans, that's Paul and Joanne in Mr. and Mrs. Bridge, and Beau said he was headed to Wyoming working with Costner in Dances with the Wolves, but after this, it was enough. "Here, here, "let's blow this pop stand upon your return," Ashlee said, tired of Hollywood. Keller mentioned that I would call Mom and Dad if we six could come up and catch some baseball, and Carole could get her Broadway fix by seeing shows at the Muny.

With Carole and Beau gone, the days after the accident and subsequent deaths shaking everyone to the core, preliminary reports were coming from the coroner's office, and it was inconclusive. Ronald Komblum, successor to Thomas Noguchi, who was infamous for his celebrity autopsies on Robert F. Kennedy, John Belushi, Natalie Wood, William Holden, and Marilyn Monroe, released his report on May 26th. Komblum made the startling announcement on the four deceased. After police investigation and discoveries both at Zach and Kylie's and Kane and Tyler's apartments, a slow, drawn-out nightmare was soon becoming a horrifying reality. Long suspected, there were massive amounts of alcohol, cocaine, and LSD found in their bodies. Case closed, and it is time for everyone to get back to normal and lead better lives. Police were still investigating, continuing their search in apartments and asking questions. Lots of cancelled checks signed by Kane or Tyler were found proving the extortion claim as questions presented to Janine and Ashlee concern the sexual escapades between the four and often the six. The ladies wanted it to all go away; the sooner, the better. Janine and Ashlee were still shocked by answers to everyone's burning questions, often wondering if they could have prevented this. Cole told them not to worry about it. Dive into work for the next few months and stay busy, then come around the 4th of July and tell the steno pool to FUCK OFF and Arrivederci because they were leaving in late July for St. Louis, baby! LOL! Let's give these ladies much-needed closure.

Plans started shaping up; Janine and Keller called their parents to get the house ready for six retired employees of the Hollywood system and get some baseball tickets and Muny musical theatre tickets for Carole. Dad Wallace just chuckled; he would have believed it when he saw them on their doorstep. Rennie said they had four extra bedrooms; they would take NO for an answer; they were staying with them: no ifs or buts; end of discussion. Beau checked the baseball schedule, and Carole checked the Muny schedule. It was set: no ties for work, the sextet decided to fly to St.

Louis and spend two three weeks; they would go to the zoo, the Muny, the Cardinals games, shopping, restaurants, and of course, kid at heart, Cole wanted to go to Six Flags.

With retirement from the Hollywood system behind our sextet, it was time for FUN FUN FUN, and the first thing on their agenda was to leave Los Angeles behind. It was Friday, July 20th; the sextet was awaiting their flight from LAX to St. Louis, and even though it's not either exotic or breathtaking oceanfront views, it's a trip to remember.

As the plane was beginning its descent into St. Louis, Cole acted like a little kid in a China shop, looking out his window and seeing the view of the Gateway Arch and Busch Stadium. Cole told Keller he was so happy that he and Janine still had their parents, and this made him, Carole, and Beau honorary "adopted" children. Carole was getting gitty after seeing countless shows on the Great White Way of Broadway in New York City; now it's time to compare how touring companies do Broadway musicals. Gathering their luggage and getting the rental car to accommodate six, Janine called Mom and Dad Wallace, saying they were heading their way. The Wallace parents lived in West County by Chesterfield Mall. Arrival couldn't be sweeter. Instead of the eight eating out the first night, Mom Wallace had a nice spread catered with lots of comfort food to feed an army. The discussion over dinner turned sad, and Rennie and Geoff offered their condolences to Janine and Ashlee for the loss of Kane and Tyler. It was good to be back in Missouri for Keller and Janine; surely not the cold winters nor humid summers, but anxious about taking their friends on the tour of a lifetime. Janine asked Mom if there was anything at the Muny Carole might be interested in. Mom Wallace said she had two shows picked out to see, Brigadoon and No, No, Nanette. The latter had veterans of stage and screen, Van Johnson, Carol Lawrence, and Marge Champion in it.

The gang was getting settled in St. Louis and figuring out what to do on their first full day after a scrumptious meal catered by Mom and Dad Wallace. Mom and Dad said there were plentiful things to do; Mom said she would take the gals to Chesterfield Mall and Plaza Frontenac shopping and lunch on Saturday while Pop can take the boys to the Planetarium, the Zoo, the Arch and other historical places downtown. Beau said he would check the baseball schedule and figure out when would be a suitable time to see a Cardinals game. Looks like the Cardinals were playing the Padres on the 21st and 22nd and their all-time rivals, the Cubs, on the 24th and 25th. Since the gang didn't have any timetable to get back to Los Angeles and Hollywood, Mom and Dad Wallace asked them to please extend their stay till at least part of 2nd week in August. They were so enjoying them visiting, never running out of things to do, even if it was just sitting around doing absolutely NOTHING! The Muny season was in full swing, and Mom Wallace got tickets for the ladies to see No, No, Nanette on opening night on August 6th. It was set; all would kill two birds with one stone: the ladies would go to the Muny, and the men would go to the Cardinals game. In between, Cole asked if they could go to Six Flags. How could they not resist?

Everyone was enjoying themselves in St. Louis. Beau remarked that even being nearly three hundred miles down the interstate going south was Memphis; it's too bad they couldn't sneak in and sneak out to Beale Street and or Graceland. Beau was happy with the fact that being part of a new family with the gang. Especially now they are retired from the Hollywood studio system and now free to do whatever they damn, please.

Cole was happy to experience Six Flags; he rode the log flume ride at least four times during the four hours they were there. Beau and Keller enjoyed the planetarium and the zoo, going up in the arch, and seeing a baseball game, which was especially fun.

It was time for our sextet to fly back home to California; since there was no more work, what would they do with all this time on their hands? Cole still volunteering at the pantry; maybe he could twist some arms to help with the food portion of it. Cole made so many new friends, caregivers of HIV patients, and patients themselves; it was continuing to be a rewarding experience.

With fall in the air, you know what that means: new

television shows and lots of movies upcoming for the holiday season were capturing our sextet's and America's hearts. Studios were still wondering why Paramount released The Godfather Part III. Kevin Costner's Dances with Wolves was bringing much attention to the guys, and two romantic movies, Ghost and Pretty Woman, were the ladies' fancy. Godfather Part III was drawing them in, and Goodfellas by Scorsese was making a big push as well.

The television season was off to a bang; if they weren't at the movies, they were home glued to the boobus tubes. They were watching comedies like Murphy Brown, Designing Women, the Cosby Show, Cheers, Seinfeld, and the ensemble courtroom drama L.A. Law.

The holiday season was going to be a sad one; their wounds slowly began to heal. With Tyler and Kane out of their lives, Ashlee and Janine became stronger women and soon realized how lives can be turned upside down. Let's hope the "up" feeling of the movies the gang chooses to attend brings joy and happiness to their lives.

Chapter Thirty-Three

1991 roared in hopes of being an "up" year for everyone with good feelings about life. Everyone can sleep late and do whatever they damn please by doing even if it was nothing. The studio system waited until the first of the year when it awarded the six "perks" of luxury. Ashlee kept her lifetime tickets to the Oscars, Beau received lifetime tickets to the Technical Awards, Carole received anytime round-trip tickets for two to New York and Broadway tickets, Janine received lifetime tickets to any theatre in Los Angeles, Cole received a lifetime membership to American Film Institute, and Keller received lifetime tickets to the Grammys.

With retirement in full swing, nothing changed, so they began their predictions on who would get Oscar gold. The guys were rooting for Dances with Wolves, and the ladies leaned on newcomer Julia Roberts to pull off magic with Richard Gere in Pretty Woman.

AND THE OSCAR GOES TO...

Is this the last time real married Newman and Woodward in Merchant and Ivory's Mr. and Mrs. Bridge appear in the same film? Would the mob movies of Goodfellas and the end of the Godfather saga strike a chord with Academy members? The nominations were announced on February 13th, and the guys were spot on; twelve nominations were given to Dances with Wolves, seven to Godfather Part III, six to Goodfellas, and five to Ghost. It was announced that Billy Crystal would host, and honorary Oscars would be presented to Myrna Loy and Sophia Loren.

The Technical Awards were presented by Geena Davis on March 2nd, giving Beau an opportunity to take advantage of his post-retirement benefit and Keller out of the house as Cole continued his pantry volunteer gig. Before the ceremonies were being held, Carole took Ashlee and Janine to New York City for a long girls' weekend, which included a shopping spree at Macy's and Saks Fifth Avenue to buy outfits for the upcoming ceremony. The 63rd Academy Awards were scheduled for March 25th, and the ladies were almost late in taking the earliest flight to Los Angeles. Ashlee called Cole, telling him they would meet at the ceremony, but there was a weather delay at La Guardia. The ladies arrived a few minutes before the men; awkward seeing ladies with luggage and dressed for the ceremonies waiting for Beau in his car to the valet and putting their belongings in the trunk. LOL. I'm sure the celebrities arriving on the red carpet were shaking their heads in confusion but laughter, too.

Everyone was getting situated inside the Dorothy Chandler Pavilion, with musical director Bill Conti hitting the right notes for announcer Charlie O'Donnell getting a cue announcing Karl Malden. Malden, then president of the Academy, welcomed the prestigious guests as the previous year's Supporting Actor, Denzel Washington, waiting in the wings to present Best Supporting Actress. Being quite a diverse five nominees this year, as Washington announced the winner of Whoopi Goldberg for Ghost, history certifying her as the second African American female to win since Hattie McDaniel won for Gone With the Wind in 1939. A few minutes and awards passed; the previous year's Supporting Actress, Brenda Fricker, graced the stage, presenting Best Supporting Actor to Joe Pesci, who won for Goodfellas. Appearing to be an oddity for Godfather Part III to go down in history for a sequel nominated for seven awards and not receiving one. The highlight of the evening had to be the honorary Oscars presented by Angelica Huston and Gregory Peck to Myrna Loy and Sophia Loren, respectively. In the tradition of previous years, the supporting categories begin the show and impatiently await the more important awards in between the glitz of musical numbers and not-so-important awards. The previous year, Best Actor Daniel Day-Lewis walked on stage to present Best Actress; being a diverse list, a veteran list passed new blood given to Kathy Bates for Misery. Before Jessica Tandy, the previous year's

AND THE OSCAR GOES TO...

Best Actress presented Best Actor to Jeremy Irons as real-life Claus Von Bulow in Reversal of Fortune prevented Kevin Costner a clean sweep as Tom Cruise and Barbra Streisand presented the two final awards of Best Picture and Best Director to him for Dances with Wolves. These two wins placed Costner in a prestigious company as the fifth director to win for his directorial debut, as well as being nominated both for Best Actor and Director. It was a very good night for Costner's film, which received seven wins out of twelve nominations and rounding out multiple wins for Dick Tracy with three of seven nominations and Ghost winning two of five nominations, respectively.

Being a long day for the ladies, the ladies were glad to be in their own beds; Janine and Ashlee were doing their best not to be reminded of the events from a year before. Beau was letting Carole sleep in by starting his new exercise regime, and Cole was anxious to hear all the Broadway dishes but letting the other two sleep in as well before calling them.

The sextet was itching the travel bug again, but given Cole's HIV status, would an international trip be an advantage or disadvantage? Keller asked Cole to talk to his doctor about it, and then they could go from there. Cole was doing quite well; everyone was pleased with his progress, his weight had slightly increased, he was eating right, his T-cell count was stable, and he was like a new man. Cole's doctor told him international travel was ok; just have some fun. Beau was letting the exercise go to his head, loving the routine, but lately been short of breath and confided to the boy mum is the word.

Starting the selection process, the sextet began going through brochures and deciding where to go. Would it be a Hawaiian vacation, a cruise either to the Caribbean, the Baltic, or the Mediterranean? So many destinations, so little time, err, or as the gays say, so many men, so little time. The sextet was leaving Los Angeles behind since Cole was given the green light to travel internationally. It was time to make some plans, and they did! They would fly from Los Angeles to Rome. Spend a few days there seeing the sights, catch a bus to Florence, and capture views of Tuscany before heading to Venice. From Venice, catch a ship cruising a twelve-day journey through the Mediterranean. In between, Greece and more of Italy and end in Barcelona; all there at their doorstep. This trip is exactly what the doctor ordered! Lots of things to see, and the start of each day was just a memory to last in their heart of hearts forever. The Mediterranean cruise boasted sights like the Vatican, the Colosseum, St. Peters Basilica, the Sistine Chapel, and Trevi Fountain to Mykonos, Crete, Rhodes, Santorini, and in Barcelona, the Gaudi Cathedral, and then a few days on the beaches of Sitges—lots of new memories created and able to share with others.

Upon the sextet returned home, the weather started to heat

up. In the middle of June, Cole and Keller got a phone call from a friend of Barbra Streisand. Cole thought it was a joke and asked Keller to check it out. James Newton Howard was doing music for The Prince of Tides, Streisand's latest directorial feature. Newton Howard was curious to know there were a few changes to the original score soundtrack, and the six would drive to South Carolina for a sneak peek before release. Keller inquired if Streisand was going to be there. Newton Howard remarked there were two songs Streisand had to do vocals on but was unsure if she would record them there or in Los Angeles. Streisand said she would record in South Carolina but would like to see Cole and Keller. Newton Howard mentioned bringing your friends a great idea and asked Streisand to join them for a Q&A and perhaps a personal mini-concert. The sextet was off for a driving vacation to Beaufort, South Carolina, and see the views of Fripp Island and St. Helena Islands. Everyone was in luck; Newton Howard was able to get Streisand to join them for a few days. A dream come true, Carole was just pinching herself as The Way We Were was her favorite movie of all time, and Ashlee remarked that What's Up, Doc had to be the zaniest screwball comedy of all time. Taking two trips in one summer was surreal, and getting to meet Barbra Streisand was icing on the cake!

There was quite hyped buzz for Oliver Stone, his direction of a huge ensemble on JFK; Barry Levinson brought the life of gangster Bugsy Siegel starring Warren Beatty; Ridley Scott showed fans a woman buddy picture with Susan Sarandon and Geena Davis in Thelma and Louise, Jonathan Demme got creepy with Silence of the Lambs, animated features made a comeback and Streisand's newest masterpiece. What will be on the lips of our sextet as well as the real voice of Academy members? Will Streisand finally win a Best Director award by a woman?

Chapter Thirty-Four

R inging in the new year of 1992, an election year, no doubt as critics and entertainment writers busily discussed who and what the 64ᵗʰ annual Academy Awards predictions were going to be. First, muddling through an onslaught of critics' awards from cities like Los Angeles and New York and countless other awards like the Directors Guild, Screen Actors Guild, and, let's not forget, the Golden Globes. These awards claim to be a predecessor paving the way to possible nominations on February 19ᵗʰ and presented weeks before the Technical Awards on March 7ᵗʰ and the actual Oscars presented on March 30ᵗʰ.

The Golden Globes were presented on January 18ᵗʰ, 1992, at the Beverly Hills Hilton. One of the big surprises taken away from this was Nick Nolte for The Prince of Tides beating out favorite Anthony Hopkins for Best Actor in a Drama, and Jodie Foster won Best Actress in a Drama for The Silence of the Lambs. With these awards divided between comedy and drama, I wonder how the Foreign Press would award their winners with a diverse group of nominees. Bette Midler won Best Actress in a Comedy or Musical for her film, For the Boys, Robin Williams won Best Actor in a Comedy or Musical and Mercedes Ruehl won Best Supporting Actress for The Fisher King, respectively, and veteran actor Jack Palance won Best Supporting Actor for City Slickers.

It was a month and a day until February 19th, when the nominees for the 64th Academy Awards were announced with a few surprises. Bugsy received ten nominations, eight for JFK, seven for Prince of Tides and Silence of the Lambs, respectively, and six went to Beauty and the Beast, Thelma and Louise, and Terminator Two: Judgment Day. There were a few notable snubs: Streisand was overlooked for Prince of Tides, Kathy Bates for Fried Green Tomatoes, and Mark Rydell, director of For the Boys. This year was a family affair as the mother and daughter duo Diane Ladd and Laura Dern were nominated for Best Supporting Actress and Actress in the film Rambling Rose. Best Director Nominee John Singleton made history as the first African American and the youngest in this category for Boyz n the Hood. Our sextet was over-anxious to catch a few films before attending the ceremony in March. Cole wanted to see Bette Midler in For the Boys, playing a 40's actress-singer who teams up with a performer (James Caan) entertaining the US troops, loosely based on Martha Raye and Bob

Hope. It was well-received, but the box office numbers were low. Keller and Janine had expressed an interest in Silence of the Lambs despite the cannibalism theme. Beau was looking forward to JFK, and Carole and Ashlee were looking forward to Fried Green Tomatoes.

On March 7th, Tom Hanks hosted the Technical Awards, and of course, Beau was ecstatic about attending, asking Keller to go. Keller jumped at the opportunity; he wasn't helping at the pantry with Cole, but it was an enjoyable time to meet Hanks as well. This would provide time for the ladies to see movies in which they had expressed interest. Cole, staying busy at the pantry, depending on the day he would hand out food or sometimes with the counseling, hardly being available to see movies. Weekends were better for him. Once in a blue moon, some clients needed emergency weekend advice; Keller didn't seem to mind; it was good to see Cole content and happy in his life. Cole did make it a point to see For the Boys with the ceremony weeks away. A week before the ceremony, the sextet were at Carole and Beau's for dinner, the discussion about who would win the Oscars; they were more divided this year than others. Cole was adamant Prince of Tides and Bette Midler were going to win, Keller and Janine spoke their case for Silence of the Lambs, Beau was for JFK, and Carole was staying out of it.

The night arrived, and everyone was waving their magic wands and seeing whose predictions would be awarded the prizes of gold. The sextet were dressed to the nines and ready for a fun night despite razzing each other. As the sextet were walking the red carpet, lo and behold, they ran into Streisand. Streisand huddled to them like long-lost pals. Cole interrupted the huddle and commented how sorry he was she hadn't been nominated for Best Director. Babs told him it was ok; she was thrilled and super happy for Nolte.

Announcer Les Marshak announced Billy Crystal, hosting for the third consecutive time, roared the audience. Crystal had everyone, especially Anthony Hopkins and Jodie Foster, in tears of laughter as prison guards accompanied him on a stand-up stretcher parodying Hopkins' Hannibal Lecter. It was too funny!

Tradition starting the ceremony, Best Supporting Actor was presented to Jack Palance for his comedic turn in City Slickers, an easy win for him and a sentimental lifetime achievement. Best Supporting Actress went to Mercedes Ruehl for the Fisher King, a semi-tough category, competing against two veterans and two newbies. After Ruehl received her award, Spielberg came to the dais and announced the Irving G. Thalberg Memorial Award to his bestie and sometime collaborator George Lucas. With the ceremony running smoothly, going unnoticed if Oscar history would be made. Sure enough, Silence of the Lambs dived into Oscar history, tying 1934's It Happened One Night and 1975's One Flew Over the Cuckoo's Nest to sweep all five major categories: Actor, Actress, Director, Picture, and Screenplay from previously released material.

AND THE OSCAR GOES TO...

The upset of the evening was that everyone's favorite, Nick Nolte, lost Best Actor to Anthony Hopkins, who reigned supreme. Jodie Foster became the youngest to win two Best Actress awards at age twenty-eight.

Whew! What a night! It was great the sextet attended and ran into Streisand, and being gracious to meet them made the night complete. Certainly, it could've been better if Prince of Tides won some accolades, but alas, the "horror" film took it all.

Summer was lurking; it looked like the sextet was staying put with occasional side trips to Las Vegas, Palm Springs, San Diego, San Francisco, Seattle, Portland, and many other destinations nearby—no international flying or sailing on the highest of high seas. Lots of choices for our viewing pleasure were coming our way.

A River Runs Through It	Malcolm X	Glengarry Glen Ross	The Unforgiven		Howards End
Crying Game	Aladdin	Enchanted April	Dracula	A Few Good Men	Chaplin
Passion Fish	My Cousin Vinnie	The Bodyguard	Hoffa	Basic Instinct	The Player

Clint Eastwood was bringing back the West by not only starring but also directing and producing The Unforgiven. Biopics on Chaplin, Hoffa, and Malcolm X were stirring buzz for Robert Downey Jr., Jack Nicholson, and Denzel Washington, respectively.

The family drama, A River Runs Through It, directed by Robert Redford and Kevin Costner, was The Bodyguard to Whitney Houston and showed promise, too. A satire about Hollywood by Robert Altman boasted an all-star ensemble with The Player, an all-male ensemble assembling in the executive boardroom with backstabbing in Tony award-winning Glengarry Glen Ross; Jack Nicholson shined twice in Hoffa and the military courtroom drama directed by Rob Reiner, A Few Good Men, and Al Pacino did the unthinkable turn as the retired but cantankerous blind Army lieutenant in Scent of A Woman. Ridley Scott brought Sigourney Weaver back one more time for Alien III.

Whew, with that list and many more, it is going be hard to see all these excellent performances and attempt to predict a who's who. Especially for the national critics' awards, Golden Globes, and most importantly, the task of the Academy voters better get their thinking caps on determining the nominees in March 1993. The sextet was excited by so many on this list and more, and they certainly had their work cut out for them. So many choices, so little time. Little time would be an understatement. They had all the time in the world since retiring. What else would you do besides eat, sleep, and repeat? LOL. I am sure in the fall after their trips are done, they will start going to the movies so they can start wondering who they will pick in their annual Oscar predictions.

No hustle and bustle at the airports but long lines at the gas pumps. Some of the breathtaking views of the western part of the United States were to die for. Beau had enough room for everyone, driving this new Ford Exposition, the F-150 Eddie Bauer concept, and Keller broke down and got himself a GMC Typhoon, a new high-performance SUV, to help take turns when needed.

It was quite a win-win situation for the sextet to travel together and still have the times of their lives together! They were roaring in laughter as Cole reminded everyone that FUCCCCCCCK, he will be sixty, that is right, the big 60; Carole and Ashlee cracked up the most. Don't remind us, we are right there behind you!

Ford Exposition F-150

GMC Typhoon

Singing show tunes, telling jokes, playing trivia, reminiscing about old times when it was just four until Janine and Keller moved to Los Angeles, and as the years kept rapidly passing them by. It had only been almost three years since the tragic, horrific deaths of the two bastards who gave grief to Janine and Ashlee and the others as well. It was the biggest blessing in disguise, with time certainly healing the wounds suffered by all.

As summer ended, fall filled the airwaves with another television season, providing entertainment not just for our sextet but everyone else. Coupled with so many movies yearning to capture their hearts, the differences in our favorites switch it up from drama to comedy. It was odd to point out that when they couldn't get the Oscar buzz, they had to flip it on the other side of the coin to be buzz-worthy in another medium. One would be surprised to see, no matter what the accolade given to them, their job was complete but making us viewers happy with a smile. Is receiving an Oscar or Emmy a notch on the belt, or is it worth having a nomination amongst their peers as the goal? At the end of the day, think about it, keep working, be satisfied with the roles given, and give it your best shot. It was funny seeing how action star Burt Reynolds turned his career around with Evening Shade, Candice Bergen with Murphy Brown, and lo and behold, veteran musical stage actress Angela Lansbury making Murder She Wrote her own after Jean Stapleton bowed out.

With new films coming out every year, there is always butting of the heads to see before the Oscar nominations are revealed. Either going alone or group or a duo, take the time to discuss what has been seen. What needs to be seen and go from there? It's like a yearlong discussion about movies, television, the movers and shakers from their personal lives to the roles they choose to refuse, and it's all fun. Even better when it's near nomination and after, weighing in on the highs and lows, lots of flack might be said: why should the sextet be any different than other viewers or celebrities who attend movies? They are entitled to say what they want about movies or anything else; it's a free country.

With few months remaining in 1992, the country had just elected a new president, readying to take office in January. William Jefferson "Bill" Clinton, former Arkansas governor, beat President

George H.W. Bush in November with many Hollywood supporters. Coupled with handsome good looks and liberal views, Clinton and his team were in for the long run; one wonders what the world will be like in the next several years.

Our sextet is now on the hunt for the next big movie to weigh in, as there are several out there. If you are a hopeless or hopeful romantic like the ladies, glued in Howard's End, Enchanted April, Scent of a Woman, and the family drama tugging at the heartstrings was Redford's spectacular A River Runs Through It. The men turning all macho tuned into Clint Eastwood's The Unforgiven, Reiner's legal drama, A Few Good Men, noting you can't stop Eastwood and/or Cruise and his ensemble cast. Cole was gitty as the animated feature Aladdin made its round and couldn't get the theme song out of his head. Peabo Bryson and Patti Austin were hitting the right notes. The biopics of Chaplin and Malcolm X were getting feedback, too. Who knew problem child Downey Jr. could act, especially under the direction of Sir Richard Attenborough? Despite its mixed reviews, Chaplin soared in accomplishing what it was set to do. Spike Lee showed more complexity with Malcolm X, receiving criticism from both sides. Lee spoke out many times to percolate the notion that it was his story, and he knew people who were there, so right or wrong, and at the end of the day, nobody would stand in his way of making the film.

Chapter Thirty-Five

T he newest US President, Clinton, accompanied by his
Hollywood and television friends, brought in a new era of
politics mixed with some down-to-earth Arkansas charm versus the
Texas charisma of George H. W. Bush. The released films in 1992
vied for constructive criticism and brought lots of smiles and jeers
to the table. Anxious to get the frustrations out will be the National
Critics Association, coupled with the Foreign Press Association,
which helms the Golden Globes and Screen Actors Guilds and is
mostly a peer voting for its direct competitors. Those awards aren't
a love-hate fest. They mostly sum up what is who indeed on their
mind as their favorite at that moment. Having the best of the best is
the Oscar nominations.

The 50th annual Golden Globes were presented on January
23rd, just a few weeks before Oscar nominations were announced.
There are no big surprises, given the caliber of films released and

the fierce competition. The nominees, being in such awe and complexity of such deep friendship and respect for their fellow nominees, rarely showed any animosity towards the other in their acceptance of an award. The Foreign Press Association votes for the winners through early buzz from experts. For example, Scent of a Woman beat favorite The Unforgiven for Best Picture Drama; there was silence. Clint Eastwood triumphed in a win for Best Director over Redford, Reiner, and veterans Ivory and Altman. Al Pacino won Best Actor Drama, and Emma Thompson won Best Actress. Best Actor and Actress Comedy were won by Tim Robbins and Miranda Ricardson, respectively. Best Supporting Performances were presented to favorites Gene Hackman and Joan Plowright. The best Comedy was Robert Altman's satire homage to Hollywood in The Player.

The nominees were announced on February 17[th,] with two movies securing nine nominations apiece, hoping for a race to finish on March 29th. The Unforgiven and Howard's End had the edge. The Unforgiven, with its nine nominations, Eastwood was recognized as the seventh actor for Best Actor, Director, and Picture. Gene Hackman, a previous Best Actor winner, was nominated for Best Supporting Actor. Al Pacino, a perennial favorite to the Oscars, was nominated in both categories for the sixth time in Oscar history. Six went to The Crying Game, a critically acclaimed film that covered themes during the backdrop of the Troubles, which was an ethno-nationalist conflict in Northern Ireland. These conflicts were often mentioned as a "low-level war" fueled by political and nationalistic historical events by ethnic and sectarian dimensions, not a religious conflict between Protestants and Catholics. The Crying Game was considered a critical and commercial success despite the controversy it brought to the table. Animated features continued its appearance and secured five nominations. Four went to A Few Good Men and Scent of Woman, and three to Chaplin.

Within six weeks before the ceremony, it was announced the ceremony would (again) be produced by Gil Cates and yet hosted (again) by who else, Billy Crystal. Three special honorary awards will be presented: Federico Fellini, two Oscar winners, and two lovely ladies, Audrey Hepburn and Elizabeth Taylor. Sadly, Hepburn passed away months before the announcement was made. The ceremony was scheduled for March 29th, and three weeks prior, on March 6th, Sharon Stone hosted and presented the Technical Awards. Beau and Keller attended as usual, with Cole busy in the pantry. It gave them opportunities to interact with old and new show business and meet the beautiful Stone, who briefly discussed her career.

Box office receipts were hit and missed this year, the week of Oscar nominations, the top five nominees combined for a total of $252 million, which meant an average of $50.4 million. Leading the top five was A Few Good Men, grossing $120 million. Second was

The Unforgiven $75.2 million. Third was Scent of a Woman, $34.1 million. Fourth, The Crying Game grossed $14 million, and last, Howards End $8.7 million.

Oscar day is here, Monday, March 29th, 1993, and the sextet was excited to start their day with lunch. Cole and Keller invited everyone over for Eggs Benedict, hash browns, bacon, turkey sausage, and, not forgetting, a pre-Oscar party without mimosas (champagne with orange juice or cranberry juice) and bloody Mary with olives, okra, pearl onions and jalapeno for garnish. Around 2, everyone left to say they were going to take a nap and shower. Keller reminded everyone to be ready around 5:45 or 6. Hugs to all, be gone because Keller had a surprise for Cole. Cole was attempting to clean the kitchen, moving around to turn the dishwasher on, shutting the refrigerator door, and placing condiments in. He noticed Keller naked as a jaybird. Cole thought he was seeing double. Keller motioned Cole to follow him to the bathroom.

Leaving a trail of clothes from the kitchen to the bathroom, Cole didn't think twice. The boys were going to make love in the shower for the first time in ages. Cole had a new lease on life, doctors telling him he was undetectable but still needed to play it safe. For all not knowing, if HIV+ is undetectable, it means having a viral load too low to measure, and if continuing to take medications, this gives the individual to live a long, healthy life. Cole asked Keller if he was sure about making love, and Keller told him more than ever. The boys began kissing passionately and making love like two rabbits. This way, kill two birds with one stone, make love, shower, and change. LOL. Now, it was time to get ready and go pick up their friends with two big smiles on their faces.

Oscar night was always special for all six, sitting and relaxing and being themselves. The quartet noticed the boys were extremely gitty when a nosy body, Ashlee, broke the ice, "OK boys, out with it. Why so happy tonight? Don't try any bullshit being excited to see Eastwood or Pacino. I know this isn't right," Janine chimed in as well, "I see it clearly as a bell now. It's on their faces!" Carole spoke up, "No, say you didn't because we know what you did, you fucked after we left, didn't you?" Beau, rolling his eyes, let out a roar of laughter and chuckled with TMI TMI (too much information). By the end, all six were laughing so hard they were crying. Beau sighed and finally said, "All I can say is it's about fucking time!" After that comment, everyone started to laugh again. Cole finally spoke, too. "Yes, bitches we fucked, and it never felt so good. Thanks for your concern!"

Keller pulled in the valet of the Dorothy Chandler Pavilion with Ashlee eyeing the red carpet, getting her mini binoculars from her purse, and started throwing out celebrities' names she was ogling. A few names to mention were some of The Unforgiven Men, Eastwood and Hackman, Scent of a Woman's Pacino and Chris O'Donnell, and Howards End, Emma Thompson, to name a few.

The fourth time, Cates and Crystal producing and hosting, respectively, almost didn't happen. Crystal had earlier weeks prior contacted Cates and said he would have to decline due to his hectic yet busy schedule making two movies, Mr. Saturday Night and City Slickers II: The Legend of Curly's Gold, back-to-back. According to columnist Army Archerd from Variety, to lure Crystal back, Cates sent him a funeral wreath with a poem. "The show and I are dead without you!" followed by the head of a fake dead horse like one featured in The Godfather; Crystal relented and accepted. It goes without saying, an offer Crystal couldn't refuse.

Inside the auditorium, everyone was rapidly assembling when orchestra leader Bill Conti started the music. First, a female and new announcer, Randy Thomas, introduced the new Academy President, Robert Rehme, who gave the standard remarks welcoming guests to the ceremony, leading to the introduction of Geena Davis, who presented a montage arranged by producer Gil Cates. Cates cooperated with Oscar-winning documentarian Lynne Littman to celebrate women in film. Keeping with the theme, "Oscar Celebrates Women and the Movies," Cates assembled some attending sixty-seven female Oscar winners for a photo at the start of the presentation.

When the montage ended, tradition reversed itself. Previous year's Best Supporting Actor, Jack Palance, walked on stage to start the Oscar presentations to present Best Supporting Actress. Marisa

AND THE OSCAR GOES TO...

Tomei was a "surprise" to everyone as she was awarded Best Supporting Actress over heavyweights Redgrave, Richardson, Plowright, and Davis. Mercedes Ruehl appeared minutes later to present Gene Hackman, the favorite for Best Supporting Actor, over two veterans and two newbies. Al Pacino defied the odds and finally received his first Best Actor Oscar, beating Eastwood, Washington, Downey Jr., and newbie Stephen Rea. Best Actress went to Emma Thompson for Howards End, passing by Sarandon, Pfieffer, Mary McDonnell, and the best ever sexy Catherine Deneuve. It was a pure coincidence that Thompson's co-star in Howard's End, last year's Best Actor, Anthony Hopkins, presented her with the award. It was Clint Eastwood's night scoring both Best Picture and Best Director to prove the Western genre will be riding a comeback with The Unforgiven. For music buffs, Alan Menken, winning both Best Song and Best Original Score, became the third person to win two Oscars in two consecutive years.

Without giving it a second thought or a benefit of the doubt, the studios race to get their films shown, assuring everyone checking their lists twice. Let's dive in to see what will be shown to our sextet to bicker and hurry to the theatres teasingly. It's never set in stone when a movie is released; ones earlier in the year tend to get lost in the shuffle, and a new lease on life adds more box office money. This opportunity, when being re-released, assists in momentum going forward with more critical praise and accolades into the next year. These are:

Schindler's List	*What's Love Got to do With it?*	*Six Degrees of Separation*
The Piano	*What's Eating, Gilbert Grape?*	*Fearless*
Remains of the Day	*The Fugitive*	*In the Line of Fire*
In the Name of the Father	*Age of Innocence*	*Short Cuts*
The Firm	*The Wedding Banquet*	*Sleepless In Seattle*
Philadelphia	*Farewell, My Concubine*	
Mrs. Doubtfire	*Shadowlands*	

With the Oscars done, it's time for a vacation. Woohoo, our gang is going on a cruise. A Baltic cruise is in the works for early May. The Baltic cruise will begin in three to four days, leaving from Copenhagen, Warnemunde, Germany; Tallinn, Estonia; and St. Petersburg, Russia; Helsinki, Finland; and ending in Stockholm, Sweden. This will be fun! Flying from Los Angeles to Copenhagen is a twelve-hour flight, and finding the perfect hotel is an adventure. Before embarking on the cruise, the sextet got rooms at the Nimb Hotel, situated in one of the most beautiful attractions, the Tivoli Gardens. For three days, they saw the most breathtaking attractions ever, ranging from the Hop On Hop off tours, the War Museum, King's Garden, Gefion Fountain, etc. The architecture was fascinating to see, and the glory of seeing it up, close and personal, was a dream come true. Three days passed quickly. It was time to board the cruise ship and head to its first docking of Warnemunde and Rostock, which is one of Germany's major shipping centers. While there, they saw the Berlin Wall, Potsdam Square, Reichstag, and Alexanderplatz. The ship left at 10 pm and headed for a full day of sea before docking in Tallinn, Estonia, where it was Toomkirk Cathedral, St. Nicholas' Church, Town Hall Square, and Catherine's Valley. The next two days were spent in St. Petersburg, Russia, for two days filled with what is promised to be more breathtaking than ever: the Hermitage, the Alexander Column, the Peter and Paul Fortress, the Senate Square, etc. From Russia, the cruise headed to Helsinki, Finland, where the sextet saw lots of attractions and told Helsinki was such a modern city with an absence of high-rise buildings, plenty to see there for the day. Some of the few attractions are as follows: Kaivopuisto (Wall Park), Lutheran Cathedral, Mannerheim Museum, and, for the hearty and physical fit, a hike up to Sibelius Monument. Dinner with the captain and others was the highlight of the cruise last night before reaching their destination, Stockholm, Sweden. Taking in three more days of sights before the flight home to Los Angeles. With no hidden agenda, it was a busy Stockholm filled with lots of adventures, which included the Vasa Museum, Skansen Open-Air Museum, Skokloster Castle, City Hall, and Swedish Museum of Natural History. On a grand scale, the sextet secured a room at the Grand Hotel, which is infamous for occupying an enviable spot on the waterfront overlooking the Royal

Palace and Old Town.

Leaving the Baltic behind was hard on the sextet landing at LAX; there were a few things they needed to start seriously thinking about. Beau was having issues, needing to get to the doctor as soon as possible without alarming Carole. Ashlee told Janine to swear to secrecy as well, found a lump on her breast while on the cruise, and Cole was finally feeling fatigued from the sightseeing excursions.

Once returning, Cole went back to volunteer at the pantry. Carole, being curious, anyone for New York City. Beau, being sneaky, was able to get Carole and the ladies to see Broadway. Despite being ecstatic about Jurassic Park pending a release date, Beau needed to see a doctor. Pronto! Cole and Keller offered to go with him. Beau wasn't a smoker, but he was doing his exercise regimen of jogging, walking briskly, etc., finally inquiring what was causing his symptoms of shortness of breath and chest pains. Beau was fighting the chest pains off as indigestion. When the trio arrived at the doctor's office, Beau was fighting the other two by saying, "I got this and not a word to the ladies until I find out anything, ok!" Mum was the word, not easy for Cole to do, as he was the biggest blabber mouth and worry wart out of the whole bunch. Anyway, Beau went in and sat impatiently with the other two until they called his name. Walking towards the door to go into the exam room, Beau hugged Cole and Keller. Cole whispered in Beau's ear, "You got this bitch, go on!" Beau walked down the long hallway and settled in the exam room as the nurse got a urine sample checked. The doctor checked him and concluded Beau had had little heart attacks and needed to do a stress test to find out if there was any damage. In the interim, the doctor suggested a prescription of nitro tablets for any time there were chest pains; this would curb the issue for now. As the doctor concluded his exam, a nurse came to take blood to check cholesterol and other pertinent numbers important to his case. Beau was horrified by the news, asking the nurse and his friends to join him as the doctor laid down some ground rules for a regimen going forward. The doctor said Beau can exercise but not as vigorously, watch his diet, keep up with doctor appointments, blood testing for cholesterol, etc. Beau was now faced with telling Carole upon her return from the ladies' trip to New York City.

Looks like while Cole and Keller were assisting Beau on the mend, the ladies were in New York City having a fun time seeing shows. Carole was excited being the ladies this time as she really needed to finally address some issues. Carole, once outspoken as Ashlee, never changed. Had been quiet for a long time about what really went down a few years back when Kane and Tyler were alive. Things were bothering her; Carole knew something was wrong with Beau, too, but couldn't put a finger on it. Before you know it, Carole was ranting and raving, explaining to Ashlee and Janine she was sorry for being quiet until now. Ashlee and Janine responded they didn't feel compelled to explain anything to anybody for the odd sexual behavior they displayed. Carole mentioned she felt left out in the cold. Ashlee began to sob a bit when she began her and Janine's downward spiral. "I don't know where to begin, Carole. I really don't, and I am very sorry it seems we stopped talking." Janine chimed in unison that Kane and Tyler had this magic spell cast over them, begging them not to tell a soul when Keller found out; he was furious. Keller was so mad that he was at the point of hurting Kane and Tyler just a few days before the accident. As the three ladies cried, they realized they were late for dinner and a show. Their first show was a revival of Damn Yankees, and tomorrow night was Grease. Carole was missing Beau, something terrible, especially after the short but tense tiff before the ladies left for their trip. Damn Yankees and Grease were great, but it was time back to Los Angeles. Carole explained to Janine and Ashlee she feared the worst coming home to Beau; Ashlee reassured her things would be ok as she had something to tell her. Ashlee told Carole not to worry; she needed help in getting an appointment with her doctor. Dumbfounded with a silly look on her face, Carole said, "Yes, anything, sweetheart; once we get back, I will hook you up with my doctor, ok?" Janine chimed in and said, "We are friends forever, stuck like glue; nothing will ever come between us."

The sextet was back together in late May and turning slowly into June, and no more travels until possibly next year. Memorial Day weekend promised fun for everyone. Janine and Ashlee told everyone they were hosting a big dinner and an improvised picnic. There would be grilled hamburgers, hot dogs, bratwurst, sauerkraut, the whole nine yards, and held at their apartment. Before the festivities began, Carole and Beau had their talk and made a pact. Nothing was going to come between them, and they promised to help each other get through Beau's medical crisis. Ashlee announced at the party she was seeking medical assistance and wanted everyone's prayers; she found a lump in her breast. Cole said, "OK, bitches, let's not all this get us down, we are together for the NOW and the FUTURE!" As the "fake" picnic was underway, everyone was having a grand time when Keller proposed it was time for all to get back in the groove for movies.

Movies, what's a movie? LOL. Is that thing on a reel, and do you put it on a projection object like a projector? Oh, that thing, it's been way too long. All six chimed in to say there was plenty more as the summer was new, and then the fall and winter would bring many more as well. Beau asked if anyone was interested in the dinosaur Jurassic Park film and The Firm with Tom Cruise. Cole and Keller were interested in The Fugitive, and being big music fans of Streisand, there was the biopic of Tina Turner coming as a must-see. What's Love Got to Do with It proved to be the best medicine as the music and the acting over the top had the sextet singing Ike and Tina's music. It really resonated with the ladies concerning the subject of spousal abuse. There was a common thread for Keller and

Janine as St. Louis was a backdrop to the storyline. The ladies expressed interest in Remains of the Day, The Age of Innocence, and In the Name of the Father. Tom Hanks was doing a 360-degree turn away from comedy in the drama Philadelphia, which was turning heads, but being HIV+, Cole wasn't sure he wanted to see it; it wasn't coming out until near Christmas.

Ashlee finally made a dreaded appointment with Carole's doctor. Carole and Janine went with her for emotional support. Carole's doctor was very thorough with the examination and did a biopsy. The medical team told Ashlee to play the waiting game and get results in a week to ten days. Ashlee was a nervous wreck waiting for the results. Given the location of the lump, it appeared to be negative, but a lumpectomy was needed. Ashlee was so ecstatic with the news she splurged and took the ladies out for a nice lunch and drinks.

As the holidays were surging forward, the sextet felt all needed some comic relief. Robin Williams provided the ticket for all in the form of Mrs. Doubtfire. It was so good; they saw it twice. Nearing the end of the year brought heavy drama about a German industrialist providing for many Polish and Jewish refugees from the Holocaust in Spielberg's Schindler's List.

1993 left everything from laughter to tears with this roster for our sextet, which was combined from the fun Baltic Cruise and the tears of sadness praying for relief for the concerning health of

AND THE OSCAR GOES TO...

Beau and Ashlee. Beau's promise sticking hopeful to bring awareness.

Chapter Thirty-Six

W hew! Looks like we all survived another year; it was fun, especially the Baltic cruise, and there were many places to visit; who would imagine in a million years a trip certainly for a lifetime full of dreams? Sadly, they are getting into the prime of their middle-aged years, and despite all the ailments they are suffering from, they LIVE for the moment, as tomorrow is never promised. Don't take life for granted; keep loving one another and take each second, minute, hour, day, week, month, and year one at a time! Everyone seemed to be constantly reminded of treasured memories working in Hollywood with heavy A-listers from behind the scenes to front of the scenes. It's sad how ageism had forced them out of jobs a few years back and the studios taking fresh talent from "kids" out of school. These were the ones probably born with silver spoons in their mouths, still living with mommy and daddy, had surging debt, and driving fancy cars; they couldn't possibly afford the insurance or the car payments. LOL

1994 was to promise everyone good health coupled with fun fueled by movies, travel, and always being number one on the list, as well as companionship filled with love for each other through thick and thin. It's been that since the beginning of their friendship when it was just a quartet. It certainly has grown and lessened over the years, and hopefully, there will not be any more turmoil to change that. Sadly, how things could turn on a dime! Bringing in the New Year over at Beau and Carole's was fun; the sextet finally realized they didn't need any new friends after the turmoil of a few years past. Let bygones be bygones, and keep a cheerful outlook. If only there wouldn't be any more sadness in the world, but life can't be a bed of roses and perfect all the time.

The first of 1994 brought some sad news from the Heartland of Missouri. Apparently, Dad Wallace had fallen over the holidays and broken his hip; Mom Wallace reached out to her children and asked if they would come home. Cole told Keller he would stop volunteering at the pantry and accompany Janine and him as well as Ashlee offered to be with them as well. Beau and Carole offered to fly up when needed. With Beau's heart condition, he asked Keller and Janine if they would understand; they accepted their love and words of encouragement by offering to pass them on to their parents. Janine called the airlines, seeing a flight out as soon as possible. Picking American Airlines, Janine found four tickets with an open return, hoping for the best; they would be able to return in time to attend the Oscar ceremonies, which were slated for March 21st.

Mom Wallace was beside herself with worry, trying to get the house in order and getting the foursome to Missouri quickly. There were other pressing issues that needed to be discussed as well. Mom neglected telling our brother and sister duo; Dad Wallace also had pneumonia, and she was suffering from a few ailments, too. The four arrived on the earliest flight from LAX and headed straight to baggage claim and rental car for the drive to West County. Pulling away from the airport, you could hear a little sobbing in the backseat from Janine. Ashlee asked Janine if she was okay, reaching over to comfort her and wrapping her arm around her. Janine mumbled she was afraid their mother was hiding something from them. And right she was.

When Cole pulled up in the driveway, there was someone different standing at the open door; neither Keller nor Janine recognized them. The four walked the sidewalk to the front door, the person greeting them with a cracked smile to say, "Welcome home; I am Esther Van Camp, your parents' nurse and caretaker." Janine ranted, "See, I told you Mom was hiding something." The four walked into the house, finding Mom Wallace sitting in her favorite chair and Dad nowhere to be found. Keller said, "Mother dear, where is Dad?" Mom told them he was in the back bedroom resting. Janine dropped everything and ran back there, crying out, "Dad, we are here!" Mom stood up; Esther got the walker by the dining table and raced down the hall. Mom said, "Keller, go follow your sister; your Dad is resting on oxygen for pneumonia; he won't be able to hear anything." The duo quietly went into the back bedroom and stood by their dad's bedside as he rested comfortably. After a few minutes, Esther walked in with their mother; Janine said, "Why did you keep this from us now? And look, you are with a walker; what the hell is wrong with you, Cris's sake!" Mom mentioned t had had a stroke around Thanksgiving last year and needs the walker to walk. This was going to be a rough trip for the Wallace family, and thank God Ashlee and Cole were there to help pick up the pieces. With all the unpleasantries being disclosed, the duo, their mother, and nurse walked back into the living room. Esther stated she had sandwiches and a pitcher of sweet tea; did anyone care to have any? To give Keller, Janine, and Mom Wallace time to talk, Ashlee and Cole put everyone's luggage in the guest bedrooms and assisted Esther with serving lunch. Mom Wallace told the duo she didn't intend to keep anything from them and wanted to wait till the right time. When was going to be the right time?

This is so sad! While the others were placing the plates in the dining room, Esther said lunch was served. The group gathered around the table, holding hands and saying grace; Cole mentioned in prayer t they should bless the Wallace house family and hope the four begin to heal from family strife and love each other more deeply. As the five sat in total silence, you could hear Mom Wallace letting out a little sniffle, mentioning she didn't mean to hurt anyone. "Enough with the suffering wife routine, Mother," Janine yelled out to add, "Did you expect us to bring you an Oscar, too!" Keller seemed annoyed with all this and mentioned the two need to bury the hatchet now and not be displayed in front of everyone. Cole and Ashlee nodded to relate. We are family, after all. Look at what we have all been through in the last few years. Ashlee said, "Janine, please give your mother the benefit of the doubt." You can see the writing on the wall Mom Wallace was trying to protect her children from sadness. You can only hope this mother-daughter feud will blow over. Keller and Cole couldn't get over the banter; Keller was beginning wondering Janine was acting out because their mother gave more attention to him, and dad gave more attention to her. Is there something to talk about there? Let's not open any more cans of worms, please.

It had been a few days, and things around the tense Wallace household, Ashlee and Cole, were doing their best to remain neutral and calm, but everyone appeared to walk on eggshells. Dad Wallace hasn't said two words since they arrived and has been sleeping the whole time. Cole and Ashlee told Janine and Keller they were driving downtown St. Louis, allowing time to spend with their parents. What a relief, thought Keller; this could get ugly, and shit hit the fan. Keller is restless, not sleeping well since arrival. Keller started taking Melatonin, but it wasn't helping; Cole needed to be comfortable as well, trying not to wake him by tossing and turning.

Ashlee and Cole were entering the Wallace home; the family was having yet another pow-wow at the dining table. Cole said, "Did we interrupt something, or shall we leave and come back in an hour or so?" Janine said, "No, it's ok; I think we resolved what we came here to do, right Mom." Mom Wallace was sitting at the table with a Kleenex box near her with a small pile already wet. You could see she and the brother-sister duo were crying. Keller announced to Ashlee and Cole their mother agreed to place Dad Wallace and herself in a rehab facility, mentioning it would be best if the two returned to Los Angeles. The next few days were crucial; Janine and Keller needed to find a place for their parents, and a realtor sold the family home, and the parents settled in an unfamiliar environment. Cole and Ashlee were shocked beyond disbelief. The next morning, Janine and Keller went to check Delmar Gardens and the Fountains of West County. Upon their return, they had an appointment with Callie Maloney. She was going to stop by and look at the house to see how much they could sell it for. The sooner, the better.

Back in California, Carole and Beau were busy seeing movies while the others were still in St. Louis. Carole got a note from Ashlee saying she didn't know exactly how much longer they would be there and couldn't believe the drama. It was so sad, especially when it didn't turn out to be a cheerful trip, hoping they could come to a truce. Ashlee mentioned she and Cole were innocent bystanders, and it was horrifying to see the change in Janine. Janine didn't mention she was having hot flashes; maybe that is why she was so hateful towards her mother. It's still no excuse; Janine shouldn't be treating her mother like that. Keller should step in and have his say, but it looks like Janine has her mind up. Sell the family home, get rid of their parents, throw away the key, and bring the money back to Los Angeles. February was here, and winter was wreaking havoc on Janine's plan; the housing market wasn't so good, and houses weren't selling; she told Keller they should go back to Los Angeles for the spring and return in May. Keller thought it be a promising idea as well, time to catch up with the entertainment scene. Catching up on some quick movies gave Cole an opportunity to catch up with pantry clients; Ashlee needs to see her gynecologist and reunite with Beau and Carole. Having it all set, Janine laid the law down on Nurse Ratched, I mean Esther. Janine explicitly told Esther at any time she and Keller needed to return, they would be on the next flight, and for now, their family home wasn't on the market, nor were they going into assisted living.

The 66th Oscar nominations were announced on February 9th. Twelve were given to Spielberg's newest masterpiece, Schindler's List, eight to The Piano and Remains of the Day, seven to In the Name of the Father, and five to Philadelphia and The Age of Innocence. Holly Hunter and Emma Thompson became the first two actresses to be nominated for both Best Actress and Best Supporting Actress. Jane Campion became the second woman ever to be nominated for Best Director. Young adults shine brightly for Best Supporting Actor and Actress nominees Leonardo DiCaprio for What's Eating Gilbert Grape and Anna Paquin for The Piano, respectively. Two beautifully made Asian films, Taiwan brought us Ang Lee's The Wedding Banquet, and Hong Kong brought us Chen Kaige's Farewell My Concubine for Best Foreign Film to much critical acclaim. The Best Song category brought a nomination to Bruce "the Boss" Springsteen for his song "Streets of Philadelphia" from Philadelphia. The announcement was made that two honorary Oscars would be bestowed to Paul Newman and Deborah Kerr. We will now have to wait till March 21st to see who will win. Time for everyone to get their thinking caps on and start their predictions.

Judging from the 51st Golden Globe Awards, looks like their winners might predict what lies weeks ahead in the Oscar ceremony. One will wonder if these have any significance or are set in stone; let's see. Tom Hanks and Robin Williams won the Best Actor awards; Holly Hunter and Angela Bassett won Best Actress; Tommy Lee Jones and Winona Ryder won Best Supporting Actor and Actress, respectively; Schindler's List won Best Drama and Mrs. Doubtfire won Best Comedy or Musical and Best Foreign Film went to Farewell My Concubine.

It had been almost a month since the quartet returned from

St. Louis, and Wallace's caretaker, Esther, hadn't written or called. No news is sad news, I suppose. Janine, still stubborn, was relatively quiet during this time, and others hoped she would snap out of it soon. Keller was busy helping Cole at the pantry and exercising, while Beau helped Carole had a keen watch on him. Beau, as you remember, always attended the Technical Awards with Keller by his side; this year was no exception. Laura Dern, daughter of Bruce Dern and Diane Ladd, continued the tradition of host and presenter on February 26th.

With a month to go before the actual Oscars were presented, there were a few movies the sextet had yet to see. Cole put on a brave front seeing Philadelphia; it swept him away, coming home in tears. The ladies were blown away by Holly Hunter in The Piano and by the smarty pants law secretary in The Firm, which was based on the novel by former Mississippi lawyer John Grisham. It was a delight, too, for the sextet gathered, seeing the family drama What's Eating Gilbert Grape – tour de force performances from Johnny Depp and Leonardo DiCaprio.

Before leaving and picking everyone up for the ceremony, Keller called his parents in St Louis to check on them. Esther answered and said they were doing well, just missing him. Keller told Esther might be able to get away for an April visit; he would check with Cole and see if he wanted to come with him. Esther advised Keller not to bring his sister unless it deemed necessary for her to look for places for their parents. Keller said he had not mentioned his parents or, let alone planned another quick visit. Once at the pavilion, Keller gave the valet his keys; they hopped out and headed down the red carpet. The ladies were excited to see Tommy Lee Jones, Hanks, and DiCaprio as the men were scoping out to see Pfieffer, Hunter, and Bassett, to name a few. This was going to be a sad night, especially after Cole's sad experience seeing the film Philadelphia. Before the telecast, producer Gil Cates was in a predicament. Billy Crystal was busy trying to find a suitable replacement. After asking Steve Martin, Bette Midler, and off-on again host Johnny Carson, all of whom had said no, he found his new heir apparent in Whoopi Goldberg. Critics were already panning the host even before Goldberg took the stage. It was a first in two cases: the first woman and the first African American solo host. Despite the negative backlash, Cates stood by his choice, addressed Goldberg was highly recognizable, had millions of fans, and with her outrageous humor, she would be fine and wanted to do it.

The end of the discussion need not stop there; Goldberg pulled off a wonderful job by being deliciously elegant, uncharacteristically restrained without the bawdy humor and an ability to make it funny. Schindler's List cleaned up nicely, winning seven of its twelve nominations, including Best Picture and Best Director. Tom Hanks took home Best Actor, delivering an eloquent acceptance speech dedicating his Oscar to a former teacher, bringing the audience to tears. Holly Hunter and Anna Paquin received Best Actress and Best Supporting Actress as the mother-daughter duo in The Piano. Tommy Lee Jones won Best Supporting Actor for The Fugitive. Everyone was shocked to the core when the two earlier heavily favored Asian films lost to Spain's Belle Epoque. Bruce "The Boss" Springsteen brought Best Song honors home.

Oscars out of the way, it was time for the sextet to decide if anything was going to top their vacations in the past. Keller was determined hell or high water; returning to St. Louis with or without Janine was his top priority. Looks like the friends will have to do their best not to take sides and let the two siblings duke it out and agree on what is best for their parents. Thank goodness they are retired now and whenever is needed for their parents' concerns or wherever they decide to see the sights from abroad or stay in the good ol' USA.

The newest and earliest movies were yearning to bust open the gates for everyone to ponder thoughts on what the 67th Oscars will look like coming March 1995. Was there something in the air that could lure some of our sextet out of retirement? Will the steno pool dangle a package in front of Ashlee? It would be interesting seeing Carole go back to help in the makeup and writing departments. Beau and Keller were done with their technical duties by resting on their laurels and enjoying attending the Technical awards every year, meeting, more importantly, the technical artists they worked with, making acquaintances of the new breed, as well as meeting with the host/hostess of the ceremonies. Cole didn't seem to tire in his niche with the pantry; his expertise in working with the other HIV patients was drawing high praise from the Human Rights Campaign. Here are some movies to see in 1995:

Forrest Gump	*Four Weddings and A Funeral*	*Nobody's Fool*	*Speed*	*Hoop Dreams*
The Adventures of Priscilla, Queen of the Desert	*Ed Wood*	*Interview with the Vampire*		
Legends of the Fall	*Quiz Show*	*Pulp Fiction*	*Madness of King George*	*Bullets Over Broadway*
True Lies	*Wyatt Earp*	*Little Women*	*The Shawshank Redemption*	

Speaking of decisions, our sextet will deliberate on traveling or staying home and waiting. We do know for certain Keller will be making a trek to St. Louis to see his and Janine's parents. It is still unclear if Janine will tag along; Keller is hoping she will bury the hatchet of animosity between her and Mom Wallace.

Easter holiday was coming around the corner, and Keller was reminiscing about past holidays with his parents in St. Louis, mentioning to Janine, hoping getting a rise out of her. In silence,

Janine's heart was aching trying to stay firm with her brother about going to St. Louis. Little did Keller know that Janine and Ashlee had irons in the fire as well; pretending she didn't care was getting on Keller's last nerve. Keller was tired of arguing with her, and Cole sensed something was troubling him. Finally, Cole had enough of seeing Keller in tears; he was going to Janine himself. Cole called first because he didn't know what time the ladies woke up; Janine told him to come over for lunch and she would fix a garden salad. Ashlee had gone to the studios to have lunch with steno pool friends, so it was a perfect time. Keller was out and about with Beau, jogging and exercising at the gym. Cole entered the apartment. He knocked. Janine yelled out, "I'm in the kitchen; come on in and have a sit." Janine walked out of the kitchen with two bloody Marys.

Janine said, "So, my dear, what did you want to talk to me about? I am sure it's about a family feud." Cole said, "Well, honey, I hate to see Keller so upset. Why you torture him so!" During the conversation, you could hear a pin drop of silence, and then, you could hear an occasional cry from Janine. Cole said, "Janine, dear, you may as well drop the Oscar routine; you aren't going to be nominated this or any other year; you certainly aren't Oscar-worthy." That brought a little chuckle from Janine, "You and your goddamn Oscars," she said. Cole said, "Well, besides the pantry volunteer, my doctor appointments, keeping up with Keller, and movies are and will always be a part of my life." Janine remarked,

"Gotcha there, honey!" As the duo at their salads and drank their bloody Marys, Janine remarked, "Don't tell my brother, Ashlee, and I are flying up to Missouri on Good Friday to spend Easter weekend with the folks and Nurse Ratched." "Ashlee is determined the nurse is doing something wrong with Mom and Dad," Janine remarked, clearing the table. Cole stated Nurse Ratched always seemed nice around me. Janine thought for a second. Don't tell them we are coming and show up on different days to surprise; maybe we can catch her in devious ways. Cole nodded to think it might be an innovative idea, and he asked Keller when he got home from the gym with Beau. Holidays were past fun times with the Wallace family; Cole said he asked Beau and Carole if they like to tag along. Janine said that would be great. Deep down in a gut feeling, Janine hoped Esther wasn't up to something.

Feeling relieved from his chat with Janine, he headed home, waiting for Keller's arrival from the gym. Cole was going to surprise him with a nice dinner of pot roast and veggies asking Carole and Beau over and discuss the possibility of joining them in Missouri. Carole was already there when Beau and Keller arrived; Cole invited her over for an early happy hour. Keller walked in and smelled the aroma, "Hmmm, what did Julia Child whip up tonight?" Cole walked over to the door to give Keller a peck on the cheek as Beau walked in behind and noticed his wife in the kitchen. Beau said, "What's up, honey? Didn't see you over there. I was about to head home to see if you wanted to catch a movie and dinner." Carole said, "Well, that would be nice; Cole has invited us for dinner and TV. Is that ok with you?" Beau nodded to say it was ok. Cole was finishing preparing dinner with Carole's help; the two gym gods were enjoying a beer. Cole said, "Well, gang, I went to see Janine today!" Keller said, "I told you not to interfere with me and my sister!" Cole relented, "Oh, hon, don't be so upset; she told me something advantageous to your family situation. Ashlee is flying with her next week." Carole mentioned it would be perfect for Keller to beat her there. Cole said, "It's been a while since Carole and Beau saw your parents. Can they go with us?" Keller nodded in unison, of course, if they wanted to.

Beau replied, "We would love to; your parents have always been so gracious." Cole said, "It's settled. I will look tomorrow, and we will beat the other two and surprise everyone." The four settled down to eat dinner; the topic shifted to what movies everyone seemed interested in. Everyone was ready for Pulp Fiction, Forrest Gump, Bullets over Broadway, Quiz Show, Four Weddings and a Funeral, and Interview with the Vampire. Cole mentioned he had heard about an Australian movie about drag queens, The Adventures of Priscilla, Queen of the Desert should be the comedy hit of the season. Can't wait for that! There wasn't much on TV; Carole helped clean up and do the dishes; the duo left to their separate cars for their way home and left the boys alone to discuss their travel plans to see the parents and get there before Ashlee and Janine.

Cole was determined to find what flights were available to the quartet. Cole called Carole to see when they were available to leave and mentioned they could leave the next day. Beau had a cardiologist appointment later that day. Cole said he would look for the earliest available tomorrow. That would be perfect. Carole and Beau went to his cardiologist appointment. The cardiologist gave Beau a clean bill: watch his stress level, eat right, and continue taking his nitro tablets for any signs of chest pain. Upon their drive home, they stopped by the boys to ensure all systems go for the next morning. Cole remarked, saved on parking, put either vehicle at the others' apartment, and hailed a cab to LAX. Nodding in unity: PERFECT! It was set; the middle of the day was cheaper to fly, so leave Wednesday and have an open date to return. St. Louis, here we come. It's early Wednesday, and the sunrise is the perfect day for a flight out from LAX to STL. Cole was getting excited about seeing Mom and Dad Wallace, even if it had been a few months. Hopefully, Nurse Ratched, err, I mean, Esther, will have them doing well, putting Keller's heavy mind and heart at ease before Janine and Ashlee arrive next week. The quartet arrived around 11:30 am Missouri time, gathered their luggage, grabbed the rental car, and headed to Chesterfield. On the way, they stopped at Steak and Shake to get some burgers and sat down to discuss their strategy for how Keller could present his parents with the care scenario. Upon pulling into the driveway of the family home, Carole noticed something rather odd. Carole said, "Keller, I know it's been a few years since Beau and I were here last, but can't help but notice the house looks rather different." Keller remarked that when he and Janine were up just a few short months, they hurriedly had it repainted a distinct color, putting it on the market, but changed their minds. Carole said, "OK, I was wondering; sorry if I talked out of turn." Keller nodded, and it was ok not to worry. As the quartet climbed out of the rental car and gathered their belongings, they were greeted outside by a rather heavyset gentleman. The man said, "May I help you?" Keller said, "I am Keller Wallace, son of Rennie and Geoff. These are my friends, and we flew in from Los Angeles to surprise them!" The man then said, "Oh yes, I have heard them speak of you, your sister Janine, and your friends. I am Chance Stewart, the nurse on duty. Ms. Esther is off today, so come in. This will be a surprise for your parents." Chance remarked the parents had lunch and were down for their naps, please be quiet. As the quartet assembled through the house, finding their respective sleeping quarters, they made their way to the den where Chance was watching the daily talk shows. Keller inquired about Chance's parents' situation since he had seen them a few months back. Chance answered that Geoff was still the same, resting all the time and not really saying much, and Rennie was always trying to help despite walking with the walker. Keller said. "My sister and her best friend should be here in the next week or so, and hopefully, when she arrives, we can sit down and come to a mutual agreement on what we need to do for our parents going forward." Chance said, "I agree. Have heard your mother's grumblings concerning Janine's rush to put them in assisted living and your opposite concerns." Chance concluded he had only been here a few weeks, but Esther explained that it was getting more difficult for her to care for both, and that's why the visiting nursing association added him to their case. It was getting to be about 2:30 in the afternoon; the quartet was impatiently awaiting Rennie to wake up when suddenly, you heard this noise coming from one of the bedrooms. Chance said, "Don't be alarmed; it's just Miss Rennie telling me she is awake." Keller inquired if he could go down the hall, and Chance nodded in agreement. Chance knocked on Rennie's door to say, "I have a surprise for you, Miss Rennie." As Rennie sat up in bed and reached for the walker, she looked up with a big grin. "Keller, you have returned to see us." Keller smiled back and said, "Yes, Mom, Cole, Carole, and Beau came with me. Hope it's ok. Sorry for the surprise." Rennie mentioned, "It's ok, your father is still the same; I am not so sure what we should do; as you can see, we had to hire another nurse." Keller remarked, "It was okay; we need to resolve our differences. I think Janine and Ashlee will be here next week." Rennie said, "Yes, I know; Janine called last night to tell me." "Believe it or not, there was a little truce in the air between the two women," Chance remarked. Rennie got her walker as the two men opened the door to let Rennie scoot into the den; as she did, Cole, Carole, and Beau stood to greet her with warm hugs and kisses. Rennie let out a little cry and exclaimed, "It's so great to see you three; sorry that Geoff and I aren't in the best condition." Beau said, "No apologies needed, Mom Wallace; we just wanted to see you two while we still had the opportunity." As Beau continued, "I guess Cole and Keller have been keeping up to speed on Carole and me." Rennie said, "Yes, Beau, you need to take care of yourself; you don't want to end up like me."

As everyone was enjoying themselves thus far, Carole and Cole mentioned they run to the grocery store to gather more food to fix an Italian feast for Rennie and Geoff. Rennie mentioned, "Geoff doesn't eat much; he sleeps ninety percent of the time; poor Esther and Chance have their work cut out for themselves." Keller and Beau came into the den from the back bedroom, seeing Geoff. Cole stood up to hug Keller, and he told Cole and Carole there was no change. Cole and Carole took off for goodies to make chicken parmigiana. Rennie remarked did I mention already how happy I am to see you four. Cole prepared the main course, and Carole made a Caesar salad, hot Italian bread, and a nice dessert apple pie. After dinner and dishes were done and put away, everyone returned to the den to watch TV. Most everything on television these days was nearing their season's end, so typically, it was a boring night. Rennie said she was ready to get some sleep, but she wanted Carole and

Cole to walk her down the hall to Geoff's bedroom. Rennie stood with her walker, and Carole and Cole sat on the edge of the bed rubbing Geoff's hands and feet; there was this sensation. Geoff opened his eyes and looked around the room. Geoff motioned for a pad and pen; Carole found one on the right of his bedside table. Geoff scribbled, not very legible, but still readable: Hi, you two!!! Suddenly, Geoff put the pad down; for the first time in months, he raised his hand with a thumbs up and a big smile on his face. Rennie saw this; she let out a big, curdling scream. Keller comes running down the hall, "Everything ok, Mom?" Rennie started to say something, but she was crying and laughing; she pointed to the bed, and Geoff looked over at Keller, scribbled on the pad, HI SON! Next thing, you know, Beau was down the hall and sitting on Geoff's bed, smiling and laughing. This was certainly a change of events; in between the combination of laughter and crying, you heard Geoff speak; it was the first time in months, Rennie said. Geoff spoke rather slowly and with a slurring tone, but it was clear and distinct. Geoff said, "It is so nice to see everyone here, and I love all of you very much." Keller was excited seeing this change in his father's condition he excused himself from the crowd surrounding the bed, crying and laughing. Janine will be ballistic with this change of events. As the days progressed, Geoff was steadily improving his speech and mobility skills were getting there, and the gang was getting more and more excited every day. It had been almost a week to the day, around 3 pm, when a couple of car doors heard shut; Cole and Rennie were having tea in the kitchen as the others were in the back bedroom watching Geoff doing his physical therapy with Chance. It was almost too painful to watch as frail as Geoff had been, but with his steady improvement the last few days, Chance was very optimistic. As Rennie strolled to the front door in her walker, she motioned for Cole to squat down behind her. Rennie opened the door and yelled out to the two in the driveway, "Well, well, what a surprise! Look who we have here!" It was Janine and Ashlee. They ran with their luggage across the front lawn towards the front door; as they scurried in, Rennie held the door as best she could, holding her walker, too. Hugs and kisses between the three, and Ashlee shut the front door behind one of the chairs; Cole jumps out and screams, "Surprise Bitches!" Janine said, "OMG, what the hell are you doing here." Cole explained the quartet had been here about a week and was happy to see them. Rennie said, "Girls, put your luggage down and come to the back bedroom; we have a bigger surprise!" Cole helped them with their luggage as Rennie led them back to the bedroom where the other three and Geoff were sitting around the bed giggling. Rennie pushed the door open as Chance was finishing his therapy session. Janine inquired who this was and what was so funny. Keller stood to embrace his sister and said, "This is Chance, an alternate nurse when Esther is off and an extraordinaire physical therapist." Chance was giggly reaching shaking Janine and Ashlee's hand, "Pleasure is all mine, my ladies!" Out of the corner of her eye, Ashlee began to snicker too and told Janine to look. Geoff was grinning from ear to ear, giggling like a little boy; he raised up his thumbs-up sign to the ladies, saying, "Good morning, my beauties, please forgive me; I just tooted during therapy; it might smell a bit. "When Geoff said the word toot, everyone got louder in laughter, and Geoff said, "Must have them damn ham, beans, cornbread, and fried taters Cole fixed last night!" Janine was so overcome with emotion that Carole, Beau, and Chance left the bedroom, leaving her and Ashlee with Keller still in the room. Fighting back tears, Janine said, "When did all this happen." Keller told them about three or four days ago he is still a little weak but getting stronger every day, talking and eating solid food. Keller added Chance had a doctor stop by Monday; he was able to give Rennie and him a big thumbs up, but don't rush his progress so fast. Feeling relieved, Janine told Keller, her parents, and friends how so very sorry she was for doubting them on their recovery and hoping there was forgiveness. Rennie told her, yes, there is forgiveness, but they can't forget what Janine was considering to be malicious. Cole said, "Girls, you two hungry? I can warm up some beans and make some cornbread quick!" Ashlee said, "Sure, that would be lovely!" The girls left Geoff to nap and walked into the den to hug everyone while Cole whipped up jalapeno cornbread and warmed the beans for lunch. Everyone gathered around the dining room table as Cole served leftovers from last night's dinner; the chatter was getting so intense you couldn't get a word edgewise. LOL. It was so good to see everyone getting along, and hopefully, bygones will be bygones. Everything was cool with the siblings and parents letting the children and their friends stay as long as they wanted. It was made a point that they were always welcome and could easily see movies there in Missouri. Alas, it's just different from being able to see them come out first in Los Angeles. It's not the same with all the glitz, glamour, and sometimes the possibility of seeing red carpet premieres holding court with celebrities. Right?

Rennie and Geoff continued their progress as suspicion of Esther was all but forgotten. Keller and Janine reeled with smiles from ear to ear for Chance as well. They wanted to assure the siblings that everything was going to be okay and that they could call and visit anytime. This would always ring true as retirement was settling in nicely with the sextet, and there were a few more places overseas to visit. Looks like Australia and New Zealand were being talked about, possibly winter 1995 or 1996 after the Oscars; it was summer down under, plus a month would be the perfect getaway.

As the sextet prepared their goodbyes, extending their visit till Memorial Day weekend, Rennie and Geoff embraced and kissed, sending them back to Los Angeles. At first, the visits seemed doomed, but they turned out to be the best. The Wallace parents had their new lease on life, content with their children living dreams in California surrounded by a circle of friends called family. Rennie told Carole, Beau, and Ashlee to welcome each other anytime and didn't need to wait for Cole, Keller, and Janine to plan the trip. Geoff added continuing to take care of each other, especially after hearing about Ashlee's breast cancer scare, Beau's heart woes, and Cole's undetectable HIV status. All was good; promises were made, especially having the others watched over closely, and nothing could go wrong.

Summer and fall passed quickly; as the quartet readied for the holidays and the movies graced the screen, Cole had another quick trip idea. Cole asked if anyone was interested in going down to Palm Springs for their annual film festival. The festival was relatively new to Palm Springs, having started in January 1990, with predictions of filled hotels and restaurants, possibly over forty thousand, and run to a new schedule of eleven days. The eleven days proved quite the commanding force drawing huge respect from worldwide filmmakers and new visitors to the Palm Springs area as a new regular place to visit or even perhaps making it their new second home. Off the sextet went breezing the highway, Palm Springs, for ten days of fun and relaxation, and here they came after spending those days detoxing. Returning home from the festival was just right; everyone was looking for their getaway to miss working behind the scenes in Tinseltown even more. At least, they still had plentiful movie adventures ready to explore before the 67th Oscars sooner than you think March 1995.

With all the buzz, Forrest Gump, Bullets Over Broadway, Pulp Fiction, Quiz Show, Shawshank Redemption, Lion King, and The Adventures of Priscilla, Queen of the Desert surrounding the circle of talk with these and many more for their watch over the next few months.

Chapter Thirty-Seven

1995 started off with a bang; overwhelming predictions were running rampant with the new arrival of director Quentin Tarantino and his rather odd dramatic but satirical viewpoint on violence and his future projects. Could it be a Tarantino surprise to everyone if he took out, figuratively speaking, veterans Zemeckis, Redford, and Allen? Could Travolta score some brownie points against a possible repeat from Hanks or a surprise late comeback from Newman? We will have to see in the next few months; care to see what the Golden Globes pre-determine the nominations due out February 14th. The Globes didn't appear to shock many as Hanks reigned supreme for a consecutive year with a win for Forrest Gump, and Hugh Grant surprised everyone with a win over much-heralded favorite Terrance Stamp.

The nominations were released on Valentine's Day, February 14th; thirteen nominations went to Forrest Gump, the fifth time a film had been nominated for that many and the first time since Who's Afraid of Virginia Woolf? A couple of scenarios could play out besides Hanks possibly winning consecutive years. Lange and Wiest, if win with Hanks, would mark the first time since Gone With the Wind. Three top acting awards would be three double wins. Also, Wiest would have the distinction of winning Best Supporting Actress directed by the same director, Woody Allen, who was showing a comeback with his seven nominations for Bullets Over Broadway, tying Pulp Fiction and Shawshank Redemption. Redford was nominated twice for Best Director and Best Picture for Quiz Show. He talked with three lesser-known producers about the 1950s Twenty-One quiz show scandals that were investigated for game fixing by a United States Congressional lawyer and received four nominations. The Disney-produced cartoon Lion King was nominated for four as well, three of which were for Best Song written by music icon Elton John with Tim Rice.

With the Oscar ceremony a little over a month away, Beau and Keller were getting excited about the Technical Awards. They were excited to hear about a change of venue, but, most importantly, the keen possibility of meeting Arnold Schwarzenegger was promoting True Lies. The awards were moved to the Regent Beverly Wilshire years before the Beverly Hilton. As the ceremony was closer, figures as fate had it, instead of Arnold, Beau, and Keller getting the next best thing, his lovely co-star of True Lies, Jamie Lee

AND THE OSCAR GOES TO...

Curtis, serving as both host and presenter.

Producer Gil Cates had the task of finding another host. Goldberg backed out due to film commitment and tried desperately to hook Crystal again but was busy with his new film, Forget Paris with Debra Winger, which he directed, produced, and starred in. Cates announced he finally decided on talk show host David Letterman by noting he was on time, well-groomed, and knew how to keep an audience awake. Since ABC has the broadcasting rights to the Oscars, it was only fitting that their chief of entertainment, Ted Harbert, weighed in on his approval as well, noting if Letterman liked the gig, this would bring a much-needed ratings boost to the show as Carson had done previously. Preparations were underway for the ceremony. The Academy Board announced its usual honorary awards: actor-director Clint Eastwood and music producer Quincy Jones, respectively.

Anxiously arrived early at the venue, changing this year to an earlier location of the Shrine auditorium. The red carpet shined to see some of their favorites, Elton John, John Travolta, Tom Hanks, and Jodie Foster. Janine and Ashlee appeared overzealous to see Travolta and the Pulp Fiction cast. The ladies predicted big wins for Tarantino, being the new kid on the block. Carole and Beau were hoping for Bullets Over Broadway and Shawshank Redemption. Cole and Keller were anxious to see costume designers Lizzy Gardiner and Tim Chapel would dazzle to promote Adventures of

Priscilla, Queen of the Desert. The men were lucky as the designers shined on the red carpet, Lizzy wearing a dress resembling an American Express card. LOL

Bill Conti orchestrated everyone's entrance as Randy Thomas again announced the president of the Academy, famed director Arthur Hiller, onto the stage to welcome prestigious celebrities and guests. Buckle your seatbelts, movie fans! Tonight, some history might be made on the horizon.

The previous Oscar ceremonies begin with the Supporting categories. Of course, without a bat of an eye and no exception to the rule, Tommy Lee Jones walked to the stage presenting Best Supporting Actress. Given the actresses nominated, it brought a newcomer to the field who would prove dominant in years to come, Helen Mirren. Sadly, her time wasn't tonight. Predictors were correct. One of Woody Allen's muses won a second time under his direction, and Dianne Wiest won for Bullets Over Broadway. Anna Paquin presented Best Supporting Actor to television character actor Martin Landau as Bela Lugosi in Ed Wood, beating out possible favorites Gary Sinise in Forrest Gump and Samuel L. Jackson in Pulp Fiction. The highlight of the evening before the top Oscars were presented was Elton John on stage performing one of three nominated songs from Lion King. Bringing down the house with his hit, Can You Feel the Love Tonight and tradition of late, pop artists with Best Song Oscar wins. Forrest Gump ended on a high note, winning six of their thirteen nominations, including Best Picture, Director and Actor Tom Hanks. Best Actress Jessica Lange won for Blue Sky.

Now, with the Oscar ceremony gone, one must remember the time for travel and the good times had by all. What will the future hold from April to summertime? Where will they decide to go this year? Will it be near or far?

Our quartet was at that age now, sixty-two for Cole, sixty-one for Carole, sixty for Ashlee, and fifty-eight for Beau. Janine and Keller are getting closer; there is something yet for them not yet done. There were talks of Australia and New Zealand. Maybe Asia, so much time, possibilities, and concerns for Mom and Dad Wallace were the number one priority. The sextet didn't want to be too far in case it needed assistance. Maybe it is best stay focused one day at a time and cherish the ability to enjoy life. Beau relished going to the gym and jogging daily, watching his heart condition. Cole was keeping up with his T-cell count, doctors were amazed by his regimen, staying active, and volunteering at the pantry. Keller stayed busy doing technical tinkering with sound engineering at some recording studios. Ashlee kept up with her yearly mammograms. Excellent job, friends! It didn't seem anything could tire Carole and Janine down for now. Carole began journalling off, she announced to the group at one of their usual dinners, thinking seriously about putting pen to paper about their Oscar adventures and calling it AND THE OSCAR GOES TO. Janine spent her downtime tracing the Wallace family tree, proving interesting and therapeutic.

Sounds like the sextet finally started delving into various projects, making their retirement time go fast instead of spending their lifetime savings traveling abroad or on other lavish material things. Their vehicles were paid off, and they didn't see anything soon capturing their eyes for anything new. Being long-standing residents, the leasing companies offered them lower rent and upgrades to their units with painting inside and out, new appliances, ceiling fans, etc., and anything just to make them more modern and livable. They were few of the long-time residents at their residences; housing was so expensive in California.

Time was certainly passing quickly, and reading the trades and other newsworthy tabloids kept the sextet abreast of what movies were upcoming. Testing the waters and racking their brains on what would secure the nominations in 1996. Here is a list of what they had to choose from:

Babe	*Brave Heart*	*Apollo13*	*Nixon*	*Dead Man Walking*	*Toy Story*
Usual Suspects	*Mighty Aphrodite*	*Casino*	*12 Monkeys*	*Crimson Tide*	*Sense And Sensibility*
Leaving Las Vegas		*The Bridges Of Madison County*			

AND THE OSCAR GOES TO…

Given these films, how could you go wrong? The caliber of the performances directed by actors turning to directing, bringing tour de forces performances were stellar. Ron Howard, a child actor, turned heads with Apollo 13, Scorsese rebounded with Casino, Woody Allen with Mighty Aphrodite, and the bold, dramatic story of self-destruction brought Nicolas Cage in Leaving Las Vegas, the comic tale from Australia about a pig named Babe, Mel Gibson directed Braveheart and the cartoonish wizardry of Disney with Toy Story. So many choices, so much time, what will everyone venture to see and make everyone's head turn? As they say, so many men and women, so little time! LOL

What else is there besides going to the movies? Park your butt on the sofa or relax in the recliner, kick back, and watch the boob tube. It looks like it's just the same ol' same on the networks these days. FOX, WB, and UPN networks rivaled competition with hits like Star Trek Voyager, Married With Children, and Melrose Place. The rivals, ABC, CBS, and NBC, fill the small screen with Roseanne, Coach, NYPD Blue, Home Improvement, Frasier, Wings, 3rd Rock From the Sun, The Nanny, Cybill, and the annual favorite newsmagazine, 60 Minutes for options.

Woe is me; the holidays are upon us again. With the films above to see for the next few months leading into 1996, what will our sextet decide to see in making their predictions for Oscar gold? Thus far, Mel Gibson was getting raves for his Braveheart box office smash, the technical masterpiece Ron Howard putting together in Apollo 13 became mesmerizing, and the performance of the year was quite a revelation by Nicolas Cage in Leaving Las Vegas. Who would know the nephew of Francis Ford Coppola had it in his genes? Bravo, simply Bravo!

The sextet decided to take a quick trip to check on Mom and Dad Wallace. Chance and Esther expressed a bit of concern over Rennie. She was slowly suffering memory loss. Especially when Esther mentions the children and friends are possibly coming to visit, Rennie nods and smiles. The sextet knew the airports would be packed during Thanksgiving, opting for the week after gobble gobble. It was not a good sign when arriving; Esther greeted them in the yard, shaking her head. Esther told Cole, Carole, and Beau to go ahead and take the luggage, as she needed to talk to Keller and Janine alone for a minute. "It doesn't look good. It's only gotten worse since we last talked," Esther said. "We at the VNA decided our work here is almost complete; your Mom has been in bed for a few weeks, and the same with your Dad," Esther continued. Esther explained they had doctors to check on them and felt it was time to place them in more advanced hospice care. Esther explained further Rennie was diagnosed with a fast-growing brain tumor that was inoperable, causing memory loss coupled with dementia and Alzheimer's. Geoff was constantly in bed and wouldn't eat or talk. It was so so sad. As the trio stood out on the front lawn, it was quiet for a quick second, and then, a big, loud, curdling scream accompanied by a flood of tears from Janine. Keller reached over to comfort Janine, and Esther hugged both tightly, walking towards the front door. The trio entered the front door, finding their four friends with open arms in the living room. Ashlee said, "Chance told us, we are so very, very sorry. I am so glad we decided to come here with you two." Fighting back tears, Keller and Janine nodded, and both said, "We wouldn't be able to get through this ordeal without all of you. We love you so very much." Cole asked Esther and Chance if they needed to run to the store and get some food. Esther thanked him by telling him they did a grocery run yesterday, stocking up to fix four or five dinners. Beau said, "We will stay as long as Keller and Janine need us. If need be longer, they would get more food." Chance replied, "That's good to know. We got a variety of goodies and are so very happy all six came; we aren't sure how much longer Rennie and Geoff will be with us." Esther mentioned she summoned the doctor to stop by since Keller and Janine were coming to town.

The first week after Thanksgiving in St. Louis was quite grueling for Janine and Keller, assuming the worst with both parents in declining health. It was a month before Christmas. The sextet decided to decorate the Wallace home one last time. The weather began getting colder, so be nice to have a white Christmas. Especially, California was not getting much snow, except in those high-elevation areas. Cole, the sole California-born and raised, was excited to see snow. There wasn't much to write home about except the colder temperatures. Christmas came by quickly as the sextet continued vigil amongst the Wallace parents. It was so sad, watching them day by day suffering, just being quiet.

Esther and Chance had their work cut out for them, watching the slow deterioration. Rennie and Geoff weren't eating and losing weight constantly. It wasn't looking good at all. Esther called the VNA on the day before New Year's Eve, asking them to send a doctor as soon as possible. Chance said Geoff wasn't breathing well the night before, and Rennie still wasn't taking her medicine. The doctor arrived at about noon. Checking on Rennie first, then Geoff's room before walking into the den where the sextet was sitting, the doctor told them the Wallaces were hanging by a thread. In addition, not meaning mincing words, Rennie and Geoff could have passed away with their conditions, and nothing more could have been done. Janine and Keller could see the writing on the wall. It was inevitable their parents were going be gone, unsure when time was of the essence. They needed to look for legal documents and agree on what needed to be done. Either way, given the circumstances they were wasting away, tragic and hard to accept them being gone also a blessing at the same time. The brother and sister duo decided cremation was the perfect solution to blend the ashes together so they wouldn't be fighting. Weird, I know, but it worked.

Chapter Thirty-Eight

1996 started as it ended, the sextet still in Missouri with Mom and Dad Wallace. Beau, Carole, and Ashlee were showing signs of restlessness by remaining positive for their friends. After all, that's what friends are for. Cole was being Cole, relished in cooking for everyone being fed and cared for. Snow began falling in Missouri, making it beautiful. Cole, the snobby son of the rich and privileged, most snow seen was holidayed in Colorado for skiing. Iowa and Tennessee natives Ashlee and Beau saw it occasionally, and Carole saw it many times in New York. The quartet, minus the brother and sister duo, were anxious about a return to California preparing for the 68th Academy Awards. Being such loyal friends, something had to give by not wishing ill will on their friends' parents. There was the sitting around, wait and see especially the weather looked like a typical Missouri winter.

Chance and Esther were alternating three days on and three

days off. It was getting tedious taking turns sleeping in the recliners with either Keller or Janine next to Rennie and Geoff's bedside. Early Wednesday, January 3rd, the house was awakened by a blood-curdling scream coming from the far left back of the house; everyone jumped up, gathering their robes and running down the long hallway leading to Rennie and Geoff's rooms. Ashlee and Carole stopped in Rennie's room, finding Janine sobbing uncontrollably as Beau and Cole found Chance and Keller at Geoff's bedside. Chance gave Keller time with Beau and Cole as he walked to Rennie's room. Within a few minutes of each other, being a complete blessing, both parents passed away. Walking out of the rooms and down the hall to the den, Cole said, "I'm going to fix a big breakfast. It looks like we need food to start the day." As four of the sextet made their way, Chance pulled Keller and Janine aside to inquire about what needed to be done. Janine said to give them a few minutes.

Cole was busy in the kitchen; Ashlee appeared to help, wondering if there was any champagne left from New Year's; there was a need to celebrate Rennie and Geoff. Cole acknowledged there were a few bottles of Prosecco. Cole finished cooking, Ashlee setting the table; Esther walked in from the back door to begin her three days. Chance was in the kitchen with Cole, telling her the sad news. Esther was devastated. Walking through the breakfast nook towards the den, Esther noticed everyone was coming in for breakfast. The duo told her how grateful they were for all she had done for them.

Keller said, "Let's eat breakfast first, then call about arrangements; there is no rush, ok?" Cole served everyone around the table and breakfast nook. Ashlee walked around pouring glasses of champagne to make a toast, "To Mom and Dad Wallace, may they rest in peace, thanks for wonderful memories, and to Chance and Esther for putting their lives on hold, always helping when needed. Love to all!"

After breakfast, dishes were cleared and done, everyone leaving Janine and Keller alone. Sorting through their parents' personal documents, looking for insurance papers, wills, etc., gives them more in-depth clues on what to do next. Janine found the number for the St. Louis Cremation establishment off Manchester Road in Ballwin. Sooner, they get the bodies out of the house, have a service for friends and the neighborhood, sell the house, and gather their childhood memories. These feats should take about a week to ten days, hopefully not too much longer, wanting to get out of Missouri before the weather gets worse. While Janine and the ladies connected with St. Louis Cremation, the men were trying to get the house sold and donations of furniture and clothes. Luckily, the housing market was doing well, and lots of families moved to West County for the Parkway school district midterm. The men lucked out and found someone willing to pay cash for the house and its contents. St. Louis Cremation gathered the bodies, telling Janine and Keller everything would be ready the following week. The memorial service was set for Friday, January 12th. Afterwards, the brother and sister could pack and ship their memories over the weekend, and everyone could leave for a California return mid of next week.

It was a sad next few weeks preparing Mom and Dad Wallace's celebration of life, packing up memories, and shipping to California. Who would have known the Wallaces were pack rats, deciding what to keep, throw away, or donate? Time was really working hard on their side, trying to get things organized, packed, sent, and set to be delivered on Monday, January 22nd, the day of their return.

The celebration of life went well, with a huge turnout as the Wallaces were one of the first families moving into their subdivision in Chesterfield; Janine and Keller attended Parkway schools and Ascension Catholic Church. Ascension had the distinction of being one of the twelve founding churches in the Chesterfield area between 1816 and 1923. Rennie and Geoff are one of the most well-loved and respected families in the area. The neighborhood children, now adults with children of their own, recently returned to the neighborhood after losing their own parents, telling Janine and Keller how lucky having them as long and were infamous for the best Halloween treats. Rennie was famous for her popcorn balls, while Geoff enjoyed dressing up startling the children stopping by for trick or treat.

Home, sweet home! Back in California, time to catch up on movies. There has been a long drought after spending the last few months in St. Louis. Such a sad occasion, but forever thankful Mom and Dad Wallace went together instead of lingering. What a blessing in disguise. Trying not to sound maudlin, the time was right. Now, the sextet are back in their homes snug as a bug and ready to predict their upcoming nominees for the 68th annual Academy Awards. At the same time, everyone was glad to be back in California to see as many movies as possible in a few weeks' time before the nominations were announced on February 13th.

The 68th annual Academy Awards nominations were released on February 13th. It was no surprise actor Mel Gibson scored ten nominations for his historical drama Braveheart, Ron Howard's Apollo Thirteen scored nine, Sense and Sensibility scored seven, along with the Australian comedy about a pig, Babe. Best Actress of two years prior, Emma Thompson wrote the screenplay pining for a nomination, could possibly be the first actress to win both. Four nominations went to Dead Man Walking, Toy Story, Nixon, and Leaving Las Vegas; three went to Crimson Tide and Batman Forever, and two to Twelve Monkeys. Woody Allen continued his comeback with Mighty Aphrodite, Clint Eastwood directed himself and Meryl Streep in the romantic drama Bridges of Madison County, and Martin Scorsese directed a star fest in the moving drama Las Vegas-based Casino.

Six weeks before the ceremony, as the nominations were held in the court of a who's who, there was controversy brewing between the Rainbow Coalition and Rev. Jesse Jackson. There was talk that a protest might occur at the ceremony as the group was objecting African Americans and other minorities were underemployed, as well as being portrayed unflatteringly on film and television in the entertainment industry. Gil Cates stepped away from producing the telecast after the negative response to David Letterman's performance the prior year. A familiar face stepped on the scene; Quincy Jones was asked to produce recruited Whoopi Goldberg for a return hosting gig. In hopes of not adding fuel to the fire, Jones agreed with Rev. Jackson not to protest at the venue but rather move to the broadcast facilities of the local Los Angeles WABC-TV. Jones later remarked that the Academy Awards wasn't the appropriate place for a protest.

In recent years, with the dominance of Walt Disney productions winning in the Music category, the academy committee decided to divide the Original score category into two categories: Best Original Score for Drama and Best Original Score for Musical and Comedy.

Beau, Cole, and Keller attended the Technical Awards on March 2nd and had the pleasure of meeting Richard Dreyfuss, who was selected as host. Beau and Keller found Dreyfuss spot on in his reference to Jaws and Close Encounters of the Third Kind's technical aspects, which were the most fun he ever had. Cole got tickled and talked with Dreyfuss in his one scene in Valley of the Dolls to Fun in American Graffiti and Goodbye Girl.

Just a few weeks left before the ceremony, upon their late return from Missouri, the sextet were unable to see films and feeling was time to catch most performances nominated for Oscars. Two specifically resonated in their hearts growing up, seeing Nicolas Cage and Sean Penn in two different arenas from their teenage comedies. Both Cage and Penn were eyeing Best Actor as an addendum to their resume, and their work was cut out for them being against Richard Dreyfuss and Anthony Hopkins. From a technical standpoint, the men were mesmerized by the techniques Ron Howard used in Apollo Thirteen and the performances given by an all-star cast. After seeing these and a few other films, they were slightly undecided on who was going to win the Oscars.

The ceremony was held on March 25th. Gil Cates stepped down as producer and music producer, then Academy president Quincy Jones and David Salzman's shoulders were hopeful, bringing a fresh look without any backlash from the possible protests. Jones reiterated that his choice for Goldberg to return as host would bring her ability to make everyone laugh with a proven elegance and dignity to the show. As mentioned in earlier chapters, nothing has changed. Best Supporting Actor was given to Kevin Spacey for Usual Suspects, and a few minutes later, Woody Allen's muse, Mira Sorvino, daughter of well-known character actor Paul Sorvino, took home Oscar gold two consecutive years an actress in an Allen film had won supporting awards. Emma Thompson took home an award for Best Original Screenplay adapted from another medium for Sense and Sensibility, making history as a previous Best Actress winner for writing a screenplay. Would she repeat a third time and a second-Best Actress on the same night? Time will tell. Poor songwriter and artist Randy Newman was a regular loser in the music category, keeping his losing streak alive by writing songs for Toy Story. LOL. Luck wasn't on Thompson's side; Susan Sarandon swiped it away from the likes of Streep, Sharon Stone, Elisabeth Shue, and Emma. Better luck next time!

Best Actor was heating up between two former winners, a deceased actor, and two actors whose teenage comedic turns suddenly showed dramatic chops; who would it be? Luck was in favor of Nicolas Cage as a washed-up alcoholic writer in Leaving Las Vegas. It was ironic for the first time since the 42nd Academy Awards, none of the performers who had won acting awards appeared in any Best Picture nominees. Mel Gibson proved critics wrong by becoming the golden boy for the evening as Braveheart took home five of its ten nominations, including two for him as Best Director and Best Picture. What a delight!

AND THE OSCAR GOES TO…

Worth noting from a financial perspective, the United States box office surpassed $333 million with an average of $66.5 million per the five Best Picture nominees. In domestic receipts, Apollo Thirteen slaughtered the competition with a gross of $172 million; next was Braveheart with $67 million, and rounding out the top three of the five nominees was Babe with $58.2 million. Quite an accomplishment, you think.

It's amazing millions and millions of dollars we moviegoers spend for a movie, refreshments, transportation, gas prices, and other miscellaneous items in our lifetime. It would pay off in the long run as we devoted fans glued to the television watching these telecasts. At least we could do is show up more to watch them and declare them a ratings winner. Ratings for a telecast can bring box office dollars to a film's revenue. Many films are given second chances. It's a win-lose situation, no matter if released, seen earlier, or sometimes re-released to give fans and possibly critics the opportunity to catch what wasn't seen the first time around.

With our sextet in their late fifties and early to mid-sixties, one can imagine what the movie business will be like in many years ahead. There will be more offerings for our audiences, with up-and-coming performers to shine and entertain us. Who knows if awards will ever be the same? There will be repeat winners, records will be broken, memories will be created and shared, you name it, the sky is the limit for everyone in Hollywood. Everyone will be out for themselves, creating movies and the ability to make us laugh and cry through the many adventures left for us to enjoy.

1996 promised a lengthy list of movies for everyone's tastes, hoping nothing would stop the sextet from searching for a blockbuster. One will never know what the future holds when preparing for another season of films. Here is a list of hopes bringing good vibes.

The English Patient	Shine	Jerry Maguire	Independence Day	Fargo
Evita	The Mirror Has Two Faces	Sling Blade	Emma	The First Wives Club
Primal Fear	The Nutty Professor	Marvin's Room	The People vs. Larry Flynt	

The caliber of these films promised a bit of this and that, from old Hollywood to some music divas duking it in varied interesting flair, certainly turning heads with ensemble pieces and e real-life stories, bringing up the challenge of showing the gripping truth of their stories.

Cole and Keller were in mutual agreement, anticipating Streisand directing and starring in The Mirror Has Two Faces, a romantic comedy with Jeff Bridges, and making choices to bring Lauren Bacall out of semi-retirement to play her mother. Music icon Madonna starred in Evita, and after years of speculation about who's who secured the rights to direct and sign the perfect star to deliver a poignant performance, it was the talk of Tinseltown. Beau was quite interested in the technical of Eddie Murphy's comedy remake of comedian Jerry Lewis's Nutty Professor. The ladies were intrigued with Emma, The First Wives Club, and The English Patient. Everyone seemed to agree the true story of Larry Flynt coming to the screen might prove worthy as quirky Fargo and odd Sling Blade, a tour de force writing, directing, and starring Billy Bob Thornton.

Besides the upcoming films, health concerns began surfacing amongst some of our sextet. Sadly, Mom and Dad Wallace were only gone for a brief time, certainly not forgotten in their hearts; it was time to focus on Beau, Ashlee, and Cole. Steadily, with alternate days, working out either in the gym or running, jogging, and brisk walking was catching up with Beau, and his cardiologist strongly suggested a new diet. Cole started having issues with a rise in T-cell count. Doctors were highly concerned as Ashlee and Carole's gynecologist found a few lumps on Ashlee's left breast and her thyroid. What needs to be done to keep our friends healthy? How about a trip to the Big Apple of New York City? Carole promised to score Broadway, Saturday Night Live, Late Night David Letterman, possibly The View and Regis & Kelly tickets for the ladies, and Keller promised Mets and Yankees baseball for the men.

First things first, Carole took the ladies to New York, and

the gents would follow in a few days. Keller and Beau took Keller to the clinic to check out his T-Cell count and other issues. After the loss of Mom and Dad Wallace, Cole appeared more depressed than usual, more so than Keller and Janine. Cole attempted to hide his depression, showing a brave front, telling Mom Wallace before her death he would pay Janine and Keller back. Rennie told Cole there was no need; the brother-sister duo were going to be well taken care of once they were gone.

The two weeks in NYC were a blast by day. The sextet was out sightseeing from the Empire State Building, Statue of Liberty, Wall Street, Times Square, a ferry ride on the Hudson River channeling Melanie Griffin in Working Girl, and eating at some of the big spots like Tavern On the Green. After some of the shows, the girls would try to catch some celebrity sightings. The men, or shall the gay men be fortunate to check out the men at the ballpark, fantasizing about what was underneath their uniform, leaving nothing but imagination. It was a perfect fit for teasing Beau since he wasn't gay. LOL, shame on Cole and Keller for trying recruitment again. Just silly old queens looking, no touching, no harm in that. LOL.

Chapter Thirty-Nine

R inging in the New Year after a whirlwind year and a half between the deaths of the Wallace parents, tending to ailments of Ashlee, Beau, and Cole, their trip to New York City and other matters of the heart took front-row center for the sextet. Early in January, Keller and Janine announced they needed a return to St. Louis for a probate hearing over their parents' estate and any possible monies due them. Carole offered to go for moral support; the brother and sister duo suggested going alone, and she could help the other three. The weather is so unpredictable this time of year for Missouri; it's either bitter cold mixed with wintry precipitation or mild, who knows, on arrival. Let's hope business can be done in a timely manner and return to the mild sunny winter in California. Hopefully, there will be good news from St. Louis and California. Carole has the task of taking Ashlee, Beau, and Cole to their appointments, and the brother-sister duo will receive some news concerning their parents' estate.

First off, Carole decided to take Ashlee to their mutual gynecologist to discuss Ashlee's finding more lumps on her breasts. The gynecologist recommended some MRIs and biopsies checking the nodules on Ashlee's thyroid, which was causing growing concern. In a nutshell, Ashlee was facing a double whammy here: breast cancer and thyroiditis, an inflammation and swelling of the thyroid gland. Ashlee was given a lifetime prescription of levothyroxine in hopes of reducing the swelling, and it was just a wait-and-see what the MRI and or breast biopsies show.

Second, Carole enlisted Beau and Ashlee to take Cole to the clinic. Cole explained he was fine; actually, he wasn't. In Keller's absence, Cole complained of being very tired and depressed, heavy night sweats, extreme weight loss, and severe cold symptoms turning into flu-like pneumonia. Not good at all, Cole was slowly developing blisters, red rashes like lesions, and other fungal infections. Embarrassed by his appearance, Cole decided it would be best to start covering them by wearing long-sleeved shirts. Given this sad news, it looks like HIV was taking its toll on our beloved Cole.

Thirdly, Carole took Beau to his cardiologist. Carole and Beau were hoping for better news after the earlier two friends had received it. Unsure, Carole was faced with three of her closest friends who needed medical assistance. Money couldn't buy it, but their long-term friendship had been such a blessing over the years. Carole didn't know how much longer she could take of such turmoil and agony. Beau's cardiologist wasn't happy with the cholesterol numbers, and after a stress test showed signs of small heart attacks and clogged arteries, wasn't too impressive either. The cardiologist suggested surgery, but Beau wasn't willing to cooperate, telling them a preference for being on lifetime heart medication, and for any sign of pain, he would take that little white pill underneath his tongue.

Keller and Janine were somewhat better in St. Louis, preparing a return to California, but after Carole's sad news on the telephone, I'm not sure if things be better. The brother-sister duo were told, in probate, they were more well off in their wildest dreams. What if I told you that the Wallace fortune was close to a couple million dollars? Keller and Janine were taken by surprise. Where did their parents get so much money over the years? Especially the astronomical amount of money their parents gave Cole for his medical bills, Keller and Janine couldn't fathom where this was from. Their family lawyer, Jerome Schwartz, said Geoff and Rennie enjoyed playing the stock market, and once they hit big, hiding from the children in secret accounts was shocking news.

Keller and Janine returned to California on the first of February, just in time to hopefully get the quartet out of their post-

New Year's blues and forget about their ailments. Keller announced, "It's movie time, and we need some cheering up around here to prepare for the Oscar nominations." Ashlee and Cole appeared to be in the worst funk, especially given the news from their doctors and specifically didn't feel movies would cheer them up. What could possibly get everyone out for a night of food, drinks, movies, etc.? Upon arrival, Carole called Janine, telling her she was fixing her famous Chicken Parmigiana and wanted the six to get together. Janine agreed to say she would talk it over with Keller on the plane ride home. Keller wholeheartedly agreed a home-cooked meal would hit the spot as it seemed while the duo was away, food was mostly takeout or hotel food. LOL. It was great to be surrounded by friends like family; sad to hear how much two to three weeks' time can change the direction of how you live your life. Hopefully, with the presence of the sextet altogether again as a unit, assisting each other in the healing process and be on the road to recovery.

Movies were far from everyone's mind, but the Oscar nominations were due soon, on February 11th. Usually, Ashlee was more excited than ever; you could see her demeanor at the dinner table, concentrating on fighting her cancer and thyroid issues. Cole, on the other hand, basically had nothing that could be done for him. Especially the doctors told Carole that if Cole developed more aggressive pneumonia and flu-like symptoms, get him to the emergency room as soon as possible for oxygen and further assistance. Keller was devastated to hear this; he couldn't lose Cole. Cole had been his lifeline confidante and prayed every night from here on out for a miracle. After all, we are all God's children, and he wasn't biased about who he wanted to join at the pearly gates and be in his flock of new guardian angels.

Depending on how everyone was feeling health-wise, come April, the sextet would attend the Oscars or just watch them at home. Everyone wasn't too excited about anything except trying to get better and enjoy life with everyone. Looking at the trade papers, the Los Angeles and New York Critics' Awards, and the Golden Globes, it looked like a slam dunk: an epic romantic war drama, The English Patient, quirky Fargo, musical Evita, perhaps comedy, Jerry Maguire or even The People vs Larry Flynt and Sling Blade might be a dark horse.

Streisand labored so hard joining the men's and women's club of directors; it is nice recognition as Cole and Keller teased in anger over the possibility. The reality was close to Cole's heart of hearts; he loved Streisand and everything she had done. Hopeful her comedy. The Mirror Has Two Faces would garner a few nominations. Streisand had done so well in getting Lauren Bacall out of semi-retirement to play her and Mimi Rogers' mother, as well as Pierce Brosnan as a swine of brother-in-law and Jeff Bridges as her romantic leading man—dream cast. Cole promised Keller hell or high water wasn't preventing him from seeing this film.

TIM J. CULBERTSON

The English Patient received twelve, Shine and Fargo received seven, five went to Evita and Jerry Maguire, a sad two to The Mirror Has Two Faces (no Streisand!) and Sling Blade. A month away from the ceremony, it was to see at least a few films nominated despite their health woes. They decided against going to the ceremony and missed seeing Streisand, Bacall, Cruise, and Madonna.

Beau decided, with his declining health, to stay home and forgo attending the Technical Awards scheduled for March 1st. NBC's Mad About You lead, Helen Hunt, appeared as hostess and presenter this year. There was word in the trades Hunt was making a film for James L. Brooks, a romantic comedy starring Jack Nicholson and 60s matinee idol Shirley Knight as Hunt's mother called As Soon as It Gets. Hunt is slated to play a single mother waitress to Nicholson's romance novelist who suffers from OCD, obsessive-compulsive disorder, and E! News host Greg Kinnear as a gay neighbor; ready for release in late 1997.

With the ceremony rapidly approaching, Janine returned Carole's favor. Having everyone over for Swiss Steak and watching the Oscars at her and Ashlee's place. Swiss Steak was one of Janine's favorite, and especially if done in the crock pot, cook it all day until juicy and tender. Cole, being the chef, well not exactly what the doctor ordered. Rest and relaxation, watching the Oscar in the comfy setting of someone else's home when they are as close as everyone is. Poor Ashlee was having a rough time, too, forgot to mention her biopsies came back positive, and MRIs gave it a more in-depth diagnosis. Ashlee had the big C and was slated for surgery in April. The doctors recommended a double mastectomy and reconstructive surgery. Ashlee laughed it off; she was going from a double D in cup size on her breasts; who knows what she would look like? LOL. Cole was trying to laugh it off as well, saying he looked like a person with leprosy. Ashlee vowed as God was her witness the sextet would reign to see at least one or two more live Oscar ceremonies before their lives were through.

Janine called the quartet, telling them to bring champagne and other alcoholic beverages if they chose to; Ashlee would provide the rest as she would slave overseeing the crock pot and making mashed potatoes, green salad, and green bean casserole. Keller and Cole were the first to arrive. Cole insisted he wanted to be in the front row of the television in hopes of catching a glimpse of Barbra Streisand walking the red carpet. Beau and Carole arrived a few minutes later with the champagne, only the best, Prosecco. LOL. Carole left the men to themselves, racing into the kitchen and catching up to dish the latest scoop with the ladies. Ashlee set the table for four, and the island bar for two as Janine diced the potatoes preparing the mashed potatoes, and Carole played cocktail waitress for the gentlemen refilling their beverages. Dinner was ready at about 5:30, which was enough time for the sextet to gather around to say a few prayers for good health concerning the trio battling their ailments. Just as they were ending the prayers with Amen, it was quiet, then Janine let out a little sob. Janine remarked, being sorry; life was so unfair right now, and nobody deserved to be ill. Dinner was finished, dishes were in the dishwasher, the table was cleared, and drinks were replenished; everyone settled in the living room, ready for the dish of who was wearing what and who was walking the red carpet.

It was a repeat performance by Gil Cates, who returned as Oscar's producer, his seventh gig after a year's absence. Billy Crystal, Cates's secret weapon good luck charm, returned for his fifth hosting duty, and musician and film composer Bill Conti served as musical director. The routine was kept in sync with the same old wondering which Best Supporting Award would be presented first. After director Arthur Hiller, the current Academy president, welcomed guests, the previous year's Best Supporting Actress winner, Mira Sorvino, appeared to present the Best Supporting Actor award to Cuba Gooding Jr. for Jerry Maguire. Gooding Jr. was becoming infamous for his film quote, "Show Me the Money," winning over possible predictors William H. Macy for Fargo and Edward Norton for Primal Fear. In between the few awards and introductions to nominated Best Picture and Best Original Score and Song, it was the previous year's Best Supporting Actor winner, Kevin Spacey's turn. Spacey shocked the audience by announcing

AND THE OSCAR GOES TO...

Juliette Binoche won Best Supporting Actress for The English Patient over what would be a sentimental lifetime award to Lauren Bacall for The Mirror Has Two Faces. The tedious ceremony rolled as The English Patient began an early sweep of their competitors for a final nine out of twelve awards; Crystal was slowly running out of jokes. Other miscellaneous awards and music numbers sped the time to when coming down to the more important awards of the evening were ready to be presented. The previous year, Best Actor Nicolas Cage presented Frances McDormand Best Actress for Fargo, being the first to win an actress directed by her husband. Following the same year, Best Actress Susan Sarandon presented Geoffrey Rush Best Actor for Shine, upsetting favorites Tom Cruise and Billy Bob Thornton. Mel Gibson presented Best Director to Anthony Minghella for The English Patient, and Al Pacino presented Best Picture to producer Saul Zaentz for The English Patient. This award for Zaentz was his third in previous years for One Flew Over the Cuckoo's Nest and Amadeus, coupled with his earlier win of the coveted Thailberg Memorial Award. This win made this trivia fact the seventh time in Oscar history, whereas a winner won an Oscar and a special award in the same year. Cole mentioned being happy to see Celine Dion step in for ailing Natalie Cole to sing a nominated song from The Mirror Has Two Faces but rather had seen Barbra and Bryan Adams do it. Oh well, you can't have your cake and eat it too. Dion didn't bring good luck to either nominated song she performed; famed Broadway music virtuoso Andrew Lloyd Webber and songwriting partner Tim Rice took the prize for a song written especially for the film version of Evita.

Box office receipts reached a high plateau on February 11, and the nominations announcement date showed off the five Best Picture nominees totaled a mere $209 million, averaging $41.9 per film. Quite a chunk of pocket change, you think. To no surprise, Tom Cruise's Jerry Maguire led the pack with $121.5 million, and a distant second, the Best Picture winner grossed $42.3 million.

With another Oscar ceremony under wraps, it was now time for the sextet to lay low, concentrate on feeling better, and enjoy what was in store for the 70th Academy Awards. Grave as the ill trio were movies need to be on the back burner. The remaining three put in their love and energy, ensuring comfortable times were ahead with ease. The next several months were going to be hard on them as everyone decided to pitch in and help the ones ill. Ashlee was contemplating having her surgery soon, Cole day to day, up and down on how he felt, and Beau was struggling with his demons if surgery was an option.

Nearing the end of the first quarter of 1997, upcoming films in post-production were looking for release dates. Bravura's performances perked interest in the trades on a who's who and what's what list, bringing smiles to filmgoers. Given what had been

AND THE OSCAR GOES TO...

ailing our sextet emotionally as well as physically, hopefully, plenty of films to ensure the ability to make us laugh and cry for the feeling-good cheerful outlook. Here are some of the films coming soon in either the middle or late 1997 to a theatre near you:

Con-Air	*Face-Off*	*Contact*	*Air Force One*	*Men In Black*	*Jackie Brown*
In & Out	*My Best Friend's Wedding*	*Boogie Nights*	*L.A. Confidential*		
The Full Monty	*Good Will Hunting*	*Titanic*	*As Good As It Gets*	*Amistad*	

The trades were touting several films and were releasing tidbits about some of the movies: this new young screenwriting team, Matt Damon and Ben Affleck about an intellectual math wizard in Good Will Hunting, a film surrounding the inside story of the pornography business starring Burt Reynolds in Boogie Nights, the early days of Hollywood mixed with intrigue and crime in L.A. Confidential, a romantic drama around the Titanic shipwreck, the list was endless. We can only hope that our ill trio, along with the rest of the sextet, can enjoy these films before the end of the year.

The ladies, Ashlee, Carole, and Janine, went together to her gynecologist appointment on Good Friday, March 28th, a few days after the Oscar telecast. To be frank concerning Ashlee's condition, the gynecologist strongly suggested she immediately be admitted to prep for surgery on the following Monday. Dr. Zachary concluded Ashlee waited too long having surgery; concerns were raised as a cautionary measure, waiting to see how her thyroid condition would heal, tests proving a deeper concern as well. Janine and Carole realized Ashlee let it go. Finally, Ashlee let the cat out of the bag. While Janine and Keller were in St. Louis, Ashlee became depressed, not a mention to Carole, Beau, and Cole. You would think, since they were the original four musketeers, sticking together was the right thing to do. Ashlee stated she didn't feel the need to worry, especially with Beau and Cole not well.

Ashlee added having suicidal thoughts upon hearing of the double whammy for mastectomy and thyroid ailments. Ashlee stopped her thyroid medication, thinking to herself it would dissolve and go away. *Wrong!* Carole called the men from the hospital, staying with Ashlee, while Janine returned to the apartment gathering clothes and toiletries. Carole was able to reach Beau; saying they were on their way taking Cole to the clinic, wheezing and coughing. What else can go wrong? Carole went back to Ashlee and Janine, who just returned. Carole was unsure about sharing Cole's news. The nurses assigned to Ashlee's surgical team arrived and politely asked the ladies to go out to the waiting area as they prepped her for surgery. As the ladies sat down, Ashlee told Janine about Cole. It had been church; you would have heard a pin drop, but then, of course, Ms. Drama Queen Janine let out her blood-curdling scream, and the others in the area just gasped. One of the nurses stopped by the waiting area, telling Janine and Carole Ashlee were heading to the operating room; they were welcome to come to wish her well. As Janine wiped away her tears and blew her nose, Carole and she put on the bravest front, holding Ashlee's hands in prayer and each kissing her on the forehead. It was going to be a lengthy procedure and constantly be updated.

Meanwhile, Keller, Cole, and Beau arrived at the clinic around 12:30, and the doctors were ready to see him. You could see Cole wasn't himself walking very slowly as his wheezing and coughing sounded worse than earlier in the morning. Keller said Cole hadn't been eating well the last few days. The last big meal he enjoyed was Janine's pot roast a few days prior on Oscar night. The doctors suggested the men sit in the visitor's area, they were taking Cole to the examining area, explaining a bit before they knew anything. Time went rather slowly; around 2 pm, the phone was at the clinic's desk, and the receptionist called Beau, saying it was Carole. Carole spoke briefly, saying nothing, yet Ashlee had only been in the operating theatre thirty minutes; how was Cole? Beau mentioned Cole's state when they brought him in, but there has been no word either. The duo exchanged I love yous and said they call when the other either heard anything. Anyhow, 2:00 became 3:30 p.m., when one of the clinic doctors appeared and discussed with the gentlemen. It was sad news: Cole had pneumonia, required oxygen, and was placed on a ventilator and resting comfortably, being fed nutrients via IV. 3:30 became 4:30; taking turns sitting with Cole, Beau excused himself to call Carole. Beau notified Carole about Cole's condition, and Carole had no news; surgery was still ongoing at about 4:15. 4:30 turned into 5. Carole and Janine went to the desk as the receptionist was getting off the phone; Ashlee was being taken to recovery. They should see her at about 6. What a relief! The receptionist added a surgeon would discuss surgery and what to expect going forward. Around 5:30, the surgeon, Dr. Manuel Stephenson, appeared. Dr. Stephenson introduced himself and explained thoroughly the procedure, what was done, why the length, and will address concerns the ladies would have. Explaining the length, Ashlee expressed an interest in immediate reconstruction, which meant being done immediately after surgery, very extensive therapeutic measures were needed, and anywhere between six to eight weeks of recovery in the hospital. The ladies thanked Dr. Stephenson for his time, telling Ashlee he should be coming around from anesthesia between thirty to forty-five minutes. In the meantime, Carole called Beau, giving details concerning Ashlee and vice versa concerning Cole. Both suggested just a few blocks from each other, letting the siblings sit with Cole, and they sit with Ashlee.

It was now about 7 pm; Beau and Janine switched places between the hospital and the clinic. Given Cole's circumstances and need for oxygen, he was being moved to the same hospital as Ashlee. The situation proved more critical than noted, and it needs to be done very carefully with everyone involved, both professionally and personally. It will be a success. This will be a welcome relief for the remaining four; upon the hospital were told firsthand, the six were bonded together forever. The hospital administration found their relationship so unique; they would do everything in their power to ensure everyone was comfortable giving them the royal treatment and moving a bed in each room. It looked like the sextet was going to be very busy now, and there was no time for movies. Not by any means were Cole and Ashlee out of danger. Poor Cole needed to breathe on his own, and Ashlee would need physical therapy coupled with counseling dealing with all the trauma in joining a support group for breast cancer survivors. Healing is the first step, and the second is being there for one another, whatever lies ahead. During the healing process, there will be many happy and sad times mixed with laughter and anger, a no-brainer.

The days slowly moved to weeks, getting closer to Memorial Day weekend. The Forrester-Guthrey duo were still hospitalized. Doctors were very optimistic about Ashlee's progress; therapy was going well, and her ability to move her arms above her head without much pain was showing significant signs. All kidding aside, Ashlee wasn't too thrilled with her new breast size; it was a reduction from a 38C to a 34D. Physical and counseling therapy was going as well as expected for Ashlee, learning the exercises from others in the same situation. Poor Cole was in sad shape; doctors were beginning inquiries with Keller and the rest of the group about making him comfortable. Sadly, even though this being a tight-knit group, something needs to be done. Since Keller and Cole weren't legally married, they found his parents and let them decide. Cole would never forgive them if the group did that. Memorial Day weekend arrived, and Ashlee was coming home from the hospital! Ashlee was given the green light by her doctors. Ashlee had a positive outlook on life; her scars were healing, and given her physical therapy progress and successful reconstructive surgery, she was free. Carole and Beau went to the hospital and picked her up; before leaving, she stopped by Cole's room to find Janine and Keller. Cole was breathing on his own now but going in and out of reality. Janine excused herself from Cole to talk to the trio. Fighting back tears, Janine explained the doctors were worried about Cole being on the ventilator; he suffered light brain damage. The brother-sister duo wished they had Mom and Dad right now, especially when deciding what to do with poor Cole. Keller was beside himself with worry; it's a legal issue that needs to be resolved. Doctors suggested with no legal rights, they release him to Keller's care and let him rest comfortably at home.

With both patients home from the hospital, the remaining

four faced a dilemma: needing caregivers to assist them in assuring care was the number one priority. They will be adjusting, especially going to the movies for now. Luckily, with the openings of video stores across California, they could rent movies or even buy some of their classics either on VHS or DVD. As for current popular films, the sextet will resort to reading about their favorites and an occasional theatre visit. It won't be the same being in an actual theatre, but the main concern will be accomplished.

Summer peaked on the horizon; what will the rest of the year bring? Keller was beside himself with worry and didn't feel like leaving the house. Being dedicated to assuring Cole gets round-the-clock care and caters to everything he needs, Janine came over, bringing food while Carole visited Ashlee. No stone left unturned, with nobody being left alone. Janine brought over some pamphlets. She stopped at the clinic and gave her some information concerning hospice care for HIV patients. When Keller saw this, he went ballistic, "I am not ready for Cole to enter hospice care; I can't afford to lose him," Trying to fight back tears, Janine told him, "Big brother, it's hard to lose someone we love, you have to let go!" Janine suggested we call the Forrester parents; they have a right to know about their son. Carole stopped by to see Ashlee. Ashlee was on the sofa watching TV when the doorbell rang. Ashlee yelled out, "It's open, and no, I don't want any!" Carole chuckled and said, "Well bitch, I aim to please, I don't have anything except love and friendship for sale."

"So, how are you feeling," Carole asked.

Ashlee responded with a thumbs up and said, "Just peachy, like a million bucks; how's the rest of the gang?" Carole noted she couldn't complain, except for Beau being stubborn and scared of returning to the doctor seeing what she and Cole experienced. Ashlee mentioned she would talk to him. Carole nodded in agreement, mentioning her worries about Keller and Cole. Ashlee said, "Yes, I wish I could go see him, but Keller said all he does is sleep." Ashlee mentioned Janine was over now trying to convince Keller to get more advanced care, like hospice, and calling his parents in Beverly Hills. Carole said, "I was afraid it comes to that, HIV cases rising and not enough medical care for patients; it's a shame our government can't do more about it."

Near summer's end, Janine took Ashlee to the doctor; they mutually agreed on a time to get out and enjoy life more, see movies, attend concerts, etc. Apparently, sitting on her butt these several months made her gain weight. The doctors said a healthy diet and exercise regimen of walking, cycling, and swimming. Ashlee was determined to get back to her old self in time for fall TV and movie season. Ashlee hadn't been on a bicycle in years; it was going to be great, giving her an opportunity to visit with Cole. When Ashlee visited, taking movies to watch, read books, and listened to music.

Cole lay motionless with Ashlee talking to him; she finally said, "You know I am tired of visiting. If you don't say something soon, I might as well pack my goodies and head home." Keller was ever so thankful for the shared friendship and having each other's back concerning Cole's declining health.

Fall was in full bloom, and the sextet, or at least four of the six, discussed the upcoming TV and movie season. Keller was adamant about staying by Cole's side; the other four go to the movies, and he stays home, watching TV and current and old movies. Certainly, it wasn't like old times, but the five could still get together for dinners and activities. Keller invited the four over for a cook-out of burgers and steaks on Halloween. This Friday evening, the five were finishing their dinners when, suddenly, there was a THUD sound coming out of Cole's room. Rushing into Cole's bedroom, finding him trying to get out of bed, looking straight at his friends and saying, "Hello." Keller sat beside him on the bed, hugging him, and said, "Oh my God, Cole, you are awake." The other four were speechless, thinking about what would happen next. Leaving their plates, the five grabbed Cole, still in his pajamas, wrapped him in a jacket, and headed to the emergency room. Arriving, they rushed Cole to the desk, and luckily, he was not busy. The attendants took him right away to a station to check him. About thirty minutes lapsed, a doctor came walking towards the five and asking questions about Cole's past medical history. Keller explained he was HIV+ not been well for several months, wasn't breathing, and his doctors, during his last visit, sent him to pass away basically. The doctor mentioned Cole was breathing well on his own and suggested keeping him overnight, being a clever idea. Monitor him, telling Keller he was welcome to stay the night in his room. Elated with this new break on Cole, Keller said he would like that, as the others said they would stop by the apartment, get him a change of clothes, clean the kitchen, etc. As the four left, the doctor led Keller down a corridor to Cole. Keller pulled back the curtain, and Cole was sitting in a wheelchair, mumbling under his breath something like when can we get the fuck out of here.

Keller told Cole the need to be patient because the doctor wanted to keep him a day or two for observation as soon as the hospital secured Cole a room, hooking IVs full of nutrients, giving him energy as Keller looked on. As the couple were in the room, Cole said he needed sleep; Keller understood, leaving him to the waiting area and gathering his clothes from Janine. Keller told Janine he was resting comfortably; she could stop by in the afternoon after his tests were done. Sadly, as Janine was about to walk to the elevator, there was a loud noise. The intercom screeched CODE BLUE to room thirteen. Keller realized it was Cole's room, starting to run down the hall; a nurse stopped him, saying he couldn't go in there. The nurse explained Cole had a seizure and was cuffed to the bed. Doctors were working on him; notify him as soon as they could. Cole grabbed Janine before hitting the elevator. Cole called Carole and said to get Ashlee and Beau, and they came as soon as they could.

Thirty minutes passed; everyone was there in the lobby, pacing the floor so as not to bump into each other in front of the nurses' station. Out of the corner of her eye, Ashlee saw two white coats slowly making their walk down the long hall. Ashlee nudged Keller, noting that white coats were headed down. The five quickly assembled in front of their chairs; one doctor was shaking his head as he spoke. "Mr. Wallace, I am afraid we have done all we can on our end; Mr. Forrester isn't responding to treatment; no other way to say this: he is brain dead." The other doctor said, "I know you two don't have legal rights. We need to let him go peacefully. Are you certain his parents can't be notified?" Choking back tears, Keller mentioned Cole's parents were in their eighties and unable to make decisions, let alone see their son. It was Cole's wish for them not to be told, and he wanted to honor it as much as it pained him. The doctors walked away; the gang comforted each other. Beau reminded there was a need for legal counsel concerning Cole's condition. Pulling back from the embrace, Keller mentioned, too, it was a shame gays weren't legal to marry; he could decide. The five were stunned by the doctors' comments hearing the inevitable Cole was gone. Keller was becoming beside himself, worried about what happened next. Apparently, in the end, Keller respected Cole's wishes and let him die with dignity and not contact his parents.

The legalities regarding the right to die caused varied reactions across the United States. One specific case, Vacco vs Quill in New York, addressed the constitutionality of its ban on physician-assisted suicide. The U.S. Supreme Court upheld New York's ban: there was no constitutional right. However, California didn't have a specific law, but the right-to-die issue was very popular as there were many discussions and legal battles related to these types of decisions. Hearing this proves stressful for Keller and his wrestling with the idea of finding Cole's parents.

Trying their best to stay brave for Keller, the remainder of the sextet sitting with Cole individually was the best thing. Even though he was on death's door and comatose, Ashlee would bring Streisand music to the hospital in hopes Cole would interact with her soothing voice, Carole would read to him, and Janine and Beau brought comic relief by telling jokes and reminiscing about years past. Keller would sit at the bedside and hold his hand, rubbing his arms in hopes Cole could feel it and wake up just one more time. Holidays were approaching rapidly, and there was no change in Cole's condition. Ashlee remarked things hopefully would be better once the holidays passed. Movies are what's needed to get out of their darkest days. Ashlee was determined to get the whole gang out. Hopefully, this will be the ticket. There was a limited release of James Cameron's epic, Titanic, a James Bond movie, Tomorrow

Never Dies, Scream 2, the second in the Scream anthology from Wes Craven, and comedy relief was in the store with Home Alone 3. The anticipated romantic comedy pairing Jack Nicholson and Helen Hunt in the James L. Brooks directed As Good As It Gets. Keller found time to get away for a few nights seeing some making him laugh and cry. Make him laugh briefly.

The holidays were melancholy; the season's movies proved to be what the doctor ordered for them, keeping vigil over Cole. The movies viewed made them laugh and cry, perfect to cure their doldrums. Keller and the rest gathered around their holiday dinner, discussing what should be done, especially with no legal rights, unable to assist in a smooth transition. You would think there is a better way. Keller told everyone he was seeing the doctors would allow him to bring Cole home again and let him spend the remainder of his days surrounded by his loved ones. This should be a clever idea because, between the five of them, round-the-clock vigil and the VNA of California assist in the medical aspect. Janine had been staying connected with the two, who did a wonderful job with their parents in St. Louis, and asked who to call in Los Angeles.

Chapter Forty

T he holidays were rough. New Year's was over but with little but not much fanfare, so now on into February, arriving rather quickly.

It was close to Valentine's Day, and Keller wanted nothing more than to have his partner home. After an in-depth conversation with doctors, it was decided, in the best interest of Keller and Janine, to take Cole home and have him surrounded by his loved ones.

Prior to the 70th Oscar nominations announcement on February 10th, the hospital released Cole on the 9th, and the day before, on the 8th, VNA stopped to set up what was needed to ensure Cole's comfort. Back to square one, the doctors said don't be looking for miracles, this time, warning Keller, this is it. Cole is at death's door. Fighting back tears, both Keller and Janine were reminded that the severity of Cole's seizure was a signal from the Lord above; it was time to let him go. Fourteen nominations went to

AND THE OSCAR GOES TO...

James Cameron's Titanic. Affleck and Damon's screenwriting debut, Good Will Hunting, scored nine nominations, As Good As It Gets received seven, and both Amistad and The Full Monty received four. A few pieces of Oscar trivia: Best Actress and Best Supporting Actress nominees Kate Winslet and eighty-five-year-old Gloria Stuart were nominated for playing the same character in Titanic. Jack Nicholson was in line for his third award, and his co-star, Helen Hunt, was vying for possible Oscar history. If they both win, it would be only the seventh time that both leading roles accomplish the feat. Titanic, resting on laurels with fourteen nominations and a possible Best Picture win, could be the first since Sound of Music without a screenwriting nomination. If it won more than eleven awards, it would be the most won in history.

As mentioned, technical awards are presented a few weeks after the announced nominees; Beau and Keller were disappointed not attending this year. This year's ceremony was held at the Regent Wilshire in downtown Beverly Hills on February 28th and hosted by a newcomer to Hollywood, Ashley Judd, one-third of country and western singing duo, , the Judds. Ashley chose acting as her occupation, and her mother, Naomi, and sister, Wynonna, chose country music; luck would be bestowed on all three having luxurious careers.

It was a given; Keller and Janine stayed home with Cole, stating she was making a casserole, and the others went without them. The trio said they would stop by before and after the ceremonies to check on Cole. Before the ceremony, Ashlee, Beau, and Carole kept their promise and were met at the door by Keller as Janine prepared salad to go with the casserole. Carole asked Keller how Cole was doing. Keller remarked he hadn't been well the last twelve hours, not breathing well and needing oxygen several times throughout the day. Ashlee remarked they would stay with them instead of going to the Oscars. Keller said no, it would be fine because Janine had made a lovely dinner, watched the Oscars on TV, and looked forward to them stopping by on their way home. The trio hugged the duo goodbye and went by Cole's room to pat his hand and kiss his forehead as a nurse sat by. As the trio was leaving, Beau said, "We will call and check in before they hand out the major awards, okay?" Janine nodded; it would be fine. The brother-sister duo and the nurse quietly ate Janine's casserole and settled in to watch the ceremony. Janine remarked to the nurse the ritual for many years; we were there watching all the glitz and glamour and what fun we had. Keller mentioned the time talking to Streisand, so many shared memories, and mentioning the times Cole ogled the handsome actors. Promptly arriving, the trio was walking towards the auditorium, one of Ashlee's former steno pool co-workers, Laurie Eden, stopped them.

Laurie said, "Hello, Ashlee, long time no see, oh my, you are looking wonderful these days!" Ashlee chuckled, "Oh, it must be the big C!" Laurie, embarrassingly questioning what the big C was. Ashlee, chuckling again, mentioned nothing much, just a round of double cancer in both tits doing wonders. Ashlee continued to say, "You ought to try it sometime; help you with your sour puss outlook on life, Laurie." Having said that, the trio turned face to face, continuing their entrance into the auditorium. Carole said, "That was kind of harsh, Ashlee!" Ashlee remarked the bitch deserved it after the years of shit at the steno pool, especially the unwelcoming of Janine after finding out about her abortion and Cole being gay.

Bill Conti, the musical director, was striking up the band, playing instrumental themes from some of the released movies while the attendees were still assembling in the Shrine Auditorium. This year, it was hosted yet again by Billy Crystal for the sixth time, produced by Gil Cates, and directed by Louis J. Horvitz. Announcer Norman Rose, unseen but heard, was asking everyone to hurry and take their seats as he prepared to introduce Robert Rehme, the Academy President who would welcome the guests and give his opening remarks. On with the ceremony, with dictated tradition, in previous years, supporting award winners presented the first award of the evening. In doing so, Cuba Gooding Jr was presenting the Best Supporting Actress Award. Predictions for this award were swaying towards the sentimental favorite Gloria Stuart in Titanic, or any of the other four nominees would welcome a win. Kim Basinger, for her stunning portrayal of a femme fatale in Curtis Hanson's tribute to the early 20's crime drama film noir, L.A. Confidential, took the honors. Producer Cates decided not to disappoint attendees and viewers this year with yet another tribute in assembling a 70th anniversary present to the Oscars by honoring seventy competitive or honorary past and present winners in a segment Dustin Hoffman introduced as Oscar's Family Album. The seventy were acknowledged one by one by announcer Norman Rose for each of their accomplishments as they were seated onstage, marking the largest gathering assembled since the 50th anniversary in 1978. In between other awards, it was time for the Best Supporting Actor Award, presented this year by the lovely Mira Sorvino. Predictors were debating it to be a two-man race between comedian Robin Williams in Good Will Hunting and comeback heartthrob Burt Reynolds in Boogie Nights. It was a delight seeing Williams take the gold in a different light with dramatic roles. Earlier, while watching at home, Janine and Keller took turns between the not-so-important awards check on Cole and the nurse sitting at the bedside. Midway through the telecast, the nurse mentioned Cole was quite uncomfortable, not meaning to upset Keller, feeling the need for him to come and sit by him. Keller entered the room and held Cole's hand as Janine was talking on the phone with Ashlee. Ashlee called midway through and told Janine about running into the bitch Laurie. Janine was trying to get a word in but finally said in a whisper, "Ashlee, I hate to ruin your evening, but I think you three need to come over quickly. Cole is taking a turn." Ashlee remarked yes, of course, she would get the other two, and they would be on their way. Not missing a beat, Ashlee fought back tears and headed back to her seat. Upon Ashlee reaching the aisle, Carole could see the tears, nudging Beau to say, "It's time, Beau, we need to go!" Beau exclaimed, "What the fuck? They are about to announce Best Actress early." Carole said, "I don't give a God Damn who wins, we need to get to Keller, and I mean NOW!"

The trio hurried out of their seats, running up the aisle to the exit as the valet summoned to get Beau's car. Racing to the car, the trio was twenty-five minutes away from Keller and Cole's apartment, speeding down the highway in total silence. Ashlee and Carole quietly prayed to themselves. Beau arrived at the apartment. Getting out of the car, the three ran down the sidewalk as fast as they could. Arriving at the door, the nurse answered the door, leading them to Cole's bedroom to find Janine and Keller holding each side. Carole and Ashlee sat on each side of them, holding their other hands. Beau stood at the foot of the bed rubbing Cole's feet, mumbling, "Come on buddy, you got this, live, damnit!" Keller told the rest of the room it was too late; it was a matter of time, and needed to let him go. The five surrounded the bed in a circle as Cole took his last breath and one large gasp as though a huge sigh of relief. Carole excused herself to get the nurse. The nurse entered and checked Cole's vitals, and as she moved away from Cole, she said, "I am so sorry, folks, Mr. Cole has expired." Janine and Ashlee held each other in a corner of the room as Beau and Carole stood with Keller massaging his arms and holding him tight, all five fighting back tears.

Keller let out a big scream, "What am I going to do now? He is free of pain, but how will I survive without him." The four left the room quietly, giving Keller time alone with Cole. Entering the living area, Billy Crystal was thanking everyone for watching the telecast as the nurse mentioned a sly comment, that damn Titanic movie won Best Picture. The group found the other winners, too. It's too bad that another sentimental favorite didn't win his first Oscar. Poor Peter Fonda, the favorite loser to his Easy Rider co-star and best buddy, Jack Nicholson, won Best Actor again. Helen Hunt won Best Actress as history has been made, with both winning leading roles in the Oscars, as Titanic won eleven of their fourteen nominations, tying with Ben-Hur. It will be interesting if any future films will tie or pass this record.

Box office receipts on the day nominations were announced

on February 10th were astronomical for a combined gross of $579 million with an average of $116 million for the top five nominees. It was no no-brainer: Best Picture winner Titanic grossed $338.7 million, making it one of the top ten-grossing films at the time. Second place went to As Good As It Gets, which grossed $92.6 million. Good Will Hunting, $68.7 million, and rounding the bottom fourth and fifth were L.A. Confidential, grossing $ 39.7 million and The Full Monty $38.7 million, respectively.

Keller didn't want to leave Cole's side after his passing. Beau went to check on him, telling him Carole would take care of the arrangements. Ashlee and Janine were on the sofa, wrapped in a tight embrace, still crying uncontrollably; Keller walked out of the bedroom, thanking everyone for being here with him. Carole needed to discuss what be done with Cole's body. The five decided the best thing to have Cole cremated and a small gathering for a memorial service. Carole called the Los Angeles County Coroner's office, sending someone right away. Waiting patiently for the Coroner's office, Janine put a pot of coffee on and asked if anybody wanted anything. The nurse was in Cole's room; she called the VNA; they were sending someone over to assist in gathering medical supplies and other items. Beau remembered seeing a billboard about Hollywood Forever; lots of celebrities have been buried there, and have been an institution since 1928. Given the time of evening, not wanting to leave Keller alone, everyone suggested sleeping on the sofa and floor. The Coroner's office arrived close to midnight; the attendants gave Keller a card. By mentioning getting some sleep and a clear mind call when deciding which crematorium to use. Keller nodded a yes. As they carried Cole's lifeless body out the door, kissing him one last time. Carole searched the closet for more linens to make a pallet on the floor, and Beau and she would sleep there. Ashlee and Janine pulled the sofa bed out, telling Keller to get some rest and that they discussed more in the morning. Janine hugged her brother and said, "Big brother, if you need anything, just holler off. If you want, I can come and cuddle with you like we did in our younger days." Keller said, "That would be nice, sis. I need getting used to sleeping alone."

The next morning came earlier than expected. Nobody got any sleep; it was about 6:45. Keller quietly crept into the kitchen, started coffee, and looked in the fridge to fix breakfast. The remaining four stood up from their sleeping positions to see Keller peering over the pass-through window to say, "Morning, everyone. Who wants pancakes?" Ashlee let out a big HELL YEAH! Janine jumped up, racing to the kitchen to help Keller. Janine told her big brother to set the table and let her finish preparing breakfast. Breakfast was done, and the dishes were cleaned and put away. The Oscar attendees would have to eat, run home to shower, change clothes, and race back to the apartment to help Keller finalize Cole's funeral arrangements. Carole told Keller while they were home, she would call Hollywood Forever and get quotes for him to discuss upon their return later in the afternoon. Janine had her car, kissing Keller bye for now, saying she and Ashlee would be back too. Keller was alone for the first time in the few hours after Cole's passing; it was sort of a relief but didn't feel like being alone. Wanting to hear music, Keller went to the stereo, selected Streisand for his listening pleasure, and sat in a chair to cry. In the background, you would see Streisand singing The Way We Were and I Found Someone flooding the gates. The phone rang, it was Janine. Janine mentioned she and Ashlee would bring some extra clothes and food to stay for a bit until Keller was ready to be rid of them. Keller said OK.

Carole called to say Beau was having a few chest pains, probably anxiety, and stopping by for a quick check with the doctor, and she called Hollywood Forever. Carole said Hollywood Forever would take care of getting the body from the coroner's office and let her know to set a time for a memorial service, possibly the first of next week. Carole and Beau arrived at Beau's cardiologist, and luckily, they squeezed him before heading over to Keller's. The cardiologist wasn't pleased with what he was hearing through his stethoscope and the readings on the electrocardiogram; he gave Beau a couple of weeks to improve; if not, he wanted him back in the office for a stress test. Beau tried to explain that the last few weeks were quite stressful concerning Cole's illness, but the doctor wasn't buying it. "You probably aren't taking any of your nitro pills, are you?" Carole chimed in, "You are right, Dr. Bierk. Beau has been lax, but we've had so much stress with our friend passed yesterday from HIV."

The doctor related his concern and offered his sympathy but wanted them back in two to three weeks. On the way out of the office, hearing Beau and Carole bicker, with Carole telling Beau I told you so. I knew he wasn't going to be happy.

Arriving at Keller's, Streisand was on the stereo, noticing the ladies returned as well. Carole embraced them and put some food in the freezer. Carole mentioned to Keller he should have plenty of food for a few weeks. Ashlee turned to Beau and said, "What did the heart doctor say?" Beau mentioned trying to elevate stress and come back in two weeks for a stress test. The five sat around the dining table playing cards when Janine mentioned when we have Cole's memorial. We should invite some from the studios. Ashlee stated don't bother. All those people there are so two-faced and backstabbers, and we saw one last night at the Oscars. Laurie, the cunt from steno pool, what a piece of work complimenting me; so plastic, I hate her fucking guts. Enough of this. It looks like things were set. Hollywood Forever told Carol their staff could finish embalming and cremation by Friday or Saturday, which is April 3rd and 4^{th,} and on Monday, the 6^{th,} their chapel could host the five for a small memorial service and give Keller Cole's ashes to take home.

AND THE OSCAR GOES TO...

Despite Cole's loss, life goes on. Keller was much a recluse, listening to music and reading all the time, and Janine and Ashlee were doing their best, ensuring he was eating right and visiting with him every other day. Carole and Beau were seeing Keller on opposite days, and in between Beau's cardio appointments, his stress test was scheduled for April 10th, the Friday of the same week of Cole's services. It wasn't looking good for Beau; he was sure of it. Dr. Bierk was going to give the talk. Beau remained calm and listened attentively to everything the doctor had to say. Luckily, Beau had Carole in for the appointment, or he is royally fucked. Dr. Bierk laid down the law to both.: Cut out red meat, eat fish, do egg substitutes, refrain from any rigorous sexual activity, take meds, and come back in a month.

In the interim, lists of movies for the upcoming season were being distributed so they could start figuring out what was going to be released in the next several months. Looks like there will be plenty to choose from. One foreign film had everyone speculating that this could be one that put Italy back on the map to prove successful in the United States as well. The film Life Is Beautiful was a masterpiece paying homage to the Italian romantic of yesteryear by famed director Roberto Benigni. Everyone was raving about it before it was even released. So many others were included:

Life Is Beautiful	Affliction	Shakespeare In Love	Saving Private Ryan	Primary Colors
A Simple Plan	Gods and Monsters	Elizabeth	The Thin Red Line	Bulworth Armageddon
The Truman Show	Pleasantville	American History X	What Dreams May Come	
Patch Adams	Mulan	A Bug's Life	The Horse Whisperer	

Those were just a few upcoming in the next several months. Hopefully, everyone can get Keller out of the house, enjoying life again going to the Grove for dinners and drinks, movies, and other fun things. First and foremost, it will be quite an undertaking; we need to ensure Beau gets a clean bill of health from the cardiologist, the mean but sarcastic Dr. Bierk. Dr. Bierk isn't playing, though. Carole was taking him seriously, but Beau wanted to keep jogging, running, working out, and other forms of exercise and not taking his nitro pills when he was in pain. Carole found his pill box full the other day, and she about had a heart attack. Carole told the others she needed help and didn't know what to do. Carole had always been the strong one for others, so stoic and didn't seem to let things bother her; deep down, you could see her hurting. Janine and Ashlee promised to help as best they could.

Late spring and early summer were around the corner, meaning the group thought about a summer getaway. Traveling to the southwestern part of the United States to see Arizona, New Mexico, and Texas before it got too hot and humid was on the agenda. Beau and Carole went to see Dr. Bierk. Bierk was pleased, urging reinforce his eating habits, use nitro tablets, and minimize his excessive exercise regimen. Beau was jogging every day, began a brisk walk instead, and quit trying to be a he-man. The gang made plans; they would pool their resources by renting an RV for the Southwest road trip. This trip should be fun, getting Keller out after losing Cole, Ashlee feeling about herself after her reconstructive surgery, Beau needing not let his heart issues bother him, and with Carole and Janine whipping the group in shape, there shouldn't be anything to worry about. The journey begins with sing-along-ranging show tunes to pop hits from Streisand, The Carpenters, Rod Stewart, Billy Joel, and others. So far, so good. Deciding to set camp around Las Vegas on the first day was a wise move; Janine started getting motion sickness from the altitude of the mountain, but she was fine. The laughter from the gang traveling was infectious great Keller was having a fun time, smiling, laughing, and telling jokes. Over to Phoenix for a few days to Albuquerque and then Dallas. Beau mentioned getting to Dallas, they must see Dealey Plaza to get his Kennedy fix. In Albuquerque, they ate Green chili turkey cheeseburgers at the Owl Cafe and Mexican food at Sadie's; instead of traditional rolled enchiladas, they were flat, and instead of beans, there were potatoes. Traveling east of Albuquerque before leaving, stopped at Sandia Peak and did the tramway. From Albuquerque, the five decided to drive to Dallas. Breaking up the trip, they stayed overnight in Amarillo.

Upon arrival in Dallas, the friends decided to go to Dealey Plaza and tour the Sixth Floor Museum. All in all, it was a great trip. Beau was excited to see where Kennedy was assassinated, Keller thoroughly enjoyed himself, giving the four a big thank you for helping him get his life back on track, and Ashlee enjoyed breathing the mountain air of Sandia Peak. Before leaving Dallas, they had to have their share of Tex-Mex eating at the original El Fenix off McKinney Avenue, Dickey's Barbeque walk around the West End Marketplace and downtown area seeing Neiman Marcus.

Heading back to California, they headed in the RV with a new cheerful and happy outlook on life. Seeking normalcy and adjusting to their old routine of watching movies. Proving to be their escape mechanism, Beau and Keller were bonding over Saving Private Ryan with their electrifying war scenes by saying Spielberg found his niche in the war genre. Armageddon, a space flick laced with family drama, brightened up the screen surprised with a twist of Aerosmith singing the theme song. Adding a spice of nepotism to the mix, Liv Tyler was in the movie, and Dad Steven Tyler was doing the theme. Come on! LOL

AND THE OSCAR GOES TO…

The year ended with apparently everyone in good health and prepared for the holidays. All was good! Beau was getting good vibes from Dr. Bierk and Ashlee from her oncologist, no lumps on her new boobies. All is good. Janine and Ashlee were offering to do Christmas and New Year's dinner over at their place, making it a bit easier on Keller. No argument there.

Chapter Forty-One

D espite their loss, 1998 ended on a positive note. The five remaining friends had a great summer, and the holiday sped up, preparing for an interesting 1999. Among the movies, there looked like a few surprises come Oscar time. Foreign films were making a resurgence, proving to be a fixture in filmgoer's lists of must-sees. Roberto Benigni warmed hearts and soothed souls; the war movie genre paved a path for men to see movies again, and women admired historical drama with their stories and costumes.

On a personal level, Keller was more outgoing than ever, attending a grief support group for HIV at the resource center. Ashlee was on her way to doing a support group at the breast cancer center and being a sponsor for other women suffering from the disease. Janine continued her busy genealogy research, warming her heart concerning her and Keller's ancestry. Carole and Beau were enjoying being together, taking side trips to the East Coast to see

AND THE OSCAR GOES TO…

Broadway plays and musicals, and yes, Beau was watching his heart issues.

The Oscar nominations were announced on February 9th, and the Technical Awards were going to be held again at the Regent Beverly Wilshire, with Anne Heche hosting. Beau and Keller made a promise to each other they would attend after a few years of absence. Attending, meeting up with their friends who had heard about Cole, being kind in offering their condolences, and checking on Beau's health scare were thoughtful. What were the odds? Shakespeare in Love scored a lucky thirteen nominations, eleven for Saving Private Ryan and seven for Life Is Beautiful, the brilliant Italian film by Benigni. Benigni's film was the first to be nominated for Best Picture since Z in 1969, coupled with seven nominations, the record for most for a foreign film. A few extra bits of trivia: Benigni became the second director to direct himself, coupled with a Best Director and Best Actor nomination since Laurence Olivier in Hamlet in 1948. Benigni was the fourth person to secure nominations for acting, directing, and screenwriting for the same film. Two different films characterizing Queen Elizabeth I of England gave nominations to Cate Blanchett and Judi Dench in the Best Actress and Best Supporting Actress categories for Elizabeth and Shakespeare In Love, respectively. Two political comedies from Warren Beatty and John Travolta, Bulworth and Primary Colors, respectively, showed Oscar promise.

Five weeks away from the Oscar ceremony, we were giving our friends ample time to view the films and performances nominated. It was like old times: honor Cole with a toast and celebrate both Ashlee and Beau's clean bill of health.

The Oscar ceremony was on March 21st at the Dorothy Chandler Pavilion with Whoopi Goldberg as hostess, her third time at the dais with Gil Cates and Louis V. Horvitz producing and directing respectively yet again. The ceremony was on Sunday for the first time; Academy President Rehme was hoping for much better television ratings and viewership, given last year was the highest rated ever. Sunday night traffic and fewer transportation issues aside, Beau made it to the venue a little earlier than anticipated. Being the first ceremony without Cole, it was sentimental; before heading out of the car to the valet, Keller mentioned doing a shot of tequila before parking the car. LOL. The group gave the valet keys and walked down the sidewalk, glancing over the red carpet to see if they recognized anyone. Beau mentioned seeing Tom Hanks and Rita Wilson and noticed the glamorous Sophia Loren. Arriving earlier than normal meant one thing: hit the cash! Alrighty then! Inside the pavilion, the cash bar nearest to the restroom and auditorium entry was their first stop for bubbly. Bill Conti started his preliminary music warm-ups, hurrying the crowd to their seat, a loud voice over the PA system; instead of Norman Rose, Randi Thomas made a return to the voice-over. "Will all attendees please take your seats!" The gang was excited for Goldberg; what would she crack jokes at? Thomas introduced Academy President Reheme, continued the tradition of welcoming guests and viewers, turning over and introducing Goldberg dressed in a costume like Elizabeth poking fun at the actresses Blanchett and Dench.

The ceremony began with its continued tradition. One of the Best Supporting category winners was announced. Last year's winner, Kim Bassinger, announced James Coburn won. This category nominated two previous Best Actor winners, two up-and-coming celebrities, and a veteran tough guy often overlooked, so it was no surprise when the tough guy prevailed, wrestling his way to victory for his role as an alcoholic father in Paul Schrader's moody Affliction. In between other presented awards, two dueling divas, Mariah Carey and Whitney Houston, appeared to sing "When You Believe" from Prince of Egypt. This beautiful arrangement was one of five nominees for Best Original Song, and it eventually won. This wasn't the first time the two had sung the song; they appeared together on Oprah a few weeks before to perform it and promote their latest music.

Contrary to belief, speculation pushed the envelope, starting rumors that the two divas didn't like each other and, afterward, put it to rest; they became friends. Gil Cates would often do tributes, not to disappoint and be different; coupled with the traditional In

Memoriam segment, there were two separate tributes. One was a separate tribute to Frank Sinatra, presented by John Travolta, and another was presented by Val Kilmer, saluting Gene Autry and Roy Rogers. After the In Memoriam segment, Goldberg and Spielberg respectively acknowledged film critic Roger Ebert and film director Stanley Kubrick as well. Robin Williams presented the Best Supporting Actress award to Judi Dench for her brief role as Elizabeth I in the comedy Shakespeare In Love. Dench was nominated amongst past Best Actress winners Kathy Bates, veteran actress Lynn Redgrave, English actress Brenda Blethyn, and Australian actress Rachel Griffiths. Despite the comedy of Goldberg, the ceremony dragged slowly, and in between the honorary Oscars given to directors Elia Kazan, presented by DeNiro, and Scorsese and Norman Jewison, presented by Nicolas Cage, Helen Hunt appeared. Last year's Best Actress winner, Hunt, presented the Best Actor award to a list of nominees ranging from Hanks, Nolte, Edward Norton, Ian McKellen, and Roberto Benigni. Benigni had previously won Best Foreign Film; hearing his name, he climbed over the seats to stand up before approaching the stage; it's a blessing he didn't hurt himself. You would wonder if Benigni knew he won when Loren walked on stage to present Best Foreign Film. After all, both are Italian! Hunt announced Benigni as the Best Actor winner, receiving his second Oscar of the evening, and remarked that he had run out of English, bringing laughter from the audience. By given Best Actor, Benigni was the first to win in a non-speaking-English role. With a few more awards and tributes in between, it was time for the Best Actress to be presented by Nicholson. The nominees ranged from veteran Streep, foreign actresses Australian Blanchett, English Emily Watson, Brazilian Fernanda Montenegro, and rising star ingénue Gwyneth Paltrow. Paltrow was announced the winner. Kevin Costner presented Best Director to Spielberg for his war drama, Saving Private Ryan, and ending the evening after almost four hours, Harrison Ford presented Best Picture to Shakespeare In Love. Tradition usually awards both to the same films; apparently, it was a surprise to select few, which included celebrities and critics alike.

Box office receipts from the top five Best Picture nominees the day nominations were announced on February 9th combined a gross of $309 million, averaging $60.4 million per film. It was no surprise that Saving Private Ryan exceeded their expectations, amounting to $194.2 million in domestic box office sales by slaughtering its competition. Best Picture winner, Shakespeare In Love, grossed $36.5 million, Thin Red Line $30.6 million, Elizabeth $21.5 million, and Best Foreign Film, Life Is Beautiful, rounded out the top five with $18.4 million. Caching! Box office was over the top in the last few years, and dollars kept rolling in.

Here we are about to face a new year, a new century, an election year. 2000, hard to believe forty years of friendship with this group hard to believe. Several months to go until 2000, given the wide variety of films to see and discuss, their potential was on the radar. Some of these were:

American Beauty	The Hurricane	Boys Don't Cry	The Insider	Sweet and Lowdown	
Magnolia	Music of the Heart	Tumbleweeds	The End of the Affair	The Green Mile	Fight Club
The Sixth Sense	Girl, Interrupted	Being John Malkovich	The Matrix	Topsy-Turvy	

Given this roster of films, one must remember that life is short, and you never know what is going to happen. That is why you count your blessings; tomorrow is never promised. Take one day at a time; wake up smelling the coffee and the flowers because life isn't taken for granted. Enjoy every second, minute, hour, day, week, month, and year to the fullest, as it is your last. Life changes in an instant because, who knows, whatever happens, it is for a reason, and it will have a profound effect on all our lives.

April showers bring May flowers. Janine woke early to work on her genealogy research and started coffee when the phone rang. Answering it in her cheery voice, the person at the end of the line said it was the Oncology Center of Los Angeles inquiring where Ashlee was. Janine mentioned she was asleep and asked if needed to wake her. The representative said she should have Miss Guthrey call at her earliest convenience and reschedule; she missed her 8:30 appointment. One would wonder, after all the years in the hustle and bustle of the steno pool, Ashlee would have kept her sense of urgency. Not! Ashlee had not been totally honest with the group. They were having such a wonderful time saluting Cole's memory of her recovery, and Beau just didn't see the time to tell.

Janine wrote down the number and went about her research. At about 10 am, the sleepy head woke up and headed straight to the coffee. Janine said, "Morning, sunshine!" Ashlee mumbled a good morning to you, too. Janine chuckled to say, "What do you want to do today? See a movie, lunch at the Grove, what's on your agenda?" Ashlee said she first wanted her headache to go away and was taking some Tylenol. Ashlee walked into the bathroom; looking in the mirror, she checked her breasts and a lump she had noticed a few weeks before but, of course, no mention to the others. Ashlee went ahead, brushed her teeth, gargled, and showered to examine her body further. While showering, Ashlee noticed a lump on her throat as well, fearing the worst; her thyroid was acting up again. Finishing drying herself off, Ashlee ran to her room and put on her clothes. Then, acting if nothing was wrong, she got a cup of coffee and said, "Janine, how's the research going?"

Janine says, "Not too bad, so when do we need to go see the oncologist again?" Ashlee said, "Don't pull this crap, what is today?" Janine mentioned it was the 10th of May. Ashlee then said,

"Oh shit, I missed it!" Janine remarked that while Ashlee was playing Sleeping Beauty, the oncology center called to say she missed her earlier 8:30 appointment and asked her to call and reschedule. Janine wondered if Ashlee was going to say something was bothering her. Ashlee said I was going to wait till after the Oscars and hoped it would go away before the appointment. Janine went on to say, "We can't keep secrets; we need to reschedule now, ok?" Ashlee apologized and went to the phone to call. Lucky for her, she could be seen later that afternoon at three if it were ok. Perfect! "I am so sorry; I thought it would be best if I tried to handle this alone. I didn't want anyone alarmed," Ashlee said. Mentioned they can go at three today; as Janine mentioned, let's call Carole and ask her to go with us for women's support. Ashlee went on to say it wasn't going to be a good day. Carole was taking Beau back to the cardiologist. Janine said, "What about Keller then?" Ashlee mentioned not to bother him; he has been through so much, so let him enjoy his quiet time.

About 2:30, the girls had lunch and it was time to drive to the oncology center. Ashlee appeared very nervous as Janine tried to calm her by trying to make her laugh, but it was not working. Ashlee, "Janine, it's not working. I know I should have gone sooner!"

Janine recanted, "Honey, don't worry, it's going to be ok." Arriving at the center, Janine parked the car, letting Ashlee outrunning to the office, telling her she would meet her in shortly. As soon as Janine got to the clinic office, she noticed Ashlee wasn't in the reception area. A nurse said she had already taken her back for testing. Ashlee felt alone as the doctor examined her and mentioned to him this had happened since January. Dr. Baines said you shouldn't have waited because the nodules on her throat were abnormal, as well as the lumps on her breasts. Dr. Baines added he was certain her cancer had returned and said, "We have two options: 1. We can do chemo and radiation or 2. just let it ride its course; what would you prefer because I am giving you six months to a year?" Given the options Cole faced with his HIV, Ashlee was scared and didn't exactly know how to feel. Ashlee began to cry; Janine, in the reception area, heard the sobs, and she recognized them. Immediately, Janine knew something was wrong as she began to pray. Ashlee maintained her composure, walking down the long hall to the reception area, where Janine was waiting with open arms. The two ladies embraced, leaving the clinic, and went to the parking lot for the ride back home. The silence was golden on the ride home, and it couldn't be any quieter; you could have heard a pin drop. Once home, Ashlee explained to Janine what Dr. Baines mentioned about possibly having only six months to a year and a combination of chemo and radiation could help, but she was afraid it had spread. Janine mentioned we will get through this with the help and love of friends, not to worry!

Meanwhile, Carole was at the cardiologist with Beau, hoping for better results. Beau had been complaining of severe back and chest pains lately, usually meaning angina pectoris; it's what the nitro pills were for. Waiting patiently in the reception area amongst other heart patients was making Beau impatient and nervous as hell, and finally, around 3:45, a nurse came to the door, "Beau Madison, Mr. Madison, we will see you now." The couple stood up to head towards the door and down a long hallway to the examining room. Within a few minutes, cardiologist Dr. Garris appeared and inquired being Beau's problem. Beau and Carole explained the pain and n sweating profusely after his exercise. The doctor inquired if any stress, depression, and/or a sad event occurred. Beau explained that he was still grieving the death of a good friend and a fellow gal pal undergoing cancer care; other than that, he and Carole were happy in their marriage, enjoying traveling with friends and together just the two of them. Dr. Garris explained to Carole and Beau he is a prime candidate for a bypass and should have a consultation with a surgeon. Carole begins to cry upon hearing this news. Dr. Garris said he could refer Beau to Dr. Zambrano and strongly suggested talking with him as soon as possible. Sadly, the couple walked out of the office again, down the hall, out the door to the car. Sitting in the car, Carole reached over to hug Beau and said, "You want me to drive, sweetheart?" Beau said, "Sure honey, if you don't mind, it's all yours!"

After the day our two friends had at the doctor's, it calls for drinks and dinner. Carole and Beau stopped by Keller's and told them what happened at the doctor's, and he was literally shocked to hear what had been going on. Carole tried to explain having so much on his plate; there was no adding to it. They didn't want to upset him. Keller called Janine to say the trio was headed to the Grove; Ashlee and her would meet them about 6 pm, depending on traffic. Janine mentioned Ashlee had a bad report from the doctor as well and will be there in a few days. Keller explained to Janine they were heading close to where the accident happened several years ago, and would that be unsettling for them. The restaurant was Chez Jay, famous for their surf and turf complete with New York Angus steak and lobster tail as well other noted items: patty melt, smoked salmon melt, and not mention seafood salad with a "secret" dressing, mixed greens, bay shrimp and king crab legs. YUMMMM.

Traffic was busy; close to 6:30, everyone was thirsty and hungry after the long day. Finally, everyone was settled at their table and the server arrived to tell them the specials and asked if anyone wanted a drink. Beau spoke first; everyone needs a glass of champagne and a bloody Mary for starters and bring us calamari rings, shrimp cocktail and parmesan truffle fries to share. As they waited on their drinks and appetizers, Keller said, "I am so terribly sorry everyone had a sad day at the doctor; please don't spare me from the unsettledness. Honestly, I am ok!" Everyone wants to protect Keller; he is like a baby brother you wish he could spoil with lollipops. Ashlee said, "I am sorry to keep everything you all, and here Janine is living with me; it's a wonder she didn't notice." Carole added, "We are family; it's been such a tight-knit group forever; we just need to trust each other more than ever."

"Here here, let's not make this night sad about forgiveness, drink and eat up like we haven't before," Janine said. The server asked if everything was ok and ready to order entrees. Beau said they were clearing the table for another round of drinks and then ordering. In about ten minutes, the server had the table cleared, and everyone had a fresh cocktail; before ordering, there was one round of business that needed to be taken care of: the men had to go to the restroom, and the ladies had to powder their noses. Who wants to go first? Ashlee chuckled in laughter to say, "You men and your teeny-weeny bladders, go relieve yourselves! Poof! Be gone!" Keller said, "Well, you bitches better hurry up because when we get back, dinner will be ordered, and we aren't leaving this place till everything is gone, food and drink and dessert and all." LOL.

In a split second, the server stopped by the men we were talking to, and he said, "Gents, would you like to order the entrees for the table?" Beau said, "Yes, we are ready. Are you ready?" LOL. Here we go; we would like Chicken Marsala, Swordfish, Salmon, Chateaubriand Filet Mignon w/ sides of rice pilaf and loaded baked potato. For dessert, two sticky toffee puddings, three cheesecakes, and espresso vodka martinis for after-dinner drinks. That was enough to keep us full and not wanting anything for the next two or three days. The meals, drinks, appetizers, and desserts were delicious, and now it was time to figure out who was the most sober to drive two cars and five people home. This was so much fun, as Judy Garland sang, "Forget your troubles, get happy." This is one meal to cherish for a lifetime. Too bad Cole wasn't there, he was such a kindred spirit and their guardian angel of all angels. Rest in peace, my friend! We miss you so much!

Luckily, everyone made it home to their respective apartments in one piece. Carole and Beau gave Keller a ride to his place but didn't leave right away. Keller invited them in for a quick cup of coffee. Carole was fine; she was more worried about Beau and Ashlee. The pact wasn't broken; Janine and Ashlee didn't reveal their sad news.

Everyone must remember to be strong for each other; it's a path we must take to survive and try our hardest to live our way in such a way to be loved. Regardless of what happens from here on out, this journey has been filled with so many adventures, and no matter the ups and down or the peaks and valleys, we are survivors. Call it what you may; it's the place we end in the afterlife. Our dreams weren't shattered; they were real to live out the best moments in life one day at a time.

The ladies made it home successfully; Ashlee called over to Keller's to ensure he made it home safely at the hands of Carole and Beau. Janine had already gone to bed; she passed out cold in bed. Keller mentioned to Ashlee the three of them were having coffee before their drive home. "Oh, how I wish I were there with you three. Keller, you have been such an angel to keep us together after losing Cole, I can't begin to thank you enough. It's been a blessing to have you and your little sister, Janine, join our clique. I will forever be grateful to you. I love you so much! Goodnight!" Keller placed the phone back in the cradle as he said back to Ashlee, "Goodnight sweet princess Ashlee, I love you so!" Little did Keller realize this would be the last conversation he would have with Ashlee. Janine was out of it she couldn't hear a thing. Ashlee went into the kitchen to a bottle of Vodka from the liquor cabinet and stumbled into the bathroom for her Seconal bottle. Ashlee hadn't been sleeping of late and often took Seconal to ease her sleeping. Ashlee had both bottles in each hand and was lying on the bed but before she laid down, she grabbed some stationery from her nightstand. She wrote:

Janine, Beau, Carole and Keller,

It's been a fun ride for the six of us, but I feel a part of me died when Cole passed; I missed him terribly, more than ever imagined. Cole was like a big brother to me and made me feel so welcome when I came to Hollywood from Iowa. Cole was my strength, my knight in shining armor, and my protector. Thinking this is the only way to join him in the heavens above is to do the same as my sweet Momma did. Momma may have been a bitch to me, but she did love me as I love you all from the bottom of my heart. Have fun at the Oscars in 2000!

Love, Ashlee

After writing the note, Ashlee placed it by the coffee maker because, usually first thing Janine is making coffee. Walking back into her room, Ashlee took the Seconal bottle, emptied the contents into her left hand, and grabbed with her right hand the Vodka bottle outstretched her left to her mouth, taking a few quick swigs of the Vodka bottle and laid across her bed for her final sleep. Ashlee was gone in the next hours before dawn. The early morning sun through Janine's window didn't faze her. Still, she lay in bed with her clothes still on, curled in a fetal position. A few more hours passed, and Janine glanced at her clock; the digital read 10:15. Janine screamed out, "It's late. Oh my God, Ashlee, you awake." Not hearing anything, she went into the bathroom to take a leak before starting the coffee. Janine noticed it odd Ashlee's bedroom door was shut all the way, usually, she left it open so they could talk to each other to sleep. Not this day. walking into the kitchen, Janine yelled again, "Ashlee, wake up; coffee will be ready in five minutes." Janine walked closer, finishing the coffee, she saw the note. Janine read it silently, then read it out aloud; it raced through her mind. Certainly,

Ashlee didn't do what I think she did. She couldn't have. Racing to Ashlee's room, she knocked, pounded on the door and walked in to find Ashlee still in clothes from the prior night. Janine checked for a pulse; Ashlee wasn't breathing, and her body was cold to the touch. Janine screamed out, "Ashlee, how could you?" First things first, Janine called Keller. Keller was in and out of slumber and walked over to grab the phone in the living room, only to find Carole and Beau on each end of the couch sleeping soundly.

Keller answered the phone; it was Janine crying hysterically Ashlee is gone, Ashlee is gone. Keller said, "Are you sure? Let me wake Carole and Beau up, and we will be over, ok? And don't touch anything else." Keller woke Carole first since she was more sober than the rest of the gang. Carole woke up fast; she said, "What is it?" Keller told Carole to wake Beau up first then he would say. Carole woke Beau up; it took a while, but finally, he was wide-eyed. Keller mentioned we need to get Ashlee's; Janine just called. Ashlee has taken an overdose and is unresponsive. Carole started crying hysterically, running to the bathroom with a washcloth to wipe her and Beau's faces. Keller said, "I can't believe this is happening; it just can't be true." Carole told Keller he could drive as she and Beau were still trying to stay alert.

Keller sped as fast as he could to Ashlee's apartment. Janine met them at the door, crying uncontrollably, leading them to the bedroom. Carole checked Ashlee's pulse as well, feeling cold to the touch; she slapped Ashlee's face a bit, nothing, no heartbeat, nothing. Keller told Janine to call 911 and go down to the apartment manager's office. Janine did as she told; a few minutes lapsed, and Janine and the manager returned as the paramedics arrived. The paramedics told everyone to go into the living room while they worked on Ashlee. Thirty minutes passed, and one of the paramedics walked out to deliver the sad news. Ashlee was gone. The lead paramedic inquired if Ashlee had been depressed of late; Janine related that she found out from her oncologist yesterday she had only six months to a year left as her cancer had spread. When hearing this, the trio was at a loss for words, especially given they didn't talk much about their medical woes; all caring about was having fun. Carole mentioned that's why Ashlee was happy in wanting to have the best time ever and Keller related the strange phone call last night. All the pieces of the puzzle were slowly coming together. The paramedics wheeled Ashlee's body out of the bedroom and told the four she would be at the coroner's office for an autopsy and released in two to three days.

NOW, THERE WERE FOUR

Dumbfounded and numb, everyone is stunned, shocked beyond disbelief. Usually, when a death occurs, one is mad at the Lord for taking their loved one, then the questioning of Why? How? We might wonder if this death of our friend is different than when Cole passed away a year earlier. Ashlee's death was sudden and unexpected, as Cole's was inevitable given his illness. One thing we must take away when someone passes away as grief is universal, and we experience it in diverse ways. Allow me to end this by helping others who have experienced loss. Swiss-American psychiatrist Elisabeth Kubler-Ross developed five stages of grief, but over many years, others have added two to seven more stages to make a better sense of dealing with death, and they don't happen all in order; you experience it various times in your life:

1. Denial-Most common as the survivor carries on initially as if nothing ever happened
2. Anger-The feeling you didn't do enough or had planned something with your loved one
3. Bargaining-The feeling of "what if" not doing enough to keep them here
4. Depression-The sadness surrounding the loss
5. Acceptance-You have carried on with your life and gone on

Over the years, other clinical studies have added shock and testing, as others added guilt, confusion, loneliness, hope, and renewal. On the other end of the spectrum, there are three C's as well from Kettering Health Organization:

1. Choose-We choose the time to grieve
2. Connect-Stay connected with others
3. Communicate-Tell your loved ones how you are feeling

AND THE OSCAR GOES TO...

English researcher and clinical psychologist Therese Rando developed seven steps to handling grief:

1. Recognize-Understand what happened
2. React-Let the emotions out
3. Recollect-Remember the memories of the past
4. Re-Experience-Review what was done and what was felt
5. Relinquish-Put the loss behind you, accept what has happened
6. Readjust-Return to your normal routine
7. Reinvest-Form new friendships and relationships

Enough of this, the verdict was in; it is true Ashlee Guthrey passed away from suicide, a combination of alcohol and an overdose of Seconal, the exact same thing her mother passed from. It is so sad; one would think she didn't want to suffer from cancer and felt necessary to end her life. Ashlee always thought more of other's needs ahead of her own and didn't want her friends to watch her wilt away like a flower and take care of her as seen with Keller and Cole. Now, our friends are left with the decision of what kind of "sendoff" they should give their beloved Ashlee. Ashlee had no living relatives; her mother passed away years after they arrived in Hollywood, and she only had the remaining friends here. Carole suggested her mother bury her. Janine and Keller were suggesting cremation like Cole; this way, they can have something to be reminded of her. Decisions, decisions.

TIM J. CULBERTSON

While our friends decide on how they will remember Ashlee, here are some expressions to uplift your heart in case you have experienced loss and need some reassurance

STRENGTH doesn't just appear. It's something

we develop over time through

our ability and perseverance

to overcome obstacles.

It grows with each challenge we face

EMBRACE IT … we've earned it

FRIENDSHIP is a PRICELESS GIFT

That cannot be bought or sold

But its value is far greater

Than a mountain of gold

For gold is cold and lifeless,

It can neither see nor hear

And in the times of trouble

It is powerless to cheer

It has no ears to listen

AND THE OSCAR GOES TO...

No heart to understand

It cannot bring you comfort

Or reach out a helping hand

So, when you ask GOD for a GIFT

Be thankful if HE sends

Not diamonds, pearls, or riches

But the LOVE of

REAL TRUE FRIENDS

LIFE IS A CONSTANTLY CHANGING THING. LIFE CAN SEND YOU THROUGH SO

MANY UPS AND DOWNS. LIFE CAN BE QUITE DIFFICULT AND UNPREDICTABLE.

LIFE CAN BE CRAZY AND EXTREME. THROUGH ALL THE TRIALS

AND TRIBULATIONS LIFE MAY SEND YOUR WAY, YOU CAN ONLY TAKE IT ONE

STEP AT A TIME, ONE MOMENT AT A TIME. YOU CAN ONLY SMILE AND HOPE

FOR THE BEST POSSIBLE OUTCOME BASED ON THE

CIRCUMSTANCES PRESENTED

IN FRONT OF YOU. THINGS DON'T ALWAYS TURN OUT THE WAY YOU WOULD

HAVE HOPED THEY WOULD. FATE AND DESTINY HAS A PLAN FOR ALL OF US ALL.

WE MAY NOT UNDERSTAND WHAT THE PLAN IS OR WHY IT IS. WE JUST RIDE IT OUT AND SEE WHERE IT LEADS US.

LIVE LAUGH AND LOVE! SMILE EVERY DAY! HOLD PEACE IN YOUR HEART!

THE NOTION OF 1 STEP FORWARD 2 STEPS BACK ISN'T ALWAYS A BAD THING,

BECAUSE IT GIVES US TIME TO BREATHE AND THINK AND PROCESS THE STEPS

WE HAVE TAKEN IN LIFE.

KEEP MOVING FORWARD!

IN LIFE,

YOU WILL FALL OUT WITH PEOPLE THAT YOU NEVER THOUGHT

YOU WOULD. GET BETRAYED BY PEOPLE YOU

TRUSTED

WITH ALL YOUR HEART. AND GET USED BY PEOPLE YOU WOULD

DO ANYTHING FOR. BUT LIFE ALSO HAS A BEAUTIFUL SIDE TO IT.

YOU WILL GET LOVED BY SOMEONE YOU NEVER WOULD HAVE.

FORM NEW RELATIONSHIPS WITH PEOPLE THAT WILL ESTABLISH

MORE MEANINGFUL AND STRONGER RELATIONSHIPS.

AND OVERCOME THINGS YOU NEVER THOUGHT YOU GET OVER.

WE ALL HAVE CHAPTERS THAT END WITH PEOPLE

AT SOME POINT IN LIFE. BUT TAKE PRIDE IN KNOWING

THAT THE VERY BEST PART OF YOUR BOOK

IS STILL BEING WRITTEN

These four thoughts ring true for everyday life when faced with valuing your friendship with others. Perhaps these will give an uplift on life's outlook when dealing with love and the death of a loved one. Enjoy!

The friends have decided on what to do with Ashlee's remains. After deep soul searching, Carole gave in, being reminded of the love-hate relationship Ashlee had with her mother. Makes perfect sense now; it would be nice to have a part of Ashlee and their shared beautiful friendship in her heart. Carole told Janine she called Hollywood Forever, the same place they had Cole's ashes and memorial. Janine nodded in agreement; it would be perfect. Carole realized after her marriage to Beau caused a drift in their friendship with the location of travels and vacations sealed the deep bond. Their love for movies made it stronger. It was good when Keller and Janine moved to Hollywood, and their friendship strengthened. The six were a talented group of people bonded by love, trust, compassion, and Hollywood. Nobody would ever take it away from them. Despite their opinionated references on how to live their lives, Carole never once raised a finger or was embarrassed by the way Ashlee lived; it was her life that let her enjoy it, and Lord, she did. Lots of memories flooded back to Carole as she made Ashlee's arrangements. Ranging from their first meeting to discussions concerning Ashlee's harassment claims, their location trips, group vacations, happy hour, and dinners at the Grove. The list was endless. One thing Carole was glad she didn't partake in the sex parties. Carole was more conservative and finally happy she met her match, meeting Beau. Carole had waited her whole life for Prince Charming, and despite his stubbornness concerning his health, she let him live the way he wanted.

Months were slowly passing after Ashlee's sudden death, and it was a question of how they could honor her legacy. Carole had other things on her mind as well; she wanted to make sure Beau was healthy and urged him to consider the bypass. Beau had been feeling a bit better, but the loss of Ashlee left him depressed; he couldn't grasp it with losing Cole, too. We have the right to grieve the way we want; there is no timetable as it is with you your entire life. Beau did give in and told Carole to call and make an appointment with the cardiologist. Carole, being the ever-attentive partner, did as she was told. The doctor was booked, but there was a chance they could slide him in a few weeks before Thanksgiving. The receptionist on the phone mentioned they were seeing more and more patients after the holiday rush; some were to feel the guilt after eating so much and not exercising, causing discomfort of sorts, especially not eating right, clogging those arteries. LOL, It was all set—Cardiologist appointment on November 18[th,] 2 pm, the Thursday before Thanksgiving. The Wednesday evening before the appointment, Carole called Janine and Keller, saying she wanted to fix Thanksgiving dinner at her and Beau's place.

Earlier in September, Janine and Keller both wanted to exorcise their demons of the loss of Cole and Ashlee by finding an apartment together. It was only fitting; Keller alone in the same place shared with Cole for little over a year, and Janine had been alone in Ashlee's for a few months. The brother and sister duo found a two-bedroom two-, half-bath den of nearly fifteen hundred square feet in West Hollywood. Keller felt the need for Janine to have an office; she was still doing the Wallace family tree genealogy. The apartment had a nice kitchen and dining area; they could cook more and not be in arms away helping each other prepare meals.

Carole and Beau were hungry. They decided to take a detour before heading to the cardiologist's stop at Inn Out Burger for a quick sandwich. Beau was feeling a little light-headed; before they left, he took a handful of pain meds without telling Carole not to alarm her. The journey began with the duo singing with the radio blaring; neither cared, they couldn't carry a tune; it was releasing and having fun. Blaring on the radio was Marc Anthony's I Need to Know. They decided to go a little out of their way on Highway 10 near Culver City, have their burger, and drive down near Santa Monica pier to look at the water, then to the cardiologist appointment. It was around 12:30, having plenty of time, music blaring, singing, lunch in their bellies, and about to reach Santa Monica pier, Beau started grabbing his chest. Beau was experiencing chest pains as Carole tried turning the blaring radio, looking down in her purse for his nitro pills. Beau's right hand flew up in pain off the steering wheel, pushing Carole towards the passenger door. Trying to move closer, Carole was still looking down in her purse, then looking up and over to Beau clutching his chest; you heard a curdling scream; both looked at each other to say their "I LOVE YOU's" and the car heading off the Santa Monica pier into the water. Beau's car hit the guard rail and into the water head first, and the music blaring Celine Dion's That's the Way It Is.

Pedestrians ran to the scene as fast as they could, but it was too late. One person ran to the nearest pay phone on the pier and told them to call 911. By the time first responders arrived, it was too late; the car was submerged in the water and sticking straight up; it looked like Carole and Beau died on impact from the trauma of hitting the guard rail; Beau had a heart attack, and Carole drowned. There was nothing to be done but stand and wait for the fire department; they arrived as fast as they could, pulling the wreckage and the bodies to shore. Beau was slumped over the wheel as Carole was thrown to the other side. Carole's purse was found; one of the responders opened it to find inside miscellaneous items, most importantly her rosary and address book. The pages were wet, but some numbers were hard to figure out, but near the end read the W's. Wallace was listed, after all these years, still having Mom and Dad Wallace's information listed as Keller's as well. The responder handed it to the police on the scene, and he walked over to the nearest place where the previous pedestrian was called Keller. In big letters above, Keller's name was ICOE, which, duh, means In Case of Emergency. Keller and Janine stopped what they were doing and raced to the scene. Janine reminded Keller this was the exact spot where Tyler, Kane, Zach, and Kylie died; isn't it ironic? Upon arrival at the scene, the wreckages had been pulled up on the concrete slab on the pier. Police were everywhere, and as they parked the car walking up the pier, it was too much to bear, walking down the sidewalk, a policeman was heading their way. Detective Sanchez introduced himself, and apologizing for their loss, he motioned Keller and Janine closer to the wreckage. Horrific as the scene was, the two now had the displeasure of identifying the bodies of Beau and Carole Madison. Hollywood is a cruel place; you live, you die. The brother and sister were alone in Hollywood, left with four dear friends and their parents gone! Life is like a bowl of cherries, but once you enter this world, keep smiling, enjoy it to the fullest, and make the most of it! You may never know who will walk in your life, but you better damn well be sure they stick around. Life is too short! This was the last thing Keller and Janine, both Beau and Carole, gone. What will they do now?

THEN THERE WERE TWO

Epilogue

Keller and Janine decided to cremate the lovebirds. They found a nice curio cabinet to house all the ashes of their loved ones. When the cabinet arrived, they had the delivery driver pit in the corner of Janine's office. Janine was determined to finish the genealogy report on the Wallace family. As one door closes, another opens. In life, there are no promises, no guarantees. The only way in and it's by birth, and the only way out is death. In the following weeks after this horrific chain of events, near 1999's end and the holidays around the corner, Janine and Keller were beside themselves how they were going to carry the legacy of four important people they met years ago. It was their legacies that brought out the best of them, and believed in them when others wouldn't. Ashlee took them under her wing and invited them into the world called Hollywood. Cole gave Keller an unconditional love he would never believe possible. Despite Cole's promiscuous ways, he did love Keller very much, just a funny way of expressing it. Lastly, Beau and Carole, lovebirds, showed everyone how to stay grounded, stay true to oneself, love everyone, treat everyone with respect, and give everybody an opportunity to gain experience and love. Movies were their lives; it was like a blood transfusion blended in their veins; everyone wasn't perfect by any means; they chose the path to live in love, who they wanted to love on their own terms. Footloose, fancy, and free, nobody was going to stop them from being who they wanted to be, not what others wanted them to be. These people were better at knowing each other, coupled with a hard work ethic, making each other a better version of themselves. This is their story! Read 'em and weep.

REST IN PEACE

Cole Forrester 1933-1998

Ashlee Guthrey 1935-1999

Beau Madison 1937-1999

Carole Ziegler-Madison 1934-1999

Reference Page

Wikipedia

Chat GPT

Chris Strodder's Academy Awards Book of Lists: An Unauthorized, Unofficial and Unprecedented History of the Oscars Parts I and II

Kendric Falcon's Big Book of Winners, Losers and Honored Complete guide through all Academy Awards Ceremonies 1929-2023

Elisabeth Kubler-Ross On Death and Dying

Kettering Health Organization Three C's of Grief

Therese Rando The Six to Seven R's Adjustment to Loss

Appendix

ACADEMY AWARDS WINNERS 1929-2024

Disclaimer: In 1929, the first Best Picture award was divided into two categories: Best Picture and Best Unique and Artistic Picture. However, entertainment historians always consider Wings the first Oscar Winner for Best Picture. And Sunrise still needs to be noted, just on a slightly lesser scale. On another note, the Best Supporting Actor and Actress awards were first presented in 1937.

Best Picture, Best Director, Best Actor, Best Actress, Best Supporting Actor, and Best Supporting Actress are here for your reference.

1929

Best Picture   Wings

Best Unique and Artistic Picture   Sunrise

Best Director   (tie) Frank Borzage, Lewis Milestone

Best Actor   Emil Jannings

Best Actress   Janet Gaynor

1930

Best Picture   The Broadway Melody

Best Director   Frank Lloyd

Best Actor   Warner Baxter

Best Actress   Mary Pickford

1931

Best Picture   All Quiet on the Western Front

Best Director   Lewis Milestone

Best Actor   George Arliss

Best Actress   Norma Shearer

1932

Best Picture   Cimarron

Best Director   Norman Taurog

Best Actor   Lionel Barrymore

Best Actress   Marie Dressler

1933

Best Picture	Grand Hotel
Best Director	Frank Borzage
Best Actor	Wallace Beery
Best Actress	Helen Hayes

1934

Best Picture	Cavalcade
Best Director	Frank Lloyd
Best Actor	Charles Laughton
Best Actress	Katharine Hepburn

1935

Best Picture	It Happened One Night
Best Director	Frank Capra
Best Actor	Clark Gable
Best Actress	Claudette Colbert

1936

Best Picture	Mutiny on the Bounty
Best Director	John Ford

AND THE OSCAR GOES TO...

Best Actor   Victor McLaglen

Best Actress   Bette Davis

1937

Best Picture   The Great Ziegfield

Best Director   Frank Capra

Best Actor   Paul Muni

Best Actress   Luise Rainer

Best Supporting Actor   Walter Brennan

Best Supporting Actress   Gale Sondergard

1938

Best Picture   The Life of Emile Zola

Best Director   Leo McCarey

Best Actor   Spencer Tracy

Best Actress   Luise Rainer

Best Supporting Actor   Joseph Schildkraut

Best Supporting Actress   Alice Brady

1939

Best Picture   You Can't Take It with You

Best Director   Frank Capra

Best Actor   Spencer Tracy

Best Actress   Bette Davis

Best Supporting Actor   Walter Brennan

Best Supporting Actress   Fay Bainter

1940

Best Picture   Gone with the Wind

Best Director   Victor Fleming

Best Actor   Robert Donat'

Best Actress   Vivien Leigh

Best Supporting Actor   Thomas Mitchell

Best Supporting Actress   Hattie McDaniel

1941

Best Picture   Rebecca

Best Director   John Ford

Best Actor   James Stewart

Best Actress   Ginger Rogers

Best Supporting Actor   Walter Brennan

Best Supporting Actress   Jane Darwell

1942

AND THE OSCAR GOES TO...

Best Picture   How Green Was My Valley

Best Director   John Ford

Best Actor   Gary Cooper

Best Actress   Joan Fontaine

Best Supporting Actor   Donald Crisp

Best Supporting Actress Mary Astor

1943

Best Picture   Mrs. Miniver

Best Director   William Wyler

Best Actor   James Cagney

Best Actress   Greer Garson

Best Supporting Actor   Van Heflin

Best Supporting Actress Teresa Wright

1944

Best Picture   Casablanca

Best Director   Michael Curtiz

Best Actor   Paul Lukas

Best Actress   Jennifer Jones

Best Supporting Actor   Charles Coburn

Best Supporting Actress   Katina Paxinou

1945

Best Picture   Going My Way

Best Director   Leo McCarey

Best Actor   Bing Crosby

Best Actress   Ingrid Bergman

Best Supporting Actor   Barry Fitzgerald

Best Supporting Actress   Ethel Barrymore

1946

Best Picture   The Lost Weekend

Best Director   Billy Wilder

Best Actor   Ray Milland

Best Actress   Joan Crawford

Best Supporting Actor   James Dunn

Best Supporting Actress   Anne Revere

1947

Best Picture   The Best Years of Our Lives

Best Director   William Wyler

Best Actor   Fredric March

AND THE OSCAR GOES TO...

Best Actress	Olivia de Havilland
Best Supporting Actor	Harold Russell
Best Supporting Actress	Anne Baxter

1948

Best Picture	Gentleman's Agreement
Best Director	Elia Kazan
Best Actor	Ronald Colman
Best Actress	Loretta Young
Best Supporting Actor	Edmund Gwenn
Best Supporting Actress	Celeste Holm

1949

Best Picture	Hamlet
Best Director	John Huston
Best Actor	Laurence Oliver
Best Actress	Jane Wyman
Best Supporting Actor	Walter Huston
Best Supporting Actress	Claire Trevor

1950

Best Picture	All the King's Men

Best Director   Joesph L. Mankiewicz

Best Actor   Broderick Crawford

Best Actress   Olivia de Havilland

Best Supporting Actor   Dean Jagger

Best Supporting Actress   Mercedes McCambridge

1951

Best Picture   All About Eve

Best Director   Joseph L. Mankiewicz

Best Actor   Jose Ferrer

Best Actress   Judy Holliday

Best Supporting Actor   George Sanders

Best Supporting Actress   Josephine Hull

1952

Best Picture   An American In Paris

Best Director   George Stevens

Best Actor   Humphrey Bogart

Best Actress   Vivien Leigh

Best Supporting Actor   Karl Malden

Best Supporting Actress   Kim Hunter

AND THE OSCAR GOES TO...

1953

Best Picture   The Greatest Show on Earth

Best Director   John Ford

Best Actor   Gary Cooper

Best Actress   Shirley Booth

Best Supporting Actor   Anthony Quinn

Best Supporting Actress Gloria Grahame

1954

Best Picture   From Here to Eternity

Best Director   Fred Zinnemann

Best Actor   William Holden

Best Actress   Audrey Hepburn

Best Supporting Actor   Frank Sinatra

Best Supporting Actress Donna Reed

1955

Best Picture   On the Waterfront

Best Director   Elia Kazan

Best Actor   Marlon Brando

Best Actress   Grace Kelly

Best Supporting Actor	Edmond O'Brien
Best Supporting Actress	Eva Marie Saint

1956

Best Picture	Marty
Best Director	Delbert Mann
Best Actor	Ernest Borgnine
Best Actress	Anna Magnani
Best Supporting Actor	Jack Lemmon
Best Supporting Actress	Jo Van Fleet

1957

Best Picture	Around the World in 80 Days
Best Director	George Stevens
Best Actor	Yul Brynner
Best Actress	Ingrid Bergman
Best Supporting Actor	Anthony Quinn
Best Supporting Actress	Dorothy Malone

1958

Best Picture	The Bridge on the River Kwai
Best Director	David Lean

AND THE OSCAR GOES TO...

Best Actor	Alec Guinness
Best Actress	Joanne Woodward
Best Supporting Actor	Red Buttons
Best Supporting Actress	Miyoshi Umeki

1959

Best Picture	Gigi
Best Director	Vincente Minnelli
Best Actor	David Niven
Best Actress	Susan Hayward
Best Supporting Actor	Burl Ives
Best Supporting Actress	Wendy Hiller

1960

Best Picture	Ben Hur
Best Director	William Wyler
Best Actor	Charlton Heston
Best Actress	Simone Signoret
Best Supporting Actor	Hugh Griffith
Best Supporting Actress	Shelley Winters

1961

Best Picture	The Apartment
Best Director	Billy Wilder
Best Actor	Burt Lancaster
Best Actress	Elizabeth Taylor
Best Supporting Actor	Peter Ustinov
Best Supporting Actress	Shirley Jones

1962

Best Picture	West Side Story
Best Director	Jerome Robbins & Robert Wise (joint)
Best Actor	Maximilian Schell
Best Actress	Sophia Loren
Best Supporting Actor	George Chakiris
Best Supporting Actress	Rita Moreno

1963

Best Picture	Lawrence of Arabia
Best Director	David Lean
Best Actor	Gregory Peck

AND THE OSCAR GOES TO…

Best Actress	Anne Bancroft
Best Supporting Actor	Ed Begley
Best Supporting Actress	Patty Duke

1964

Best Picture	Tom Jones
Best Director	Tony Richardson
Best Actor	Sidney Poitier
Best Actress	Patricia Neal
Best Supporting Actor	Melvyn Douglas
Best Supporting Actress	Margaret Rutherford

1965

Best Picture	My Fair Lady
Best Director	George Cukor
Best Actor	Rex Harrison
Best Actress	Julie Andrews
Best Supporting Actor	Peter Ustinov
Best Supporting Actress	Lila Kedrova

1966

Best Picture	The Sound of Music

Best Director	Robert Wise
Best Actor	Lee Marvin
Best Actress	Julie Christie
Best Supporting Actor	Martin Balsam
Best Supporting Actress	Shelley Winters

1967

Best Picture	A Man for All Seasons
Best Director	Fred Zinnemann
Best Actor	Paul Scofield
Best Actress	Elizabeth Taylor
Best Supporting Actor	Walter Matthau
Best Supporting Actress	Sandy Dennis

1968

Best Picture	In the Heat of the Night
Best Director	Mike Nichols
Best Actor	Rod Steiger
Best Actress	Katharine Hepburn
Best Supporting Actor	George Kennedy
Best Supporting Actress	Estelle Parsons

AND THE OSCAR GOES TO...

1969

Best Picture	Oliver!
Best Director	Carol Reed
Best Actor	Cliff Robertson
Best Actress	(tie) Katharine Hepburn & Barbra Streisand
Best Supporting Actor	Jack Albertson
Best Supporting Actress	Ruth Gordon

1970

Best Picture	Midnight Cowboy
Best Director	John Schlesinger
Best Actor	John Wayne
Best Actress	Maggie Smith
Best Supporting Actor	Gig Young
Best Supporting Actress	Goldie Hawn

1971

Best Picture	Patton
Best Director	Franklin J. Schaffner
Best Actor	George C. Scott (refused)

Best Actress   Glenda Jackson

Best Supporting Actor   John Mills

Best Supporting Actress   Helen Hayes

1972

Best Picture   The French Connection

Best Director   William Friedkin

Best Actor   Gene Hackman

Best Actress   Jane Fonda

Best Supporting Actor   Ben Johnson

Best Supporting Actress   Cloris Leachman

Best Picture   The Godfather

1973

Best Picture   The Godfather

Best Director   Bob Fosse

Best Actor   Marlon Brando (refused)

Best Actress   Liza Minnelli

Best Supporting Actor   Joel Grey

Best Supporting Actress   Eileen Heckart

AND THE OSCAR GOES TO...

1974

Best Picture   The Sting

Best Director   George Roy Hill

Best Actor   Jack Lemmon

Best Actress   Glenda Jackson

Best Supporting Actor   John Houseman

Best Supporting Actress   Tatum O'Neal

1975

Best Picture   The Godfather: Part II

Best Director   Francis Ford Coppola

Best Actor   Art Carney

Best Actress   Ellen Burstyn

Best Supporting Actor   Robert De Niro

Best Supporting Actress   Ingrid Bergman

1976

Best Picture   One Flew Over the Cuckoo's Nest

Best Director   Milos Forman

Best Actor   Jack Nicholson

Best Actress   Louise Fletcher

Best Supporting Actor	George Burns
Best Supporting Actress	Lee Grant

1977

Best Picture	Rocky
Best Director	John G. Avildsen
Best Actor	Peter Finch (posthumous)
Best Actress	Faye Dunaway
Best Supporting Actor	Jason Robards
Best Supporting Actress	Beatrice Straight

1978

Best Picture	Annie Hall
Best Director	Woody Allen
Best Actor	Richard Dreyfuss
Best Actress	Diane Keaton
Best Supporting Actor	Jason Robards
Best Supporting Actress	Vanessa Redgrave

1979

Best Picture	The Deer Hunter
Best Director	Michael Cimino

Best Actor   Jon Voight

Best Actress   Jane Fonda

Best Supporting Actor   Christopher Walken

Best Supporting Actress   Maggie Smith

1980

Best Picture   Kramer vs. Kramer

Best Director   Robert Benton

Best Actor   Dustin Hoffman

Best Actress   Sally Field

Best Supporting Actor   Melvyn Douglas

Best Supporting Actress   Meryl Streep

1981

Best Picture   Ordinary People

Best Director   Robert Redford

Best Actor   Robert De Niro

Best Actress   Sissy Spacek

Best Supporting Actor   Timothy Hutton

Best Supporting Actress   Mary Steenburgen

TIM J. CULBERTSON

1982

Best Picture	Chariots of Fire
Best Director	Warren Beatty
Best Actor	Henry Fonda
Best Actress	Katharine Hepburn
Best Supporting Actor	John Gielgud
Best Supporting Actress	Maureen Stapleton

1983

Best Picture	Gandhi
Best Director	Richard Attenborough
Best Actor	Ben Kingsley
Best Actress	Meryl Streep
Best Supporting Actor	Louis Gossett Jr.
Best Supporting Actress	Jessica Lange

1984

Best Picture	Terms of Endearment
Best Director	James L. Brooks
Best Actor	Robert Duvall
Best Actress	Shirley MacLaine

Best Supporting Actor   Jack Nicholson

Best Supporting Actress   Linda Hunt

1985

Best Picture   Amadeus

Best Director   Milos Forman

Best Actor   F. Murray Abraham

Best Actress   Sally Field

Best Supporting Actor   Haing S. Ngor

Best Supporting Actress   Peggy Ashcroft

1986

Best Picture   Out of Africa

Best Director   Sydney Pollack

Best Actor   William Hurt

Best Actress   Geraldine Page

Best Supporting Actor   Don Ameche

Best Supporting Actress   Anjelica Huston

1987

Best Picture   Platoon

Best Director   Oliver Stone

Best Actor   Paul Newman

Best Actress   Marlee Matlin

Best Supporting Actor   Michael Caine

Best Supporting Actress   Dianne Wiest

1988

Best Picture   The Last Emperor

Best Director   Bernardo Bertolucci

Best Actor   Michael Douglas

Best Actress   Cher

Best Supporting Actor   Sean Connery

Best Supporting Actress   Olympia Dukakis

1989

Best Picture   Rain Man

Best Director   Barry Levinson

Best Actor   Dustin Hoffman

Best Actress   Jodie Foster

Best Supporting Actor   Kevin Kline

Best Supporting Actress   Geena Davis

AND THE OSCAR GOES TO...

1990

Best Picture	Driving Miss Daisy
Best Director	Oliver Stone
Best Actor	Daniel Day-Lewis
Best Actress	Jessica Tandy
Best Supporting Actor	Denzel Washington
Best Supporting Actress	Brenda Fricker

1991

Best Picture	Dances with the Wolves
Best Director	Kevin Costner
Best Actor	Jeremy Irons
Best Actress	Kathy Bates
Best Supporting Actor	Joe Pesci
Best Supporting Actress	Whoopi Goldberg

1992

Best Picture	The Silence of the Lambs
Best Director	Jonathan Demme
Best Actor	Anthony Hopkins
Best Actress	Jodie Foster

Best Supporting Actor	Jack Palance
Best Supporting Actress	Mercedes Ruehl

1993

Best Picture	The Unforgiven
Best Director	Clint Eastwood
Best Actor	Al Pacino
Best Actress	Emma Thompson
Best Supporting Actor	Gene Hackman
Best Supporting Actress	Maris Tomei

1994

Best Picture	Schindler's List
Best Director	Steven Spielberg
Best Actor	Tom Hanks
Best Actress	Holly Hunter
Best Supporting Actor	Tommy Lee Jones
Best Supporting Actress	Anna Paquin

1995

Best Picture	Forrest Gump
Best Director	Robert Zemeckis

AND THE OSCAR GOES TO...

Best Actor   Tom Hanks

Best Actress   Jessica Lange

Best Supporting Actor   Martin Landau

Best Supporting Actress   Dianne Wiest

1996

Best Picture   Braveheart

Best Director   Mel Gibson

Best Actor   Sean Penn

Best Actress   Susan Sarandon

Best Supporting Actor   Kevin Spacey

Best Supporting Actress   Mira Sorvino

1997

Best Picture   The English Patient

Best Director   Anthony Minghella

Best Actor   Geoffrey Rush

Best Actress   Frances McDormand

Best Supporting Actor   Cuba Gooding Jr.

Best Supporting Actress   Juliette Binoche

TIM J. CULBERTSON

1998

Best Picture	Titanic
Best Director	James Cameron
Best Actor	Jack Nicholson
Best Actress	Helen Hunt
Best Supporting Actor	Robin Williams
Best Supporting Actress	Kim Basinger

1999

Best Picture	Shakespeare In Love
Best Director	Steven Spielberg
Best Actor	Roberto Benigni
Best Actress	Gwyneth Paltrow
Best Supporting Actor	James Coburn
Best Supporting Actress	Judi Dench

2000

Best Picture	American Beauty
Best Director	Sam Mendes
Best Actor	Kevin Spacey
Best Actress	Hilary Swank

AND THE OSCAR GOES TO...

Best Supporting Actor	Michael Caine
Best Supporting Actress	Angelina Jolie

2001

Best Picture	Gladiator
Best Director	Steven Soderbergh
Best Actor	Russell Crowe
Best Actress	Julia Roberts
Best Supporting Actor	Benicio del Toro
Best Supporting Actress	Marcia Gay Harden

2002

Best Picture	A Beautiful Mind
Best Director	Ron Howard
Best Actor	Denzel Washington
Best Actress	Halle Berry
Best Supporting Actor	Jim Broadbent
Best Supporting Actress	Jennifer Connelly

2003

Best Picture	Chicago
Best Director	Roman Polanski

Best Actor   Adrian Brody

Best Actress   Nicole Kidman

Best Supporting Actor   Chris Cooper

Best Supporting Actress   Catherine Zeta-Jones

2004

Best Picture   The Lord of the Rings: The Return of
                                    the King

Best Director   Peter Jackson

Best Actor   Sean Penn

Best Actress   Charlize Theron

Best Supporting Actor   Tim Robbins

Best Supporting Actress   Renee Zellweger

2005

Best Picture   Million Dollar Baby

Best Director   Clint Eastwood

Best Actor   Jamie Foxx

Best Actress   Hilary Swank

Best Supporting Actor   Morgan Freeman

Best Supporting Actress   Cate Blanchett

AND THE OSCAR GOES TO...

2006

Best Picture   Crash

Best Director   Ang Lee

Best Actor   Phillip Seymour Hoffman

Best Actress   Reese Witherspoon

Best Supporting Actor   George Clooney

Best Supporting Actress   Rachel Weisz

2007

Best Picture   The Departed

Best Director   Martin Scorsese

Best Actor   Forest Whitaker

Best Actress   Helen Mirren

Best Supporting Actor   Alan Arkin

Best Supporting Actress   Jennifer Hudson

2008

Best Picture   No Country for Old Men

Best Director   Ethan and Joel Cohen (joint)

Best Actor   Daniel Day-Lewis

Best Actress   Marion Cotillard

TIM J. CULBERTSON

Best Supporting Actor	Javier Bardem
Best Supporting Actress	Tilda Swinton

2009

Best Picture	Slumdog Millionaire
Best Director	Danny Boyle
Best Actor	Sean Penn
Best Actress	Kate Winslet
Best Supporting Actor	Heath Ledger (posthumous)
Best Supporting Actress	Penelope Cruz

2010

Best Picture	The Hurt Locker
Best Director	Kathyrn Bigelow
Best Actor	Jeff Bridges
Best Actress	Sandra Bullock
Best Supporting Actor	Christoph Waltz
Best Supporting Actress	Mo'Nique

2011

Best Picture	The King's Speech
Best Director	Tom Hooper

AND THE OSCAR GOES TO...

Best Actor	Colin Firth
Best Actress	Natalie Portman
Best Supporting Actor	Christian Bale
Best Supporting Actress	Melissa Leo

2012

Best Picture	The Artist
Best Director	Michel Hazanavicius
Best Actor	Jean Dujardin
Best Actress	Meryl Streep
Best Supporting Actor	Christopher Plummer
Best Supporting Actress	Octavia Spencer

2013

Best Picture	Argo
Best Director	Ang Lee
Best Actor	Daniel Day-Lewis
Best Actress	Jennifer Lawrence
Best Supporting Actor	Christoph Waltz
Best Supporting Actress	Anne Hathaway

2014

Best Picture	12 Years a Slave
Best Director	Alfonso Cuaron
Best Actor	Matthew McConaughey
Best Actress	Cate Blanchett
Best Supporting Actor	Jared Leto
Best Supporting Actress	Lupita Nyong'o

2015

Best Picture	Birdman or (The Unexpected Virtue of Ignorance)
Best Director	Alejandro G. Inarritu
Best Actor	Eddie Redmayne
Best Actress	Julianne Moore
Best Supporting Actor	J.K. Simmons
Best Supporting Actress	Patricia Arquette

2016

Best Picture	Spotlight
Best Director	Alejandro G. Inarritu
Best Actor	Leonardo DiCaprio

AND THE OSCAR GOES TO...

Best Actress	Brie Larson
Best Supporting Actor	Mark Rylance
Best Supporting Actress	Alicia Vikander

2017

Best Picture	Moonlight
Best Director	Damien Chazelle
Best Actor	Casey Affleck
Best Actress	Emma Stone
Best Supporting Actor	Mahershala Ali
Best Supporting Actress	Viola Davis

2018

Best Picture	The Shape of Water
Best Director	Guillermo del Toro
Best Actor	Gary Oldman
Best Actress	Frances McDormand
Best Supporting Actor	Sam Rockwell
Best Supporting Actress	Allison Janney

2019

Best Picture	Green Book

TIM J. CULBERTSON

Best Director   Alfonso Cuaron

Best Actor   Rami Malek

Best Actress   Olivia Colman

Best Supporting Actor Mahershala Ali

Best Supporting Actress Regina King

2020

Best Picture   Parasite a.k.a. (Gisaengchung)

Best Director   Bong Jong Ho

Best Actor   Joaquin Phoenix

Best Actress   Renee Zellweger

Best Supporting Actor Brad Pitt

Best Supporting Actress Laura Dern

2021

Best Picture   Nomadland

Best Director   Chloe Zhao

Best Actor   Anthony Hopkins

Best Actress   Frances McDormand

Best Supporting Actor Daniel Kaluuya

Best Supporting Actress Youn Yuh-jung

2022

Best Picture   CODA

Best Director   Jane Campion

Best Actor   Will Smith

Best Actress   Jessica Chastain

Best Supporting Actor   Troy Kotsur

Best Supporting Actress   Ariana DeBose

2023

Best Picture   Everything, Everywhere All at Once

Best Director   Dan (Daniel) Kwan & Daniel Scheinert (joint)

Best Actor   Brendan Fraser

Best Actress   Michelle Yeoh

Best Supporting Actor   Ke Huy Quan

Best Supporting Actress   Jamie Lee Curtis

2024

Best Picture   Oppenheimer

Best Director   Christopher Nolan

Best Actor   Cillian Murphy

Best Actress   Emma Stone

Best Supporting Actor   Robert Downey Jr.

Best Supporting Actress   DaVine Joy Randolph

I had the pleasure of visiting the Academy of Arts and Sciences in Hollywood recently and saw the Oscar Experience exhibit. Below is a link you can follow to see a curated history of the Oscars.

https://oscars.academymuseum.org/?utm_source=qr_code&utm_medium=didactic&utm_campaign=gallery

Acknowledgments

My gratitude to Book Writing Pioneer and their staff, especially to Simon Akerson, Sr. Project Manager Brian J. Murdock, Senior Book Consultant, Melissa Helga, and David Banks, project manager, for taking time away from other writers to email me when I had a question or comment concerning my issues becoming a first-time author. Their knowledge about the pricing structure and other pertinent information concerning the levels of service Book Writing Pioneer has to offer, as well as the patience in letting me write on my own terms without pressure and/or deadlines, allows me to express myself in ways I never thought I could. Another big shout to Max Gorlov and his staff at How to Write Your First Novel and countless other publishing companies in their attempts to sway me with their presentations.

I would also like to thank my husband of almost thirty years, Gary LaPalombara allowing me to use the computer for lengthy periods of time away from enjoying our retirement on the beach, at a resort, at a theatre, watching TV, enjoying dinner at a nice restaurant, cooking us a nice meal or international location. I certainly couldn't do this without all of Gary's love and support. I couldn't be anyone without Gary by my side; we would be like two lost puppies looking for a new home. A deep gratitude to my friends from all over the United States and abroad for the confidence to do something I've wanted to do until now, and its WRITE A BOOK. My deepest reward in life is being the youngest of five children and the ability to accomplish something nobody in my family has ever attempted. Lots of loving kudos to my family for having the deepest faith in my living the dream (if this goes well) continuation in writing a fictionalized account (names and location changed, OF COURSE) of our lives together, describing life's ups and downs, loves past and present in between loss and despair growing up being the wonderful people we are today. I had the BALLS to do something!

I want to praise the dear Lord above for allowing me to be true to myself as a gay white male, instilling a demanding work ethic in past work, and continuing with patience and perseverance to draft a book, especially about the Oscars. I live and breathe the movies, keeping up with past and present by reading blogs about celebrities and movies. Ever since an early age, being a moviegoer and movie trivia buff, especially Oscar and celebrity knowledge, coupled with

AND THE OSCAR GOES TO...

my book and DVD Blu-ray collection surrounding me in my home office, kept me warm and fuzzy to complete this task. Believe me, it's not been easy!

Special kudos to Wikipedia and Chat GPT for allowing me to lean on them for the facts, reading their entries and replies to my questions, and acquiring more knowledge from their enormous information bank, assisting me in the creation of my own words and put down on the page at the best of my ability.

We, as citizens of the United States and abroad, have already won an Oscar for being able to live in a wonderful world regardless of how divided; at least we are alive. There is an Oscar in all of us; reach for the stars and grab the brass ring, clinging to a fantasy one day, a celebrity reads our name amongst other well-known celebrities by calling our name after those five little words.

AND THE OSCAR GOES TO

Thank you again,

Tim J. Culbertson

For further information, visit www.bookbytimc.com

Dallas, Texas

July 2024

www.ingramcontent.com/pod-product-compliance
Lightning Source LLC
Chambersburg PA
CBHW051504120626
46551CB00012B/767